NO BORDERS

More Praise for *No Borders*

'A gift to all of us who yearn for relevant theory to help us take more effective action, this is an inspiring call to join communities around the world and work for the full realization of human rights rooted in the values of solidarity and the inherent worth and dignity of all.'

Chris Crass, author of *Towards Collective Liberation*

'Borders have failed to contain a world in motion or offer a just settlement for millions of people. What is politics in the wake of this double failure? With its focus on new forms of social movement and political action, *No Borders* will prove vital reading for anyone seeking answers.'

William Walters, Carleton University

About the author

Natasha has been involved in a lot of different expressions of the struggle for the freedom of movement, in the UK, Calais and elsewhere. Natasha would like to call herself an author but isn't sure if you can do that after finishing your first book. She hopes this will be the first of many. Natasha has a PhD in politics from the University of Nottingham, Centre for Social and Global Justice. She is from the south of England and is based in Nottingham. Right now she is travelling around Europe exploring different kinds of autonomous communities.

NO BORDERS

THE POLITICS OF IMMIGRATION CONTROL AND RESISTANCE

Natasha King

ZED
Zed Books
London

No Borders: The Politics of Immigration Control and Resistance was
first published in 2016 by Zed Books Ltd, The Foundry,
17 Oval Way, London SE11 5RR, UK.

www.zedbooks.net

Typeset in Plantin and Kievit by Swales & Willis Ltd, Exeter, Devon
Index by Ed Emery
Cover design by Clare Turner

A catalogue record for this book is available from the British Library.

ISBN 978-1-78360-468-5 hb
ISBN 978-1-78360-467-8 pb
ISBN 978-1-78360-469-2 pdf
ISBN 978-1-78360-470-8 epub
ISBN 978-1-78360-471-5 mobi

Printed and bound by CPI Group (UK) Ltd, Croydon, CR0 4YY

CONTENTS

And as capital retreats deeper and deeper into cyberspace, or into disembodiment, leaving behind itself the empty shells of spectacular control, our complexity of anti-authoritarian and autonomist tendencies will begin to see the re-appearance of the Social.

Hakim Bey (2009)

Maybe this whole situation will just work itself out

Artwork in the Calais jungle, Banksy (2015)

INTRODUCTION

Locating the issue

I started writing this on the same day that reports came in of up to seven hundred people drowning in the Mediterranean Sea after an overloaded boat carrying people from Libya to Italy capsized (Kingsley 2015). This disaster was sadly not a one-off. The spring of 2015 shone a light on what was called a humanitarian crisis that, by the middle of May, had resulted in the deaths of more than 1,800 people (Di Giacomo 2015). I'm sitting here almost one year later and all the figures from 2015 are being outdone by those of this year. More people crossing clandestinely, more people dying.[1]

The figures were horrific, but this crisis didn't begin NOW. People had been clandestinely crossing the Mediterranean Sea from North Africa or the Aegean Sea from Turkey since the early 1990s.[2] This was the same struggle that had been going on for more than two decades, just on an unprecedented scale. The mainstream story was effectively the same: an apocalypse, with those on the boats signalling the presence of a vast horde of people just waiting for their chance to cross to Europe; of victims recruited by 'merciless' smugglers, the solution largely lying in 'combating illegal migration' through more controls. In this way, the 'human crisis' that was a problem for migrants became presented as a 'migrant crisis' that was a problem for European governments.

The ironic presentation of certain kinds of travellers (the ones European states claim not to want[3]) as victims of circumstance before they reach Europe and criminals set on stealing our resources after they arrive still dominates. What this discourse smuggles in unnoticed is the sense that border controls are somehow natural, timeless and realistic. What this discourse passes over, too, is how the controls that are deemed so necessary to stem the flow of unwanted migrants actually *create* the problem of 'illegal' migration.

We live in a world where the movement of the global poor is increasingly seen as a problem and restricted (Balibar 2002; Menz 2008;

Snyder 2005). In recent years in Europe we have seen the introduction of biometric passports, the expansion in the use of immigration imprisonment, and recent investigations into the use of military drones along Europe's external borders (Fotiadis and Ciobanu 2013; Statewatch 2012). None of this is a 'natural' state of affairs. Borders are a function of states. They produce territories (countries) by delimiting and securing spaces and their contents/populations (Agnew 1994). They produce an inside and an outside, insiders and outsiders, and establish a system to control whose movement is acceptable and whose is not. They create categories (the migrant worker, the skilled migrant worker, the asylum seeker, the refugee ...) and, through the process of categorization, create groups of people who carry a label of non-status (the illegal immigrant) (DeGenova 2002). Within this, migrant illegality is a (non-)status that's produced by the regime of control and conferred on an individual when their movement is seen as problematic (Squire 2011). The border regime is *productive*. It produces human illegality, even though people might use such legal loopholes for their benefit too (Ruhs and Anderson 2007; Squire 2011). As Anne McNevin says in relation to 'irregular' migration, 'without reference to the state as bounded and territorialized the notion of irregular migration would cease to be meaningful; what would irregular migration look like if there were no borders, as such, to cross?' (McNevin 2009: 70).

A few weeks after the disaster in the Mediterranean, I was in Calais, in a self-organized camp of people trying to cross to the UK. Sitting in a friend's house in the camp drinking tea together, we talked about how the number of people living there had swelled in recent weeks from a thousand or so to double that. All these new arrivals had put pressure on those already living there. My friend's group had doubled to around thirty, forming an ordered unit of people combining their resources and labour in order to feed and look after each other. Many of these new arrivals were those people who had made the headlines weeks before. Their boat-crossing had been just a fragment of their journeys. Now they waited in Calais for their chance to reach the UK and make a happy ending to what were often years-long journeys.

I mention this because this book is not really about border controls, but about how people find ways to practise the freedom of movement despite such controls. It's a book about practices for free movement, against the border. Because border controls are and have always been resisted (Casas-Cortes et al. 2015; Anderson et al. 2012). March 2015 saw simultaneous hunger strikes in eight detention prisons across the UK, accompanied by a similar wave of solidarity actions. In June that year, a camp of people trying to cross was joined by solidarity activists to form a No Border camp in Ventimiglia, on the Italian side of the border with France. The camp lasted for a further three months. These are just a few examples of the ways that people denied the freedom of movement, and those in solidarity with them, have taken action.

And then there are all the people who keep on moving without permission. Because to only pay attention to visible and organized activities 'is to see only the smoke rising from the volcano' (Holloway 2002: 159; see also Grelet 2001). Beneath that smoke is a huge number of everyday acts of non-subordination and quiet evasions carried out by people who refuse to allow borders to stop them from moving (cf. Anderson et al. 2012; Hess 2003; Karakayali and Tsianos 2012; Mezzadra 2004a, 2011; Mezzadra and Neilsen 2003; Mitropoulos 2007; Papadopoulos et al. 2008; Rodriguez 1996). As the scholar-activists who came together around the 'Migrations and Militant Research' workshops attest, the term 'migration struggles' encapsulates both organized struggles by migrants and those in solidarity with them, *and* daily strategies of refusal (because simply to be present where you are prohibited from being becomes an act of resistance, regardless of whether it's recognized as such or not) (Casas-Cortes et al. 2015). Calais is a testament to how most of the people crossing the Mediterranean in boats continue their journeys, often beneath the gaze of media or governments or us.[4]

Paying attention to these practices doesn't mean being blind to the operations and consequences of control. I have already talked about how people travelling without permission die in their efforts to cross borders. They are routinely and indefinitely imprisoned if they make it to Europe. They face numerous ways that limit their lives and bar their access to society should they manage to remain (in the UK this means no legal access to work or free healthcare, and living with the continual risk of detention and deportation). Such things produce violent and traumatizing effects. The development of mental illness after arrival is common, as is self-harm and suicide (Athwal and Bourne 2007; Cohen 2008). Yet without discounting all this, even under intense restrictions, *acts of liberation still happen.*

People protest together and affirm that 'No-One is Illegal!'; others mount hunger strikes that contest their detention; others maintain safer houses where travellers can stay; still others pass on information about the safest routes and means of passage. All these activities reflect a *refusal* to be denied the freedom of movement in different ways. These practices form part of the movement against borders, or the no border movement, and this movement is diverse.

Thinking of no borders as a refusal brings into focus how the legitimacy of border controls is also questioned, and hence the legitimacy of the nation-state. People move for a variety of reasons. I can't imagine anyone ever moves in order to challenge the state, and I'm not suggesting that every act of migration is an act of liberation. But, in the act of moving without permission, or in actively contesting controls that limit their lives, people refuse the border and oppose the state *at that moment*. The struggle for the freedom of movement is this refusal of the border. I label this a no borders politics and explore what it is as a concept in Chapter 1.

With these points in mind, the main question this book asks is, *how do we refuse borders?*

Reflections on the dilemmas of refusing the border

Thinking of the struggle for the freedom of movement as moments when people refuse the border and oppose the state – either intentionally or unintentionally – poses a challenge. Migration is an issue so deeply shaped and inscribed by the state. As Aaron Zolberg suggests, the very definition of migration – as movement across territorial borders – presupposes the existence of the state (Zolberg 1981). We may refuse the border and oppose the state, but too often it's also the state that we have to appeal to if we want to secure greater freedoms. We demand rights from the state, when it's the state that denies us rights in the first place (cf. Arendt 1973 [1951]). This paradox creates a dilemma for any struggle that opposes the state. It's a dilemma that comes up time and again in grassroots struggles of all kinds, and can be better illustrated in the case of no border struggles through a few examples.

In the UK a common way of showing solidarity with the struggle for the freedom of movement is to visit people held in detention prisons. It's a way of offering practical and emotional support to the imprisoned, and showing that they're not forgotten just because the state tries to hide them away. Groups have held numerous demos outside such prisons, while the inmates have held hunger strikes and demonstrations and taken direct action from the inside. Both have strengthened each other. Visiting people in detention is also a way of better understanding the lived experiences of those directly affected by border controls. It's the basis for taking further action against such places. In numerous cases, access to information about 'life inside' has led visitors' groups to make complaints and publish information about poor treatment, which has resulted in improvements. This has positive effects for those who are subject to imprisonment, but it undermines any aim to end immigration detention altogether, because it suggests that the problem can be solved through better treatment, and not the end of detention itself. As the state improves its immigration prisons, it has more legitimacy in refuting claims that imprisonment is against our dignity and humanity. Ultimately, detainee visitors' groups end up struggling with the idea that, while they oppose detention, what they do *also* reinforces the idea that immigration detention is legitimate.

In Greece the struggle for the freedom of movement has led to three campaigns for the mass regularization of illegalized people in the country. In each case people have debated how legalization effectively reinforces the state's right to decide. Regularization amnesties are time limited, with conditions that disqualify large sections of the illegalized population. They often pave the way for harsher migration policies too (Nyers 2010). As such, such amnesties refine and redefine the regime of control, even as they bring about real material improvements for many at that time (DeGenova 2002). Resistance to the border always seems faced with the dilemma of how to refuse the state while also engaging with it. I think this is the main dilemma of any kind of politics that seeks to refuse the state, and I return to this dilemma time and again throughout this book.

People and groups adopt different strategies to negotiate this dilemma. This can lead to conflicts between those who resist in different ways. Some resist by engaging with the state in order to secure further freedoms. People launch campaigns that demand regularization, or that demonstrate that our cities are places of sanctuary (cf. Cissé 1996; Squire and Bagelman 2012). For others, however, the very fact that such freedoms are controlled by the state *is* the site of struggle. Such differences can be a dynamic force that generates diversity in our resistance. But such differences become problematic when they are seen as absolute, incompatible and insurmountable. They risk weakening such struggles at a time when it is more urgent than ever to mount a forceful collective and diverse resistance against the steady infestation of border controls throughout our social world. How to enact a radical politics when so constrained by the state? How to find common ground when our aims sometimes appear like opposites?

This dilemma leads me to modify my question: *How do we resist borders, in a current reality in which borders proliferate?*

On method

Who's writing? This book is my attempt to understand a certain kind of struggle against the border regime, and it came about because of my own involvement in this struggle. How I came to write this book and to ask these questions is the result of an evolution in my own thinking around how migration affects me and how I want to live my life.

Ten years ago I worked for a refugee rights organization that (among many other things) lobbied government for positive changes to the refugee regime in the UK. We demanded an end to the detention of children, and at best got assurances that safeguards would be put in place to protect their welfare while in detention. We demanded an end to the destitution of refused asylum seekers, a situation that people at the end of the asylum process *still* face. We reserved our energy for refugees, but said nothing about all the other people who arrived without permission. We didn't go there, and I put that decision and distinction out of my mind. I remember we always said that we weren't a political organization, but a humanitarian one. That statement seems naïve to me now.

Lobbying didn't bring anything like the kind of changes I had in mind. It felt like dreaming small. And the uncomfortable feeling I got from focusing only on the rights of refugees never really went away. I left that organization and found myself involved in more grassroots projects supporting travellers of different kinds. I started to think, why was it that refugees were legitimate travellers but others weren't? If everybody had the right to travel, then maybe the system that prohibited that was wrong. Looking back now, that thought process seems naïve too. But we're not taught to question the very basis of the system that we live in. It was a very simple thought, but it took me a long while to reach it.

Reaching that conclusion opened up a whole new world. I started to visit Calais and spend time with other people who came to that city and who identified in some way with the idea of the freedom of movement. We distributed clothes, tents, wood and building materials to people who were stuck in that city trying to cross to the UK. We cooked food together, hung out, held parties, visited people in the detention prison there. Others opened squats where we and other people could rest. We lived together with people trying to cross. I went to my first No Borders camp in Brussels in 2009 and was blown away by how well 800 people managed to meet their needs inclusively, collectively and creatively in this wonderful temporary community. I have stayed involved in Calais, and through those experiences become connected to a vast network of people and places that continue to try to make those wonderful, collective, creative (and sometimes less temporary) communities. This thing I'm a part of, this movement, for want of a better word, feels fierce and loving. It feels like an intensity of living. It's a way of being that doesn't so much point out what's wrong with the system (although a lot of that happens too), but is other to it.

So in some sense, this book is not really about migration at all, but about a certain way of being that's other to the system; that creates or has the potential to create supportive, collaborative and non-dominating communities of people of different backgrounds. It includes anti-deportation campaigns, detention visitor projects, language clubs, No Borders camps and detention prison blockades, but it's also connected to the ways people create other communities more generally, from squatting and occupying land, to holding free parties. Migration is a point of orientation, but not the entirety of what I'm talking about here. I ask the questions I do and pose the dilemmas I do because these are issues I have come across time and again through my involvement in the struggle for the freedom of movement. And when I say 'we', I'm talking about all of us who share the feeling that the freedom of movement is everybody's freedom. It's from this standpoint that I talk. In asking these questions, I hope that we can better understand this practice, become more fierce and loving. Like Paul Chatterton, 'I want to galvanize dissent, normalize critique, and make radical alternatives seem like real possibilities for our times' (Chatterton 2008: 426).

Activist research I ask these questions and pose these dilemmas because I have a stake in this struggle. Being open about the stake you have makes for a very different kind of scholarship from any kind of 'objective' science, or even from the more subjective methods we find in the social sciences. Starting from the stake you have resonates with the idea of activist or militant scholarship (cf. Fuller and Kitchen

2004; Routledge 2004; Pickerill 2008). Activist scholarship comes out of *partisan* participation in struggle (Gordon 2012; Juris 2007). It exists to make interventions within those struggles and to strengthen them, which means working with and expressing explicit political and ideological intent (Fuller and Kitchen 2004). It comes about through long-term commitment to the struggle and those in it, and through critical engagement with what's going on in that struggle. It aims to be activist in process/method as well as in the knowledge it produces, and for that reason is often (indeed, probably should be) collaborative and reflective (Colectivo Situaciones 2007; Juris 2007). For me, activist research is partisan reflection on and through practice. It's something that people in social movements are doing all the time (Shukaitis and Graeber 2007).

Praxis The motive behind this book was a question: *How do we resist the border, in a current reality in which borders proliferate?* On the one hand, this question speaks to those struggles against the border that exist in the here and now (how can we resist?). On the other hand, it points to a possible future (is it possible to create a world free of borders?). No border struggles are utopian, to the extent that they always negotiate between an existing reality that's highly bordered, and a borderless future that appears to be always ahead of us. As one interviewee put it, 'We're always on a walk towards no borders ... It's a constant aspiration and tension' (interview, Anon. 4). It inherently involves changing the present by thinking beyond what is.

Yet this connection with what is also makes no border struggles incredibly realistic. A friend suggested that 'no borders is happening all the time, and that the time perspective for struggle is now ... that the time to live is now, with all its bitterness and defeats but also with its victories and joy' (interview, Anon. 9).

Critical resistance speaks to that intent to contest the status quo *and* bring about radical – utopian – social change (Hoy 2004). Put another way, critical resistance is about doing and imagining, practice and theory. Yet to set theory and practice apart from each other can rob critical resistance of its power. Theory detached from practice can create irrelevant abstraction. Practice without theory can create directionless action (hooks 1994).

Critical resistance, then, comes from the feedback loop between theory and practice. A word for this feedback loop is praxis. It's a grand-sounding word for something that people are doing all the time. Whenever we critically reflect on our experience and how the world could be, and we put into practice those reflections, we are engaged in praxis (Bell et al. 1990; Freire 2005 [1970]; Moss 2004). No borders, as a particular politics, is already inherently praxis-based in that it seeks to go beyond what is, think about how things could be otherwise, and then put that into practice. I have sought to mimic this process in this book, and this book is the outcome of a praxis-based approach. It has meant I have sought to weave practice and theory together. This approach is reflected in my desire to create scholarship that's directly relevant to existing struggles against the border now, and a research method that embedded me in those struggles and that used my experiences of activism as a subject of study. This approach has also compelled me to transgress the borders within theory; to not be 'faithful' to any one theory so much as to use them as tools that can contextualize and shed further meaning on a no borders politics. This has also meant I've been strategic in my use/choices, focusing on those theories which help me to elaborate on what a no borders politics means, rather than providing an exhaustive review of certain concepts. Approaching knowledge in this way enables me to draw out the tensions and dilemmas that appear in a somewhat utopian politics when practised in reality. I'm not seeking to impose a single theory upon this movement, but to shed more light on its diversity.

Scope This book is a synthesis of my PhD research, which looked at struggles against the border in Athens, Greece, and my experiences of similar struggles in Calais, France. In bringing these two things together, my aim has been to draw out themes of refusal of the border in different places, and to look at the dilemmas such practices pose for a politics that is both realistic and utopian. It has involved a mix of research methods. For my research in Athens I spent 2011 living in the city, participating in a number of struggles against the border and carrying out thirty-four semi-structured interviews with people involved in these struggles (what could be described as an activist ethnography). In the case of Calais, it's difficult to define any method as such. I've drawn on my own experiences over the last six years, which have largely been with the group Calais Migrant Solidarity. I have supplemented this with ten interviews with people involved in the No Border Network, as well as numerous conversations and email exchanges.

Why Calais and Athens? What both these cities have in common is that they represent sites of particular brutal intensity in the struggle against the border; places where people travelling without permission have had to stay, where the mechanisms of control have been diverse, creative and brutal and where people have continued to struggle for the freedom of movement in diverse and creative ways.

On the realities of doing activist research This book is far from a perfect outcome of activist research. Synthesizing a more rigorous and intentionally scholarly PhD research process with reflections on my experiences in Calais over six years (which I did not know I would do until I started writing this book) has not been easy or anywhere near perfect. I had no direct connection to migration struggles in Athens before I went there. I had chosen the city largely for scholarly purposes. At that time (2011) Athens was a major site in the European struggle against the border. It was/is also a site with a large and diverse radical political scene. I felt that made for a really interesting and exciting combination, and I wanted to be a part of that. I felt I had a legitimate claim to be there because I was already connected to these struggles through my own involvement in similar ones at home. I already had 'insider knowledge' in the sense that I saw the struggle in similar ways, shared some of the same concerns and passions.

Yet despite being involved in migration struggles in very practical ways there, being an outsider and a researcher created borders, and collaboration proved difficult. I was an uninvited visitor, and there was often suspicion. Partly this reflects my own naivety at how much movements in different places have in common.[5] Partly it reflects the difficulty of doing activist research within the structure that is imposed upon students by universities. It puts time pressures on scholars that makes developing the kinds of relationships necessary for collaboration difficult, in an environment that often pays lip-service to collaboration but rarely carries it out horizontally. Nonetheless, over time I came to regularly participate in a number of activities of a few groups that gave me some insight. I attended various left and anarchist assemblies, went to all kinds of demonstrations and rallies, got involved in a radical media collective, spent time in autonomous spaces, spent time in Victoria Square when the square was occupied by anarchists (in response to the fascist pogroms in that neighbourhood – see Chapter 3 for more information), and participated in left and anarchist blocs at some demos.

Nonetheless, this account is based on a year of being, frustratingly, at the margins of these groups, of largely *attempting* to participate.

My connection to Calais has been different, deeper. Because of that, writing about it has been much more anxiety-inducing. Having visited the city many times, spent a lot of time there and been involved in that struggle, going back there as a researcher was not easy for me, or particularly welcome for many people active in no border struggles there. There was a fuzziness to my motives (was I a researcher or was I an activist? What did it mean for me to be there and conduct research on this situation? What impression was I giving, to be involved in the No Border Network while making scholarship? Why didn't I ask people involved in the Network, or people trying to cross first?). Collaboration was limited because of these concerns, but also because I didn't fully pursue the possibilities for it, for many reasons. This means that what I have to say about this group is partial. It implies my own particular relationship to it (although it's also based on conversations with activists and texts on it). It's also geographically partial. I don't draw out geographical variations in the Network (which stretches from Europe to North Africa and North America), but focus on how it operates in Calais.

My connection to migrant communities has been different too. For groups like 'The 300' (who I talk about in Chapters 2 and 3), as well as a whole range of different migrant-led groups, access was welcome, indeed encouraged. They wanted to talk about their struggle in their own terms, to someone who was very clearly an outsider to that (in the case of the hunger strike of 'The 300', for example, I arrived in the last days of the strike). It's different among most communities of people on the move, though. There's rarely that sense of collectivity in the same way, because often there's incredible diversity among people brought together simply by shared circumstance. Indeed, terms such as 'migrant' or 'refugee' assume a large amount of homogeneity among those who come from diverse backgrounds and places and who may have little common ground beyond this label (DeGenova 2002). All this makes placing yourself within such 'movements' more complicated. More often you're in touch with a few individuals, such that your responsibility changes, from being one oriented towards a group, to being one oriented towards those individuals. For those who I was active with during the time I was researching this book I was as open as possible (given language and cultural barriers) about what I was doing and why. But I feel a different responsibility to representing their views as I do towards the self-constituted groups I talk about here.

Finally, I want to note that few if any groups agree on everything, and what is often presented to the wider public as a unified position generally has emerged from disagreements, debates and compromises that rarely appear in the final version of events. There was considerable heterogeneity in all of the groups I was involved with. Even though I infer some key logics behind each of their practices, keep in mind that such logics were an amalgam of perspectives, rather than 'one voice' as such. The result is a book that aims to share/reflect on radical knowledge, but that gained that knowledge through a confusing mix of radical and not so radical processes. What does that do to the knowledge you create? This question remains unresolved for me. What it is important for me to reiterate, then, is that the accounts of the groups I talk about in the book are my views. There is no consensus.

Writing from 'we' My ambivalent and outsider/insider relationship to these groups makes me uncomfortable with the idea that I have a right to represent them. Yet I'm more uncomfortable with the idea that misrepresenting others leaves us fearful to say anything about collective action. I'm doing it because I want to express what's transformative and subversive about this struggle and in this way strengthen it. My responsibility as an ally also involves, in my opinion, some degree of representation and taking on all the inherent difficulties and pitfalls of that.[6] I have sought to do this mindful of the responsibility I have to others in doing this.

All that said, I *am* writing from within the no borders movement, which is the movement I have a stake in. Being within the movement makes it more than just my opinion. Movements are a mesh of collaborative processes. We work on projects together, are constantly in discussions – structured or otherwise – that reflect on what we are doing and why. My reflections cannot fail to be influenced by this mesh of collaborative experiences, conversations, texts and ideas. I write with the pronoun 'we' as a way of acknowledging this; of locating myself within the thing I talk about and, in this way, of taking responsibility for it too. Using the pronoun 'we' also makes plain who it is I identify with, which is also who I'm speaking to. The result is not a common position, though. There are many who feel differently.

Defining key terms

The border and the state When we talk about the struggle for the freedom of movement, we often use broad terms to describe something that's counter to or alternative to capitalism and the state. We say that we struggle against the state or against capitalism when we struggle for the freedom of movement. We can say that border control regimes are still ultimately a regime of the state, because borders still ultimately function to define the outer limits of state power. But then what about the involvement of non-state agencies in that regime (quangos like Frontex, or corporations like Sodexho)? What about the intersection of migration with capitalism and global labour relations, or with racism, or imperialism? What about the extension of state power beyond borders (Australia locating its refugee camps in Papua New Guinea, or the UK locating its border guards in French ports)? What about the influence of trans-state entities like the European Union? All of these things change the border regime and make it more complicated than just an effect of the state or capitalism and under contemporary conditions of globalization. Laying everything at the door of the capitalist state seems naïve. To what extent do terms such as 'the state' hold up in describing this complexity?

One solution to this dilemma has been to use more specific terms. Social movements refer to imperialism, neo-colonialism, sovereignty/ sovereign power, globalization or hegemony to bring to the fore particular elements of that which brings into being the border regime. At other times that struggle might be connected with broader struggles against patriarchy, racism, fascism, sexism ... Scholars have sought to reconceptualize the state within the context of globalization (cf. Balibar and Wallerstein 1991; Hardt and Negri 2000; Held 1995; Sassen 2006). For example, Hardt and Negri's influential account of empire conceptualizes sovereign power as a universally networked order that melds the state and capitalism together (Hardt and Negri 2000). In relation to the border regime, Dimitris Papadopoulos, Niamh Stephenson and Vassilis Tsianos (2008) offer an alternative reading of the state under globalization as a system where *multiple* dominating projects and ideologies have proliferated. Post-liberal sovereignty describes the existence of state power through multiple alliances between *segments* of the state with different actors (including individuals, organizations or corporations). This conceptualization nods both to the on-going persistence of the state and to the expression of other sovereignties, such as the emerging governance of the EU, in matters of border control.

Such concepts are useful in explaining the complexity of the system within which the border regime operates, but can easily make talking about struggles against it overly complicated and in that way excluding/exclusive. And I think this proliferation in terms misses something useful and still crucial about the term 'the state'. First, for people struggling for the freedom of movement, the state (or the government) still is that 'thing' that controls their movement, or that 'thing' that they pitch their resistance against. In that struggle, the state still matters, in really tangible ways. It's the thing that makes / upholds the border, or that denies or grants status. For that reason I agree with those scholars who suggest a need to continue to account for and recognize the persistence of the state (cf. Bigo 2002; Sassen 1998; Krasner 2000). Second, and perhaps rather contrary to this, I think we need to think of the state differently.

Following in the tradition of anarchist scholars of social revolution, I think of the state not so much as a thing – as a constellation of social, cultural, economic and legal institutions and norms – but as a particular kind of relationship between people that can lead to those institutions and norms (cf. Kropotkin 1912; Landauer 1983 [1911]; Ward 2008 [1973]). In this sense, the state is more than a bunch of structures around which a familiar kind of territorialized society is organized. It's the practice of certain *forms* of social relation that are based upon relations of hierarchy and domination[7] (cf. Invisible Committee 2009; Landauer 1983 [1911]; Karatzogiani and Robinson 2010). The state is a way of being, rather than a particular organizational or spatial structure that came into being some time around the Middle Ages. We institute the state whenever we create dominating relationships.

Thinking of the state in this way is not about making any claim to an essential human spirit; that we're either inherently 'good' or 'bad'. Rather it is to suggest that we have the capacity for dominating behaviour that leads to the state, and egalitarian behaviour that leads to something else. A consequence of thinking of the state in this way is that it opens us up to imagining alternative, non-dominating ways of organizing our social reality (Karatzogiani and Robinson 2010; Ward 2008 [1973]). 'The State is a condition, a certain relationship between human beings, a mode of behaviour; *we destroy it by contracting other relationships*' (Landauer 2005 [1910]: 64, emphasis added). It also makes it possible to imagine ways of organizing that have no relation to the state at all (Clastres 1977). We might ward off or resist the state, but we might also conduct our relationships in egalitarian ways without any reference to a structure of domination. With these points in mind, then, in this book I use the term 'the state' as something of a catch-all term to describe both a structure (in all its diverse forms) and all those permutations of domination that influence the border regime and beyond.

And when I refer to the border, I'm not only talking about those lines that divide up countries. Borders, labour and sovereignty no longer map neatly onto the space of the nation-state, if they ever did (Andrijasevic 2009; Balibar 2002). As Étienne Balibar has pointed out, borders do not connote a single and unified 'effect'. They are 'polysemic' in that they present themselves differently to different people (Balibar 2002). For some, the border is a fortress, for other it almost doesn't exist. Thinking of borders as polysemic disturbs the strict binaries of inside and outside, or the idea that borders only define the space around territories (Anderson 2000). Borders are physical *and* imagined; material *and* experiential. They aren't just 'things', so much as practices that are reproduced every time we decide who is allowed in and who isn't (Casas-Cortes et al. 2015; Vaughan-Williams 2009). As Harsha Walia suggests, '[i]nterrogating such discursive and embodied borders – their social construction and structures of affect – reveals how we are not just spatially segregated but also hierarchically stratified' (Walia 2013: 9). No border struggles represent a struggle against borders in all their manifestations. These struggles occur in many places beyond what Nicolas DeGenova calls the border spectacle; 'the fetishized image of a "crisis" of border "invasion" or "inundation"' (DeGenova 2011: 104).

Talking about 'migrants' and 'activists' Talking about migration is complicated, because all the terms we could choose to use are so infused with assumptions about who or what we are speaking about that it's near-impossible to say anything about it without inferring some kind of power play. After all, inequality in power is often structured through language, to the extent that language both institutionalizes and stereotypes certain labels (Zetter 1988). The language of migration that has filtered into popular debate overwhelmingly reflects negative ideas about people who migrate without permission, often generating abject, oppressed or victimized identities that deprive them of power. 'Illegal immigrant' implies threat and criminality (Cholewinski 2007; Huysmans 1995). 'Asylum seeker' becomes shorthand for 'victim'; 'migrant' becomes shorthand for 'scrounger'. 'Refugee' excludes those who don't fit within the strict (and state-defined) bounds of persecution. All these terms are generally 'negatively gendered, racialised and classed' (Anderson et al. 2012: 75).

This book focuses primarily on what's known within dominant or state-centric discourse as 'irregular' or 'illegal' migration.[8] If I was working within a state-centric framework, I would use the term illegal migration unproblematically and define it as the unauthorized entry or on-going presence of a person within a territory that is not their state of origin (Düvell 2006; Jandl et al. 2008; Squire 2011). AnaLouise Keating suggests that '[l]anguage's creative power requires that I think carefully and thoroughly about the possible effects my words might have and the effects I desire' (Keating 2002: 523). With this in mind, then, part of the task of critical/radical scholarship is to subvert the normal language that exists. Working within what could be described as a freedom of movement framework, I find the language and concept of human illegality unacceptable in the way it implies that someone can be labelled 'illegal' simply by their presence or their movement across a border. The term 'illegal immigrant' lacks any critical engagement with the constructed nature of such value-laden statuses, or with the fact that people labelled as such contest these terms. It's one of many examples of how we are limited in speaking of the control regime in a critical way when using such language.

There have been many attempts within critical and activist debates to appropriate and challenge such terms. This task is on-going and imperfect, and most of the alternative words we use don't break out of a definition in terms of lack, which makes it difficult to overcome a sense of inequality (Nyers 2010). A person is 'illegalized', 'irregular(ized)', 'undocumented' or 'non-status'. Perhaps 'refugee' is an example where there is not a lack inherent to the term. Yet even this term is limited in creating a language that is not emasculated, brutalized, victimized or medicalized (Pupavac 2008). Sometimes the No Border Network opts for the term 'migrant', because '[c]ategories like refugee, asylum seeker, economic migrant and illegal immigrant are used to divide and control. This is why we use the term "migrant" for all' (No Borders UK n.d.). In places like Calais, though, terms like 'migrant' still don't feel appropriate because they continue to define us in terms of a status of legitimate presence that sets 'us' apart from 'the migrants' and that leaves the 'us', whoever that is, unexplored/unquestioned.

Yet how do we talk about migration in ways that don't reproduce the same socio-political processes that create the very inequalities we seek to oppose? My experience of being in places like Calais, feeling this way and talking to others about it, leads me to suggest that where we can, and where it's appropriate, the best ways we can refer to others is in ways that don't refer directly to those things that separate us in structural ways, but which refer rather in some specific way to the material reality we find ourselves in. In Calais, for example, 'people trying to cross' or 'people living in the jungle' feel more useful terms than 'migrant'[9]; in Athens 'people without papers' does the same. Sometimes a specific migration status seems relevant and important to the discussion, and in those cases I have opted to use the most appropriate and dignified term that helps to describe this.

Creating critical language also means thinking about how we term ourselves, which also involves thinking about who 'we' are. What groups such as No Borders, Calais Migrant Solidarity and the Network for Support to Migrants and Refugees do – groups that I look at in this book, that struggle for the freedom of movement and are largely populated by Europeans with papers – is generally defined as activism and carried out by people who are defined as activists. I define activism as doing which either intentionally or otherwise potentially transforms or escapes the state (concepts I explore in the next chapter). As such, anyone who does such things is an activist, and everyone who I talk about in this book is an activist.

Yet the way the term activist is usually used is not inclusive like this. It tends to set certain people and certain types of activity apart in a way that exacerbates divisions and hierarchy (Andrew x. 2000; Führer 2014). In places like Calais, the term makes it sound as if it's only those who self-define as a participant in radical social change that are activists and create such change (yet most people often apply the term to somebody other than themselves. People rarely define themselves as an 'activist', the real activist often being someone more dedicated, more radical, more …). As such it writes out all those who come to Calais to cross to the UK, and in their crossing subvert the border in a very practical sense. In one email exchange, someone involved in the struggle for the freedom of movement wrote, for me the word activist especially in the context of Calais, is not one we as a 'milieu', movement whatever should be using, unless it applies to everyone. For me, its manifestation is racially and class charged, because we don't usually afford the term 'activist' to clandestine border crossing by 'migrants' or to people who rob [squat] houses; but when no borders affiliated folk enable someone to cross (through support or whatever) or 'expropriate' (rob) tools from houses to use in 'the struggle' It's activism. (Email exchange, Anon., July 2016)

Related to that, people involved in the No Border Network put it well when they say that 'CMS [Calais Migrant Solidarity] activists have said that they have had their assumptions about activism challenged, and have had to re-conceptualise the term activist in recognition of the years many migrants have spent subverting the borders and helping one another in the face of state oppression' (Croydon Migrant Solidarity n.d.). I use the term activist mindful of these perspectives. I use it in this book largely to refer to people directly involved in certain self-defined communities for resistance, but I hope it is clear that what I mean by activist also includes people trying to cross.

What this means for this book is that I have elected to use a diverse range of terms to go beyond and to question the division between 'migrant' and 'activist'. Where I have used terminology from the discourses of control, I have used quotation marks. Where we have not found our own language, the quotation marks mark my dissent.

Chapter outlines

In Chapter 1, I lay out what I mean by a no borders politics in theory. I have already discussed the importance of praxis, both to the kind of politics that I describe here, and to the research method behind this book. A praxis-based approach effectively rules out the possibility of making 'pure' theory that is by definition abstracted from reality and doing. Being rooted in practice means dealing with messy reality, and in doing so accommodating to our thinking the things that go wrong or that don't fit into neat theory. This makes the creation of grand 'theories-of-everything' impossible, and undesirable. In that sense, a no borders politics is an anarchist politics. It shares with anarchism an approach that 'is not an attempt to put a certain sort of theoretical vision into practice, but is instead a constant mutual exchange between inspirational visions, anti-authoritarian attitudes and egalitarian practices' (Graeber 2009: 221).[10]

All of this is a long way of saying that the 'definition' of a no borders politics offered in Chapter 1 is already something that has emerged from dialogue with the practices I describe in the remainder of the book. This chapter is better thought of as offering up a number of themes or currents which are echoed across a range of practices, and which are picked up and explored in more detail in later chapters.

I start by elaborating upon the idea that a no borders politics is a refusal of the border. This idea comes from the activism of the No Borders movement, as well as from activist scholars (cf. Anderson et al. 2012; Nyers 2015; Walia 2013). I explore what a no borders politics is and could be. A no borders politics is about refusing to have our movement confined by the border regime. In that sense, a no borders politics is first and foremost a refusal of the border. This is different from resistance, by which I mean collective practices that engage in a power play or dialogue with the state and that express a different point of view through protest, grassroots and often direct action (cf. Flacks 2004; McAdam et al. 2001; Piven and Cloward 1977; Tarrow 1994). Refusal is a form of resistance, yes. But it is of a kind that also involves opposing the border indirectly; taking action in ways that effectively turn away from the state and seek to live a life as if it wasn't there (Graeber 2009).

This 'turning away' from the border has been a central part of the autonomy of migration thesis, a contribution from activist scholars that has done a lot to challenge the idea that borders are impenetrable, and people who move without permission are just their victims. I elaborate on the autonomy of migration thesis in detail in Chapter 1. Suffice it to say for now that the autonomy of migration thesis argues that people's continued movement without permission expresses autonomy from the state. It is, put another way, the creative energy expressed through the freedom of movement.

Although the autonomy of migration thesis traces a heritage to post-Marxist theories of autonomy (particularly its expression in Italian Autonomia of the late 1960s), autonomy as a broader escape from the state is far from a new idea. *That* can trace a heritage back millennia, to all kinds of experiments in living outside of a formal state structure, or without structured forms of domination (Graeber 2004, 2011). And indeed, in the current capitalist and post-colonial context there are numerous different experiments in living outside the state; from autonomous social centres, communal gardens and collective kitchens, to conscious squats, free parties and action camps. Autonomy is a concept that flows through all these different practices of escape and, as such, I give space in this chapter to exploring in greater detail what it is about autonomy that unites these practices.

Practices of autonomy represent other ways of being to the state. In that sense they are ways of being that potentially escape it. This is what I think is politically valuable about a no borders politics. It fundamentally points to 'escape routes' from the state (Papadopoulos et al. 2008). But in so doing, practices of autonomy are a threat to the state. When visible to it, the state seeks to absorb or destroy such practices. The term 'recuperation' helps to explain what this absorption or destruction means.

A term originally developed by the Situationists, recuperation means a turning back from a 'line of flight', or the recovery by the state of activities that have sought an escape from it (Chasse et al. 1969). Recuperation is the loss of the element of negation by normalizing, codifying or making sense of that escaping behaviour within dominant social reality.[11] I have talked about the dilemma detainee visitors groups often face over engaging with the state. For these groups, visiting people in detention is a key form of solidarity, and contains an element of autonomy. But detention prison management often offers such groups an ultimatum: cooperate with us or else we will deny you access. In these situations, such projects run the risk of recuperation where cooperation can not only lead to a loss of autonomy, but also some degree of re-enforcement of the detention regime. All too often such activities end up being taken over and exploited in such a way as to maintain norms, or even increase domination (Hoy 2004).

As such, a no borders politics cannot only be practices of autonomy. At various points in the history of autonomy – in the struggle for freedom of movement or for black power, or for gender liberation – people have been forced to engage with the state through more visible forms of resistance. Often this has involved a power play with the state; forms of protest that make demands on it for rights or recognition. And this brings out a key dilemma for a no borders politics: how to navigate between autonomous practices that potentially escape the state and visible practices that, in contesting the state, also validate it?

But is it the case that all acts of visibility reinforce the state and undermine autonomy? Often struggles for autonomy have also included demands for visibility within them. Take the black power movement.

Again, for many, this struggle was about autonomy, and included a radical critique of the state and capitalism. Activities that they implemented, such as pre-school breakfast clubs for children of colour, were about creating other social structures that aimed to make reliance on a state that was deliberately failing them obsolete (Katsiaficas and Cleaver 2001). Yet this movement took to the streets often, at the same time demanding to be treated as equals in US society. In the case of the no borders movement, people carry out all kinds of practices that enable them to stay invisible and free from controls. Yet, as I show in Chapter 3, at times when life becomes unsustainable because of the border regime, people have had to come together to make demands on the state. Furthermore, what is important about these two examples, what is potentially 'transformative' about them, is that they directly involved – indeed were led by – those directly affected. As Judith Butler and Gayatri Chakravorty Spivak ask, what does it mean when those denied rights nonetheless act as if they already have them (Butler and Spivak 2007)? This is not a form of protest where the oppressed are given a voice, but one where they take their voice and make it be heard.

Transformation is different from escape. I define it as a constitutive practice that brings something new into our social world (Walters 2008). Transformative practices have the potential to change the logic of the state, or what is understood as politics, or who is understood as a political actor (Johnson 2012). What all this means is that a no borders politics is not only autonomous practices, nor only visible practices, but a constant negotiation of these two things; things which are incompatible in theory but often present together in practice. Often practices of escape bleed into practices of transformation.

A no borders politics is the politics of the no borders movement, but it is a politics that reflects numerous perspectives, and gives rise to numerous different forms of action. This politics shares a name with the No Border Network, but this network forms only a part of the no borders movement. A no borders politics exceeds the No Border Network, and this book is about much more than the perspectives and practices of that network. Chapter 1 defines a no borders politics largely in terms of the actions of people who move without permission. At times, people come together to articulate collective demands, through various forms of visible resistance. However, a no borders politics conceptualizes a movement that is much more diverse than just people who move without permission and in their invisibility do not constitute themselves as a movement in the 'traditional' sense. It primarily concerns people without papers, but it is a movement of people with and without papers. Often these actions bring people with and without papers together to form groups; people struggle together against detention; they march together to assert that 'no one is illegal'. It is in these collectives that the movement for free migration does at times appear like a much more recognizable social movement.

What could be said to unite all those who take part is expressed in a common slogan; that 'the freedom of movement is everybody's right!' Yet beyond that, partly because the struggle for the freedom of movement can be read in a way that resonates with a variety of different ideologies, from anarchist to left perspectives to perspectives that appear to have no ideological basis at all, there is considerable variation. As such, Chapter 2 offers a complement to the theory of a no borders politics laid out in Chapter 1, by looking at the spectrum of perspectives of the different kinds of groups involved in this struggle, and what this tells us about their practice. I look at the perspectives on action of the main actors in this book: 'The 300' hunger strikers from Crete; the No Border Network and Calais Migrant Solidarity as a specific part of that network; the Greek anti-racist movement and the Network of Support to Refugees and Migrants as a specific part of that movement; and the Greek anti-authoritarian movement. I have chosen these four movements or groups because, for me, they express the spectrum of perspectives and practices that make up a no borders politics. In the course of this chapter I bring out what is the second key dilemma for a no borders politics: how to navigate between being together with others in their struggle for liberation while also staying faithful to what is your own struggle. This is, in most part, a dilemma of solidarity. It relates to how a no borders politics is also a constant navigation of people's different abilities to enact their liberation.

Chapters 3 and 4 each provide a case study of the diversity of tactics that different people use to practise the freedom of movement. Chapter 3 looks at Athens during the year I spent living there and participating in various aspects of this struggle. Chapter 4 looks at Calais and draws upon reflections from the various times I have spent there. In each case I wanted to draw out the ambivalence in the struggle for mobility; how this struggle brings people without papers and their supporters into contact and conflict with the state, but also how it creates new ways of being and relating to it.

In each case the people involved in this struggle face numerous practical dilemmas; from difficulties in collaboration between different solidarity groups, to difficulties in building collaborative communities between people with and without papers. In the Conclusion I reflect on what these dilemmas tell us about a no borders politics. These dilemmas raise far more questions than they answer. How do we navigate a way of being that's not 'faithful' to any political agenda? How do we continue to stay ahead of the control regime, in particular when those controls create 'data doubles' of us that predict our future movements, or force us to be immobile? How do we navigate what seems like an irreconcilable incompatibility between privilege and solidarity? How do we ever engage in a politics of rights and representation in such a way that our claim to rights doesn't rest on there being another group to whom the right to rights is denied? How do we create equality if we are largely working within a system the logic of which is unequal? How do we create communities oriented towards autonomy that also recognize how others people's autonomies might be different from ours? How do we use political ideologies in ways that also enable us to respond to the reality we face? As such, I return to the theory of a no borders politics and, in the course of the chapter, reflect on and revise it.

It has been four years since I was last in Athens, but a matter of months since I was last in Calais. In both places the situation has changed dramatically. Yet they are both still represented as key 'flashpoints' in the 'migrant crisis'. And this 'crisis' still makes headlines. With this discourse of crisis, the EU and its member states are responding with more securitization: plans to return all Syrian refugees to Turkey; borders reimposed where before they were open. In the face of all this, it's hard to imagine any room for the idea of the freedom of movement, let alone its practice. But people keep coming. They continue to need or want to move. People continue to assert themselves, and in these assertions we see that, rather than naïve dreaming, no borders is a live political project that's already here.

1 | WHAT IS A NO BORDERS POLITICS?

> Since the creation of the very first illegalised person, whenever and wherever controls have been placed on people's movements, they have been rejected ... No set of border controls has ever worked to fully contain people's desire and need to move. In this sense, it can be argued that an *everyday practice* of refusing the border has existed as long as borders have. (Anderson et al. 2012: 82, emphasis in original)

> Migration is a force of nature. (Slogan on a banner at a protest during the Cop 21, 2015)

I really like the quotes above. I like the way they both express a sense of *inevitability* in human mobility; a sense that mobility is somehow bigger than any of us. I'm generally not a fan of sweeping statements about the human condition. Yet it seems hard to deny that as long as we have walked, we have moved and explored. We spread to cover the whole world, and then we mixed about among each other. We continue to do that. For as long we have existed, we have moved, and our movement expresses so many elements of us; our curiosity, our vulnerability, how we're at the mercy of our environment, how we're arrogant enough to think we can control it. We have generally been the main limit to our ability to move in all that time. Humans have mobility in common, and yet it's perhaps our ability to move that has made us afraid of others and in need to control others' mobility.

I find both these quotes powerful and hopeful too. They point to our tenacity in acting out plans and strategies regardless of what's in the way. They speak to that connection between struggles against the border today, and a vast and venerable history of struggle. The first quote also says something about what this struggle is. It doesn't use the term resistance, which at first glance might seem the more appropriate word, but rather refusal, something that at times has been raucous and at others subtle and hidden. Refusal is a powerful and hopeful term too. It expresses the agency of those who do otherwise but are often seen as powerless. Like resistance, refusal alludes to disobedience, and is a kind of resistance. But there's something more ambiguous or undecided about refusal. It's a rejection, but one that hints at the possibility of something else or something incomplete. I would say it's a more accurate word to describe contemporary struggles for the freedom of movement that can be said to make up a no borders politics.

These quotes are a good place to start in outlining what a no borders politics is (and could be). A number of different lines of scholarship have sought to theorize the struggle for the freedom of movement, in particular the autonomy of migration approach and those approaches that have engaged with and questioned the politics of representation. This chapter lays out the main elements of these theories. In doing this, I draw out what I see as the main dilemma for a no borders politics: how do we seek another way of being from the state while having to navigate our way 'through' it?

A no borders politics is a refusal of the border and the state

Bridget Anderson, Nandita Sharma and Cynthia Wright, authors of the quote that opened this chapter, propose that everyday practices that refuse the border are inherent to a no borders politics. I agree. A no borders politics is, first and foremost, a refusal of the border and, ultimately, this book is dedicated to exploring what that refusal does and can look like in practice. A refusal of the border is an uncompromising stance. 'It doesn't express a desire for "fairer" immigration laws and policies. To the extent that borders create, perpetuate and reinforce inequalities based on unequal access to movement (and settlement), it demands their total rejection' (Anderson et al. 2012: 82).

Borders are technologies of the state, in that they operationalize a state's ability to decide on who can enter and who cannot, who belongs and who does not (Schmitt 2005 [1922]: 1). Because of this intimate connection between borders and states, to refuse the border is also to refuse state sovereignty, in some sense. Indeed, I would argue that a refusal of the border is incompatible with the state, because to think of a world without borders is inherently to imagine a world without states. As Fernandez et al. suggest, '"No Borders", *as a demand on the state*, would thus effectively be a demand that the nation-state give up its own condition of possibility' (Fernandez et al. 2006: 473, emphasis in original). In that sense I think it's necessary to extend Anderson et al.'s definition, and say that a no borders politics is a refusal of the border _and_ the state.

Anderson et al.'s notion of a no borders politics as a refusal emphasizes rejection, but in practice I think it means more than this. Refusal of the border (and the state) is a negative assertion, but it's also a positive assertion of the freedom of movement and settlement. A no borders politics is a rejection – No borders! – but it's also an assertion – Freedom of movement! In that sense refusal is a kind of resistance that is both destructive and creative. What kind of resistance is that?

Theorizing refusal

Social movement studies Social movement studies has been the main field of scholarship to specialize in the issue of what resistance is, who does it and how, so would appear to be a good place to start. If we look within this field, resistance has generally been defined as a collective practice that engages in a power play or dialogue with the state (as I mentioned in the Introduction). Resistance as contestation challenges the status quo.

But struggles like the civil rights movement in the USA, or the struggle for LGBT (and now LGBTQI) rights, or the autonomous movements in Germany and Italy in the 1960s and 1970s, did more than just contest the status quo. They also constructed a different future, based around the reappropriation of social relationships, symbolic systems and information (Melucci 1989; Offe 1985). They demonstrated another way of being to the system, to some degree. Yet this often gets sidelined in social movement studies in favour of describing the 'what' of resistance and producing a 'theory of movements' (Stierl 2012). Put another way, it has focused on social movement as a noun, rather than a verb. In doing this, that part of social movement that affects change within the political system _as it is_ is overemphasized and that part that expresses how things _could be_ is underemphasized. As a result, social movement studies remains weak in exploring movements that _refuse_ established ways of being – the frameworks of identity, rights and self-determination – or that feature people who are largely excluded from politics, as people/travellers without papers invariably are (Flacks 2004; Stierl 2012). What is most powerful about practices that refuse the border is that they do something other than contest dominant power. As I have said already, a refusal of the border is also a refusal of the state. Refusal doesn't express a desire to change those political structures that make up our existing dominant social reality so much as a desire to turn one's back on them and create a *different reality*. As such, a definition of resistance that prioritizes contestation over creativity is not enough, and this field of scholarship has been criticized for being weak in exploring *movements for liberation* that go beyond this definition (Coleman and Tucker 2011; Flacks 2004; Stierl 2012). In writing this book I had doubts that social movement studies provided what felt like useful frameworks or lenses for grappling with a diverse movement that breaks many of the existing understandings of what resistance or social movement is. For that reason I largely leave social movement studies here.

Foucault and power/resistance For me, parts of the work of French post-structuralist thinker Michel Foucault offer a much more useful way of thinking about resistance. Despite scholars' focus on power within his work, Foucault suggested that power could not be thought of separately from resistance. For him, power and resistance constituted each other (Foucault 1982: 223). Foucault saw power as multiple, diffuse and present in all social relations (Foucault 1998 [1978]), from a relationship between two people, up to institutionalized power structures like the state. In seeing power in this way, he rejected any sense that power could be held exclusively by any single force (such as the state). With this in mind, he said that 'there is no single locus of great Refusal, no soul of revolt, source of all rebellions, or pure law of the revolutionary. Instead there is *a plurality of resistances*, each of them a special case' (ibid.: 96, emphasis added).

Foucault posited that power could also not be thought of as a 'thing' in and of itself, but an effect that comes about when it's enacted upon someone/something. In other words power exists as a relation between things or people (Foucault 1982). As a relation, Foucault saw power as neither inherently 'positive' and liberating nor 'negative' and dominating, but rather as a force capable of being either (ibid.). So, although all domination expresses an asymmetrical distribution of power, not all expressions of power are dominating (Hoy 2004).

Taking all this into consideration, what Foucault means by power is broader than domination. It is, in essence, simply the ability for structures, things or people to do. It is the assertion of will. In relation, people or structures or things come up against other forces.

This relation acts as an enabler, or a constraint, a brake or a brick wall. Resistance is inherent to power, then, because power is always in this relational form. In other words, 'where there is power there is resistance' (Foucault 1988 [1978]: 95).

Thinking about power/resistance this way has a number of consequences that I think are highly relevant for conceptualizing a no borders politics. First, it enables us to think about power/resistance as a force that can be both positive and creative, and negative and destructive. Second, it enables us to think about power/resistance as something that both responds to domination and also as something that creates something other to it; something that does not rely on a relation to an external force that we oppose. Thinking about power/resistance in this way has been central to John Holloway's work too. For him resistance is the means of negating the state by creating alternative social relations 'outside' of it. It's both a negative refusal of domination – what he calls 'the scream against' – and a positive assertion of dignity – what he describes as the movement of 'power-to' (Holloway 2002: 1). 'The struggle to liberate power-to is not the struggle to construct a counter-power, but rather an anti-power, something that is radically different from power-over ... This project is far more radical than any notion of revolution based on the conquest of power and at the same time far more realistic' (ibid.: 36–7).

Uri Gordon builds on Holloway's notion of power-to to suggest a second form of anti-power. He argues that there are numerous cases where people get others to do things where there's no coercion. *Power-with* describes a cooperative and collective form of power/resistance where individuals influence each other's behaviour in the absence of a conflict of wills or interests (Gordon 2008). Power-with is an important addition to the thesis that struggles are not dependent on a relation to an external force that we oppose. At first sight this argument seems more theoretically important than it is practically relevant. After all, how many of us get to practise a resistance that is not in relation to something we oppose? However, it has practical relevance too. It requires a reorientation towards those practices that create another way of being distinct from our existing dominant social reality. It posits that resistance can take place in relation to grand structures like the state, but that resistance is not dependent on the existence of such structures for struggles for liberation to exist (Motta and Robinson 2010). Resistance is, in either case, a force that propels us forward.

From a refusal of the border to the autonomy of migration

So far I have said that a no borders politics is the practice of, or struggle for, the freedom of movement. Because it's practised largely by people who are denied this freedom, it also amounts to a refusal of the border and the state. I have also said that it goes beyond just contesting the status quo (dominant social reality), into forms of action that are destructive (in refusing the border and the state as a result) *and* creative (in practising the freedom of movement).

The idea that people who move without permission create something – that they actively affect the border control regime and aren't just passive victims swept up in its wake – has been a central tenet to a small but growing body of scholarship that has come out of conversations over the last fifteen years between activists and scholars who have reflected on, theorized and hence shaped those struggles. In this time, the autonomy of migration approach has gone from being the 'kooky cousin' of migration studies, to a central strand of critical migration scholarship. While the scholars and activists associated with the approach often have different ideas, place emphasis on different things and openly disagree at times, there are a number of main points in the approach which form a common ground. Let me summarize the main points of this approach here.

The autonomy of migration is a way of looking at mobility that takes seriously the agency of people who move. It asserts that mobility is a social fact, something inevitable, and a legitimate and common strategy (Mitropoulos 2007). As such it challenges perceptions that frame people who move either only as victims of circumstance or calculating economic subjects (Anon. 2011; Bojadžijev and Karakayali 2010; Frassanito Network 2004). To understand migration as a social movement is to see people who move as active participants in the construction of reality, not simply as people reacting to economic or social factors (Mitropoulos 2007). In other words, '[t]he border regime does not transform of its own accord, but rather obtains its dynamics from the forms of migration movements' (Bojadžijev and Karakayali 2010: 3). It's an approach that adopts the standpoint of migration, rather than control (Mezzadra 2011; Nyers and Rygiel 2012). In other words, scholars of the autonomy of migration have talked about the strategies that people use to keep moving, or the support networks that build up among people on the move, as much as they have talked about the effects of this or that migration policy. This does not mean being blind to the power of the control regime and its effects. People die in their efforts to cross borders. They are routinely and indefinitely imprisoned; face numerous mechanisms that bar their access to society, often lose their families and their sanity. But without discounting all this, we can still pay attention to how, even under intense restrictions, *resistance still happens*. To focus on mobility rather than control in this way also makes it a political stance that opposes the regime of control through active participation in the regime of migration. It is an approach but it's also a politics that requires of us to show the stake we have in this struggle.

The autonomy of migration approach focuses on the numerous forms of everyday and largely mundane strategies – from making spaces that people can live in while on the road, to travelling on false documents or utilizing smuggling routes – which people denied the freedom of movement use in order to keep enacting the freedom of movement (Papadopoulos et al. 2008). Such practices rarely appear as resistance, but nonetheless subvert border controls in their quintessential refusal to pay attention to the 'rules'. They resonate with what James Scott (1990) termed infra-politics: the undramatic, everyday and mundane acts of quiet evasion – his examples included things like slowdowns, false compliance, feigned ignorance and sabotage carried out by factory workers – that, when performed by many, change or alter a landscape of power. Such actions do not amount to outright defiance; indeed they can at times appear like compliance. But they are underwritten by 'hidden transcripts'; certain strategies or ways of behaviour that are shared among the oppressed group and understood as means of self-determination to them, but are hidden or disguised from those in power (Scott 1985).

As the name suggests, the autonomy of migration approach employs a particular reading of autonomy in the specific context of migration. It traces a heritage to Italian autonomous Marxism (Autonomia, or operaismo), which is a standpoint that reverses the polarity between capitalism and class struggle (Tronti 1964). Rather than thinking of class struggle as being determined by and in response to capitalist development, class struggle is seen as *determining* capitalist development (ibid.). In other words, capitalism is driven by efforts to overcome the insubordination of workers; to capture the 'flight' or 'exodus' of people from enclosure within capitalist work relations.

Struggles over mobility criss-cross the whole history of capitalism, from the moment when the first enclosure in England mobilized the local rural population as well as from the moment when the first slave ship crossed the Atlantic. One could even say that the friction between a politics of migration and a politics of control lies at the very heart of capitalism's history (Mezzadra 2011: 124).

The autonomy of migration posits that human agency is a *creative* force that is expressed through flight that *precedes* any form of control or domination. It constantly forces control to respond in attempts to secure its recapture (Hardt and Negri 2000; Mezzadra and Neilson 2003). People organize, implement and carry out migration all the time outside of and regardless of state intervention (Rodriguez 1996). This 'inappropriate' or unauthorized movement, this 'escape' or flight from control where control cannot take hold, is an assertion of autonomy. It brings about change in the logics of control, rather than the other way round (Bojadžijev and Karakayali 2010; Rygiel 2011).

In the essential inevitability of people's continued movement despite efforts to control it, migration constitutes a social movement where a mass of individual, everyday acts by thousands amounts to a force to which control is compelled to respond (Frassanito Network 2004; Mezzadra 2004a). Some have used the autonomy of migration to express demands for migrant rights, arguing that the movements of migration demonstrate an inherent demand for rights and citizenship (Mezzadra and Neilson 2003). However, escape has two parts to it. On the one hand, there's a part to escape that's in reference to the thing one opposes. On the other hand, there's a part to escape that's entirely self-referential; where lines of flight create entirely other ways of being 'beyond' the system; something that 'has the capacity to develop its own logics, its own motivation, its own trajectories' (Papadopoulos and Tsianos 2013: 184). To some degree these two readings of the autonomy of migration oppose each other (cf. Papadopoulos et al. 2008: 208). Let me turn now to the latter reading.

This second reading of escape emphasizes what's creative about it. Practices of escape constitute some kind of 'other' or 'beyond' to the state. They have the potential to create a *new social reality* rather than a different version of the same social reality. This happens through enacting ways of being that are fundamentally different from and at odds with those that we take as 'the norm', *and* that function through a logic that's incompatible with that of the state. In other words, escape

does to some degree, or at least potentially, manage to *keep on escaping.*
This is a point I shall return to later, in relation to recuperation. Escape
is effectively an 'abandonment' of or a rerouting from the state, however
much the notion is problematic.

No borders as an escape from the state

Escape is a concept that has appeared many times in different forms
of radical political thought. Deleuze and Guattari's (2004 [1987])
liberatory war machine can be said to give escape some kind of form.
Other analogies give escape a special dimension or a place to be. It's
described as a way of being that's analogous to being 'outside' or
'beyond' the totalizing logic of capitalism and the state (cf. Bey 2003
[1991], 2009; Bonanno 2010 [1987]; Deleuze and Guattari 2004
[1987]; Holloway 2002; Invisible Committee 2009; Scott 1990). In
some cases it appears as a movement to, or occupation of, other (kinds
of) 'spaces' or 'gaps' in the system (cf. Anon. 2011). In others it's an
exodus from that system (Hardt and Negri 2000; Tronti 1964). But
none of these terms offers any idea of what escape might look like in
practice. Indeed, they add to the sense that escape – creating an entirely
other way of being to the state – is so entirely theoretical and utopian as
to be totally impossible. It feels as if we would have to radically change
our behaviour and social organization so much as to somehow be other
than our human selves. Yet there are numerous real examples of other
ways of being to the state that bring it back down to earth.

Scholars largely from within the field of anthropology have perhaps
had the most to say about the kaleidoscope of ways that humans
have found to organize themselves without any kind of organized
structure of domination (of which the state is the example that has
come to be dominant). Perhaps most notable is the sociologist Pierre
Clastres' (1977) historical studies of numerous tribes, as well as his
own ethnographic research with the Tupi-Guarani tribe of Brazil and
Paraguay. He argued that what distinguishes so-called primitive societies
from so-called civilized ones is the absence of the state. He argued that
primitive societies organize themselves in such a way as to deliberately
ward off the state, by which he meant a structured form of dominating
behaviour that is 'the soil in which the genealogy of the State has its
roots' (ibid.: 173). Furthermore, he argued that such societies organize
themselves in this way *regardless* of whether they have any contact with
an actual state or not. In other words, he saw the state as a structure, but

posited that these structures have a basis in social relations of domination. He suggested that 'primitive' societies are organized 'by the prohibition ... of inequality', and in that way 'are societies without a State because for them the State is impossible' (ibid.: 168, 173).[1]

In many cases such societies have developed imaginative constructions of the cosmos that value practices of egalitarianism and vilify practices that accumulate power (ibid.; Graeber 2004). This has often involved constructing world views where spectres, demons and evil otherworldly beings embody these negative values and are feared (Graeber 2011). In contemporary, consciously anarchistic projects those spectres can be said to have been replaced by capitalism. But the underlying logic is similar: create a world view where egalitarianism is valued and hierarchy is not. David Graeber, who has elaborated on the political significance of much of Pierre Clastres' work, suggests that '[a]narchistic societies are no more unaware of human capacities for greed or vainglory than modern Americans are unaware of human capacities for envy, gluttony, or sloth; they would just find them equally unappealing as the basis for their civilization. In fact, they see these phenomena as moral dangers so dire they end up organizing much of their social life around containing them' (Graeber 2004: 24).

Experiments in living without or 'beyond' the state are happening all the time around us now, in our contemporary, urban 'civilization'. They are what Richard Day (2005) has labelled the newest social movements.[2] Here we are talking about a whole multitude of different struggles, from specific border-focused resistances such as the various migrant-led movements, No-one Is Illegal or No Border Networks, to the anti-summit protests that were most explosive during the 1990s. Escape is present in the various experiments in living 'beyond' the state, from the Zapatistas, to the anarchist communes of the Spanish Civil War, to the numerous indigenous tribes that have organized their societies in egalitarian ways, to various pirate communities and ex-slave colonies (cf. Bey n.d.; Clastres 1977; Marcos 2004; Martignoni and Papadopoulos 2014). It's present in a whole host of intentional communities organized around some kind of doing. It's present in 'those crucibles of human sociability and creativity out of which the radically new emerges: racialized and ethnicized identities, queer and youth subcultures, anarchists, feminists, hippies, indigenous peoples, back-to-the-landers, "deviants" of all kinds in all kinds of spaces' (Day 2005: 183).

Escape can sound completely unattainable and far too spectacular. Yet it can also sound deeply realistic and in fact quite mundane if we pay attention to all those actually existing experiments in living equally that stretch back through the whole of human history and are taking place right now. Escape isn't something people are reserving for some future time 'after the revolution' but a *practice* – a way of seeing and being – that's taking place right now.

Escape as the mobile commons If we return our focus to the struggle for the freedom of movement, then some scholars of the autonomy of migration approach have also had something to say about what this particular form of escape looks like. The mobile commons describes an 'other way of being' to the state; a realm of activity that's organized, out of necessity, largely through non-hierarchy and equality, and functions as a means through which people can pursue the freedom of movement. Dimitris Papadopoulos and Vassilis Tsianos describe the mobile commons as

> the innumerable uncoordinated but cooperative actions of mobile people that contribute to its making. People on the move create a world of knowledge, of information, of tricks for survival, of mutual care, of social relations, of services exchange, of solidarity and sociability that can be shared, used and where people contribute to sustain and expand it. (Papadopoulos and Tsianos 2013: 190)

Papadopoulos and Tsianos define the mobile commons as comprising five main areas: 'the invisible knowledge of mobility' that circulates between people to facilitate their movement (knowledge about routes, safer spaces, border crossing methods and so on) or their settlement (how to access support structures, or knowledge of local communities); an 'infrastructure of connectivity' (the use of social media or mobile devices to keep in touch and share information); 'a multiplicity of informal economies' (how to send and receive money, how to find smugglers; what's a 'fair' rate to pay; how to rent a house, etc.); connections to 'diverse forms of transnational communities of justice' (solidarity groups, NGOs, charities, political groups and so on, something I shall explore in the following chapter); and a 'politics of care' (mutual cooperation, friendships, favours that you can never return, affective support, trust, care for other people's relatives and children, transnational relations of care, the gift economy between mobile people, etc.) (ibid.: 191–2).

The mobile commons is a realm of use. It's a world built by being reproduced by people who need to access it, rather than being owned by or attributed to any individual or group. In other words, it's accessible to anyone by virtue of their participation, and exists only through the interrelationship and collaboration of people. It's an inherently collective, social 'space' that reflects a deep interdependence. It is a gift economy because it relies on reciprocity in situations of extreme dependability. It is shared and generated in the act of being mobile.

> Migration ... is by definition a process which relies on a multitude of other persons and things. This extreme dependability can only be managed through reciprocity, and reciprocity between migrants means the multiplication of access to mobility for others. Multiplying access is the gift economy of migration. This is the world of the mobile commons. (Ibid.: 190)

The mobile commons is a resource, not for getting by within the state, but for getting by outside of it. Because of this it's largely invisible to dominant society/the state, not only because being invisible is a way of remaining autonomous (Papadopoulos et al. 2008), but also because it operates according to a different logic (autonomy) that's incompatible with that of the state (hierarchy) (Karatzogiani and Robinson 2010). The mobile commons is another world.

That's not to say that the mobile commons functions perfectly. People engage in it because they have to, and not just because they are nice. There are plenty of people connected to the commons who use it to exploit others, and in situations where people are in need, many will seek out an advantage if they can. Alongside the gift economy is a very big informal economy of exploitation – anything from other people on the move who charge others for additional help in their journeys, to large, international, organized crime syndicates that are often backed up by violence. But without discounting this, the mobile commons remains largely a realm of cooperation, mutual aid and equality.

Autonomy beyond the autonomy of migration

So far I have talked about the autonomy of migration as an approach that sees migration without permission as a form of escape from sovereign power/the state, and have said that the mobile commons is a way of imagining what that escape looks like in practice. But escape is not only practised by those who move without permission – or, put another way, the struggle for the freedom of movement does not only involve and concern people who are denied it (although it does primarily concern them). The concept of autonomy here is a useful one in that it enables us to extend outwards from the autonomy of migration, to look at autonomy as a thread that connects together different forms of escape that all impact upon the regime of mobility. For that reason I would like to explore the concept of autonomy in a little more detail. In doing this I think we can make more clear the connection between the particular struggle of people who move without permission and other particular struggles that all, in their own way, undermine the state or render it redundant.

As I have said so far, the autonomy of migration thesis largely draws on the concept of autonomy from Italian Autonomia of the 1960s and 1970s. But the concept goes back far farther than that. Drawing on its Greek roots, autonomy means self (*auto*) law (*nomos*). Put another way, it's 'the custom or law of the self', or the capability of an individual to self-legislate (Firth 2010). It's a concept that's been used by numerous ideologies and theoretical perspectives, sometimes to justify opposing political ideas. For example, two of the dominant perspectives for which autonomy is a key principle – liberalism and Autonomia/operaismo – express radically different political perspectives. In this book I'm not referring to that reading of autonomy central to modern liberal thought (following Immanuel Kant) that justifies individual self-legislation and the right to private property through reason, driven by universal moral 'laws'.[3] Neither (as I have mentioned already) am I referring only to that reading of autonomy used within Autonomia that restricts it to the realm of labour relations. I'm interested in autonomy as the creation of alternative modes of being and becoming to that of the state (Cleaver 2008; Deleuze and Guattari 2004 [1987] *passim*; Firth 2012; Katsiaficas 2007). Let me now elaborate on that particular reading of autonomy.

Autonomy as the actualization of individual desire Within the various anarchist, post-anarchist, post-Marxist and post-structuralist texts that explore autonomy as the creation of an alternative way of being, there are multiple interpretations, or differing emphases.

Certain strands of scholarship have drawn out how autonomy is a practice of complete individual freedom that begins from recognizing and expressing our desires[4] and relating to others upon that basis. In that sense autonomy is a practice of expressing our own ethic, rather than any normative morality that imposes 'shoulds' on us. Autonomy here is about an engagement with our selves as beings irreducible to pre-existing characteristics of identity (Robinson 2010a). It's about exploring and embracing what's unique and different in us; what doesn't – can't – conform, or at least can't be reduced to or fitted into the representational realm. In this sense autonomy is entirely un/ anti-representational because, in expressing our desires, we become irreducible to fixed and known/knowable identities (ibid.).

Scholars such as Wolfi Landstreicher/Feral Faun (2009), Hakim Bey (2003 [1991], 2009), the Invisible Committee (2009) and Raoul Vaneigem (2003 [1967]) have all drawn out the centrality of being in the present to this radical individualist interpretation of autonomy. They emphasize creating moments of spontaneity, temporariness, pleasure, playfulness, abundance, chaos and insurrection; moments when you are completely absorbed in the present moment, and fully self-realizing. Such experiences are part of generating routes out of our own alienation under capitalism. Hakim Bey expresses how responding to our desires first and foremost is a route out of alienation when he says, '[w]hen the last cop in our brain is gunned down by the last unfulfilled desire – perhaps even the landscape around us will change' (Bey 2003 [1991]: 33).

Autonomy as a practice of collective organization Those scholars who emphasize the radical individualist elements of autonomy make autonomy appear a selfish practice. But I don't think this is what they mean. What I think they point to is rather how autonomy has at its base a self-regard upon which we build collective social structures (Heckert 2010). Anyway, it doesn't really seem that useful to think of autonomy only in individualized terms when most of our experiences of the world are collective (Castoriadis 1987). Other strands of radical scholarship have emphasized this collective dimension to autonomy. This nonetheless highlights a major tension within autonomy as it negotiates reconciling the desires of individuals with those of others in a (potential) community (Faulks 2000; Firth 2010). As such, autonomy can be further defined as the collective responsibility for organizing and constructing norms in the absence of any pre-existing shared 'laws' and in the presence of difference (Anon. 1999; Katsiaficas 2007; Colebrook 2009).

The collective organization of autonomy through prefiguration As a practice of collective organization, autonomy can be thought of as a way of building the kinds of relationships and, from there, society that you would want to see in the world. Crucially, then, it's a practice that's not about advocating change in theory, or making plans for it some time in the future, but living it right now (Gordon 2008). This also points to how radical social change is not just about big mobilizations and spectacular demonstrations, but is a day-in, day-out way of being that's embedded in everyday life (Motta and Robinson 2010). Autonomy is not so much about reproducing the social world as is, but about *prefiguring* the social world we want to live in (Day 2005). Autonomy is a practice of prefiguration, then; a big word for a simple idea. Some of the most memorable ways of thinking about prefiguration are as 'building a new world from the shell of the old', or living out the idea that 'another world is possible'.

Prefiguration is a practice of radical equality In relation to no border struggles, escape involves prefiguring a borderless world. So far I have argued that prefiguring such a social world means organizing according to autonomy, which involves starting from expressions of individual desire and then connecting to others upon that basis. This in turn means starting from a position that values each individual's uniqueness and creativity, and that treats each individual as important in their own right. In practical terms this means organizing in a way that gives voice and space to everybody. This essentially simple principle of organization has been given numerous different names to describe it: from horizontalism to direct democracy, consensus to non-hierarchy and non-domination. For me, the most suitable term to describe this practice is equality.

Equality is an unpopular term in contemporary writing on autonomy, but I think it's the best way of describing what's at the core of it as a collective, prefigurative practice. It's come to be out of favour, partly because of its association with discourses on human rights (which qualifies equality by making it a condition of those in receipt of rights granted by a state, hence implying that there are those who, without rights, also don't qualify as equal; see Arendt 1973 [1951]), and partly because of its association with Marxism (with notions of the equal distribution of resources in society, an idea that similarly sees equality as a resource for distribution). Rather than these meanings, I use equality in the way that Jacques Rancière uses it, as a presupposition between people of each other's inherent parity that's qualified by nothing so much as us all being human (Rancière 1999, 2004). 'Equality is not a given that politics then presses into service, an essence embodied in the law or a goal politics sets itself the task of attaining. It is a mere assumption that needs to be discerned within the practices implementing it' (Rancière 1999: 33).

A no borders politics other than escape

So far I have described a no borders politics as practices of autonomy, by which I mean practices that negate the state and render it redundant by creating other ways of being to it. I looked at the autonomy of migration approach as one that explores autonomy specifically in the context of people who move without permission. Because the struggle for the freedom of movement concerns and involves more than just those who move without permission, I broadened out the discussion on autonomy, seeing it as a thread that connects a whole host of different experiments in abandoning the state.

But to what extent are these experiments in autonomy ever entirely autonomous? In response to Richard Day's book on the newest social movements, Richard Thompson argues that it's unrealistic to talk about creating wholly autonomous social structures because '[t]he second they're consequential is the second they'll be noticed [by the state]. At that point, it becomes impossible to break the cycle of antagonism by will alone. *They will come after us*' (Thompson n.d., emphasis added). In other words, experiments in autonomy are rarely (if ever) entirely free from a relation to the state, or from state antagonism, and we are rarely able to ignore that antagonism. We may antagonize the state, but we are forced also to respond to the state, as a form of self-defence. This has happened time and time again, from the steady illegalization of squatting in Europe, and the tightening of laws around private property, to the infiltration by the CIA of the Black Panther movement, to the struggle between the Zapatistas and the Mexican state. We see this in the struggle for the freedom of movement when, continuing with the examples above, the EU employs Frontex special missions on the Turkish/Greek borders, or when the living spaces of people without papers are raided or destroyed.

Whether people have been forced to, or they have seen it as the best strategy, the history of struggles for liberation has been one that included demands on the state. Often this has taken the form of engagement in a politics of rights and/or recognition. From the movement of the Sans Papiers in France, to 'a Day without Migrants' in the USA; from campaigns that fight against the detention and deportation of people without papers, to struggles against police violence, resistance through forms of visible collective action have been central to struggles against the border. In most cases such struggles have made demands on the state, particularly through seeking recognition as a group, and through making claims to rights. But to what extent are demands for rights and/or recognition part of a no borders politics?

Demands for rights and recognition have played a big part in the struggle for the freedom of movement. Yet there has been a long history of criticism over the politics of citizenship within which such demands for right and recognition are made. Rights claims, for example, have been seen as essentially reinforcing the role of the state as the benefactor and grantor of rights, and reinforcing the notion that rights represent entitlements applicable to those who fit certain descriptions of being a human (cf. Arendt 1973 [1951]; Barbagallo and Beuret 2008; Bojadžijev and Karakayali 2010; Elam 1994). From this perspective, demands for rights and representation amount to disputes over the allocation of equality and therefore can only ever achieve a redistribution of that equality, rather than undermining the idea that equality is somehow qualified in the first place. As Imogen Tyler says, '[c]itizenship is a famously exclusionary concept, and its exclusionary force is there by design. The exclusions of citizenship are immanent to its logic, and not at all accidental. Citizenship is meant to produce successful and unsuccessful subjects. Citizenship, in other words, is "designed to fail"' (Tyler, quoted in Nyers 2015: 31).

Similar variations of this critique have appeared in the autonomy of migration debate. Representation can also be thought of as a bordering technology that seeks to pacify and discipline expressions of autonomy (or attempts at escape) (Papadopoulos et al. 2008). In other words, the politics of citizenship is problematic because it only ever brings people into the state. 'Of course migrants become stronger when they become visible by obtaining rights, but the demands of migrants and the dynamics of migration cannot be exhausted in the quest for visibility and rights' (ibid.: 219).

I have a lot of sympathy with these arguments, and because of them am extremely suspicious of a politics of citizenship. But when it comes to actual practices of struggle against the border, a resolute stand against such strategies seems naïve, and insulting to those who have taken part. Migrant-led struggles have often been claims for rights, and ultimately I don't want to dismiss such practices because they are philosophically problematic. In fact, sometimes to appeal to rights or recognition is the only available strategy in situations of extreme vulnerability, where people's options are highly limited. Recognizing that we are in relations of power right now means also recognizing that our situation is imperfect and that we have to struggle in our (imperfect) reality. Youssef, a long-time activist for the freedom of movement in Greece, himself of North African descent, talked about the need for pragmatism in tactics; that sometimes we must engage with the state in order to bring about greater freedoms now. 'Today, in Creta, in Chania, they will catch five people. How can I take them from the jail? I have something in the police station, OK. I have to talk with them today. OK? But tomorrow I can fuck him. He's not my friend. He's not my comrade. OK. We are talking today. Tomorrow we are fucking' (interview, Youssef). His statement reflects how many practices that refuse the border often come out of necessity. In other words they're rarely part of some intentional or 'noble' act to become a rights-bearer, say, and more often pragmatic decisions based on the need to alleviate immediate situations of oppression.

A no borders politics seeks to go beyond claims to representation and rights that ultimately stand to reinforce the state. But claims to representation and rights can sometimes do this too. Building on Foucault's idea that power can be both positive and empowering or negative and dominating, Biddy Martin and Chandra Mohanty suggest that fighting oppression involves seeing power in a way that refuses totalizing visions of it and can therefore account for the possibility of resistance, as in creating something new, *within* existing power relations (Martin and Mohanty 2003: 104). Suggesting that representation only ever brings people into power therefore means rejecting a vast range of moments when the oppressed have voiced their *refusal* to be reduced to non-beings outside of politics (Sharma 2009: 475). In other words, resistance is not only or always a reaction to the constraining effects of dominating power, but can also express power as something positive and liberating. From the Black Panthers to the Sans Papiers, demands for representation, when carried out by minority groups for themselves, can challenge the role of dominant power over that group and create new, emancipated subjectivities (Goldberg 1996; Malik 1996). Depending on who it is that acts, then, in some cases demands for recognition/rights *can* be a radical and transformative political act (Nyers 2015. See also Butler and Spivak 2007; Isin 2008; Nyers and Rygiel 2012). As Nandita Sharma suggests, in response to Papadopoulos et al.'s book *Escape Routes*,

> we must recognise that making life and fashioning our subjectivities are intimately intertwined and making 'new social bodies' ... is *not the same* as bringing people back into power through identity politics (or identity *policing*). It is important to recognise that there are significant qualitative differences between subjectivities. There are those that Papadopoulos et al. rightly discuss as bringing us directly back into power – and which account for most of the subjectivities that people hold today ('race', 'nation', 'heterosexual', 'homosexual', 'native' and so on) – but there are also those that are born of *practices* of escape. (Sharma 2009: 473, emphasis in original)

Disagreement So far I have said that, although demands for rights and representation are often dismissed as theoretically conservative, in practice they can be a strategy that brings about greater freedoms in that moment, and, depending on who acts, can transform the logic of political membership. A number of interventions in the fields of critical citizenship and, more broadly, continental political theory have explored this. Let me begin by turning to the dilemma over rights as captured by the scholar Hannah Arendt. To summarize, she argued that if all humans, by being human, have a right to rights, then without a community through which such rights can be conferred, there is no means to 'access' them (Arendt 1973 [1951]). Put another way, the question of who has a right to rights is a double dilemma: either rights belong to those who have no rights (i.e. those excluded from the political) and are effectively empty, or they belong to those who have rights (those already included in the political) and are superfluous (Rancière 2004: 302). In both cases any claim to rights appears trapped in the logic of exception/exclusion, reaffirming the logic of insider/outsider every time a claim to rights is made.

Jacques Rancière is also concerned with those to whom the right to rights is due, but approaches the issue in a way that seems to offer a route out of Arendt's dilemma. He suggests there is a third possibility: what about the rights of those who, excluded from what we think of as the political (and hence rights), demonstrate that this exclusion is false? (ibid.: 302). Rancière is concerned with the political power of the excluded, as the excluded. He suggests that it's precisely in the dispute over the existence of 'the line' between inclusion and exclusion – the political and the non-political – rather than in any dispute over where to draw the line, that politics takes place (ibid.: 303). This creates a radically different view of what politics is.

For Rancière, politics is a rare and ephemeral thing. It happens only when the part that has no part (the part excluded from political society) interrupts what we perceive to be politics, by practising an equality that makes plain a disagreement (Rancière 1999).[5] Let me break down what this statement means.

The part that has no part can be defined as the excluded: those people who are of no account to political society. Being of no account is not the same as not being there. Rather it means to be effectively discounted from politics; to be invisible as a political subject and for the things that you say to not be heard as political speech at all (ibid.: 30). Rancière gives the example of Jeanne Deroin, who, in 1849, presented herself as a candidate for a legislative election that as a woman she was unable to run in. In attempting to take part, Deroin demonstrated the contradiction of a supposed universal suffrage that excluded women. She demonstrated the presence of those not counted as properly political subjects. Rancière describes this as demonstrating the miscount: of making visible that part which is not counted as equal (ibid.: 123). This for Rancière is politics.

What politics is not, then, is the system of rules and norms that shape our social world. Rancière labels this the police order. The police order is 'an order of the visible and sayable' (ibid.: 29, emphasis added). It establishes the rules, norms, discourses, practices and institutions that structure the 'stage' upon which a certain idea of politics can take place. As an order of the visible and sayable, it determines what and who counts as a political subject; what is possible and impossible, available and unavailable, as political discourse; what is intelligible or legitimate as political community (Nyers 2008; Rigby and Schlembach 2013). Fundamentally the police order seeks to fix designations over the terms by which people are considered as counting. It attributes abstract values to particular people. For example, citizens are the ones who have rights (which can be broken down further as the ones who have freedom and equality, for instance). The abstract notion of equality becomes a 'thing' that we attain rather than something that exists innately.

Disagreement centres on expressing the equality of those outside the count, so equality is central to Rancière's conceptualization of politics. In sum, for him equality is essentially a *practice*. It's not a resource that's granted to people, but a presupposition between people of each other's inherent equality that is qualified by nothing so much as someone being human (Rancière 1999: 300). Equality is assumed to be inherently present in politics, rather than existing as a right that is the goal of or after politics (May 2010; Newman 2011). Being of no consequence, the existence of a part that has no part, indicates that equality is missing, because it points to a status that's less than equal. Disagreement comes about when this inequality is made visible, and this happens when people who are denied equality *act out their equality anyway*. In so doing they interrupt the police order. In some respect they shame dominant political society.

For me, this understanding of equality undermines the idea of big-'P' politics, as in an activity that takes place only in specific and public realms, in properly political places. Instead it suggests that politics happens in all those ways we enact equality. In the practice of equality, it also potentially points to possibilities for escaping sovereign power, into a different way of being that's not based on domination, by removing the distinction between politically qualified and unqualified life.

Disagreement is first and foremost a means by which equality is tested in practice. It's inherently about conflict rather than consensus. As such, it reflects the collision of fundamentally different ways of being. Politics, Rancière declares, 'is made up of relationships between worlds' (Rancière 1999: 42). Disagreement is therefore provocative in that it contains the potential to rupture accepted norms and values. Practices that create dissensus are a part of a no borders politics because they have the potential to express equality, which has the potential to escape the state. However, this conceptualization of politics is not really interested in the change that those seeking action are after (May 2010). It's not that this conceptualization of politics dismisses change, but rather that disagreement is not about engaging with or describing any kind of *resolution* to a dispute. As Todd May suggests,

[i]n some sense, there is already change in the very appearance of
the movement, a change in the partition of the distribution of the
sensible. If we go further than this, we risk betraying the character
of democratic politics that Rancière has posited. For if we require
political change in order for there to be a real politics, a democratic
politics, then that politics depends not on the presupposition of
equality but on the response of those who so often deny it. (Ibid.: 41)

A group previously excluded from political society that becomes
part of the inside represents a move in the boundary of the miscount
through the inclusion of a new subjectivity, rather than the removal of
that boundary. For Rancière, the resolution of a disagreement is just
a return to business as usual; a return to the police order. From this
perspective, representation, constructing knowable subjects, is a tool of
the police order (Rancière and Panagia 2000). It's a means by which
disagreement is resolved by rendering the forces partaking in social
conflict visible, knowable and controllable to the gaze of power-over.
Control encounters escape with representation, which functions by
ordering and controlling the different parts of society that make up the
visible part, based on access – but fundamentally unequal access – to
rights (Papadopoulos et al. 2008). All this makes Rancière's a distinctly
anti-representational project (Nyers 2010: 131). Yet disagreement still
has a strong relationship to a politics of rights and representation (and
indeed it has been used as a conceptual tool to explain demands for
rights and recognition within no borders struggles (cf. Nyers, 2006,
2008, 2010; Rigby and Schlembach 2013). Through the concept of
disagreement, Rancière is seeking to recast a politics of rights and
representation in a way that does away with the distinction between
the included and the excluded. 'The task of politics therefore becomes
something other than representing the unrepresented. Something
much more ambitious, difficult and radical is at work here. The task
becomes theorizing the political in relation to the unrepresentable'
(Nyers 2010: 131). The focus lies at that point before resolution,
before representation.

Acts of citizenship The concept of acts of citizenship complements
disagreement in that it looks at what can be potentially transformative
through or after representation. Both focus on how those otherwise
excluded from politics constitute themselves as political subjects,
through the transgression of the boundaries of the political and

non-political (Moulin and Nyers 2007). Whereas disagreement focuses on practices of equality that create another way of thinking about the political, the acts of citizenship approach focuses on how representation can bring into being new, liberated political subjectivities that change the logics of political membership. Acts of citizenship are described as acts that *rupture habitus*: that fundamentally disturb or change the norms and logics that underpin dominant social reality (Isin 2008).

The acts of citizenship approach sees citizenship as something that's not only a formal legal status, or something tied to the state, but equally a dynamic process/practice that can also create new ways of being and new ways of thinking about belonging (cf. Bojadžijev and Karakayali 2010; Isin 2002, 2008, 2009; Balibar 2004a; Nyers 2010). As a praxis, it's not constructed only by (already existing) citizens, but also by those (currently) excluded from it (Hill Maher 2002; Sassen 2006). In order for citizenship to be possible, abject subjects must exist that represent the other to citizenship (Isin 2002). For example, undocumented migrants are not simply excluded from contemporary forms of citizenship, but are constituted as the other to citizenship. Citizenship is constantly contested and transformed by those included and excluded by it.

Citizenship is a dynamic and dialogical process, then, and acts of citizenship have the potential not just to make new citizens, but to make new ideas about what political membership is and means (McNevin 2011). Such struggles question the very validity of 'legal' and 'illegal', 'citizen' and 'non-citizen'. As such they potentially challenge the legitimacy of the nation-state over what remains of its ability to control access to political membership.

The autonomy of migration approach and the acts of citizenship approach can be seen as two of the most important strands of scholarship in contemporary critical migration studies. Both speak to what a no borders politics is in theory. On the one hand we have the argument that freedom of movement is expressed through the autonomy of migration; a politics that is all about creating other ways of being from the state. On the other hand we have the argument that people who move without permission are forced to engage in contentious dialogue with the state and in doing so they transform the state and bring potentially new liberated subjectivities into being. Both approaches work from the perspective of mobility rather than control, and both put migrant agency rather than control as central. Yet despite these similarities, neither has spoken much to each other's concerns (or at least until recently) (Nyers 2015). Indeed, Peter Nyers, one of the leading proponents of the acts of citizenship approach, has argued that one reason for this is that the autonomy of migration approach tends to reduce struggles to some kind of zero-sum game where either mobility is primary or control is, and where the only part of struggles that count are those acts that are somehow untainted by state engagement (ibid.). In reality, struggles for the freedom of movement are much more complicated than that, and he argues that this approach could be enhanced by looking at the ambivalent relationship between the two, of which citizenship is an inevitable part.

I agree, but I can also make sense of why these two approaches have largely been so separate. I think that's because each approach is describing a very different form of being political. Acts of citizenship speaks to hybridity, tension and change within 'the system'. It works through an assumption of navigating between inside and outside. The autonomy of migration approach, on the other hand, speaks of absolutes: of seeking out another world through a wholesale rejection of this one. As Martina Martignoni and Dimitris Papadopoulos suggest, 'migration is not primarily a movement that is defined and acts by making claims to instituted power' (2014: 38). Without this sounding too much like a judgement call, it could be said that the autonomy of migration approach is less interested in negotiating with the state, or at least less interested in what's politically at stake in such negotiations. As such I'm not sure that the autonomy of migration approach denies that acts of citizenship are important, or even a part of a radical politics of mobility. I just think they see such acts as tangential to the struggle for the freedom of movement.

> Citizenship and borders are the main two (interconnected) tools for governing and controlling the autonomy of migration and at the same time they are continuously challenged and reshaped by people on the move ... This does not mean that migration is all about struggles over citizenship, though; rather, struggles over citizenship are the effects of the control of – and at the same time an opportunity for – autonomous mobility. (Ibid.: 39)

In reality, I think people on the move engage in both all the time. They carry out strategies – whether alone or collectively – that keep them invisible from state control. At other times they create themselves (or are created) as a recognizable group and make demands on the state. They engage in one or the other ways of being political. One interviewee expressed this sentiment as how the distinction between autonomy and representation is clear in theory, but distinctly blurred in practice:

> Often I find that they [autonomous practices versus representational practices] actually fit more easily together than I would think from the outset because often it's more like conceptually you find that it's hard to get your head around, but actually in practice it flows more easily than it sounds just because people have such a different position; that the people you're building political affinities with might be in a very different position from you because of their particular privileges, but actually you find yourself quite comfortably in both positions and still find affinities in both directions ... I just often conceptually find it difficult but in practice then it's not, because it just means you are building particular affinities in a direction where the position of power is so different. If you don't have a passport for example the kind of demands or tactics you are going to be making are quite different. (Interview, Anon. 7)

Different elements of autonomy and representation are often mixed in together in practice and often overlap. People on the move might hold demonstrations calling for the protection of their autonomous spaces; they might demand the right to work even as they plan the next stage of their journeys. There are bits of practices of escape in struggles that appear largely about contestation, and vice versa. Autonomy and representation are both tactics. As Martina Tazzioli suggests, '[i]n the case of unauthorized migration, both visibility and political representation form a battlefield: the invisibility of migrants' presence is at times produced by mechanisms of capture and at times it is strategically played out by migrants themselves. Representation is at the same time what is claimed by many migrant struggles, and what is dodged by them' (Tazzioli 2015: 2).

Yet ultimately I think the tension that exists between the autonomy of migration approach and the acts of citizenship approach is what's fundamentally at stake for a no borders politics. It highlights that a no borders politics is not just about escape (it can't be), but is about negotiating between transformative practices that potentially change the logics of the state and escaping practices that amount to other ways of being to it. It's not just that claims for representation undermine struggles for autonomy (so that our task is to just ignore them and focus on the autonomy part). It's that such claims seem intimately tied up with the struggle for autonomy. Yet these two things are somewhat incompatible with each other. When people move autonomously and challenge the foundations of the state, they reinforce its logics every time they (are forced to) engage in any claims to visibility or rights. Because representation, as much as it might be transformed by challenges to it, nonetheless paradoxically undermines our ability to be autonomous. Yet until we are living entirely autonomously, we have to negotiate with existent social reality. We seek another way of being to the state, while also having to navigate our position within it. In that sense, a no borders politics involves a diversity of tactics.

Conclusion

In this chapter I have sought to bring out what a no borders politics is and can be by engaging in a number of theoretical concepts that explain it better. In doing this, I progressively defined what I mean by a no borders politics. In summary, I argued that a no borders politics is first and foremost a refusal of the border and the state. It goes beyond contesting the state, by seeking to remain autonomous from it. This autonomy can also be seen as a practice of escape from the state. For those who move without permission, this escape is largely temporary and unintentional. People do not move to refuse the border and the state. It is, to some degree, an unintended effect. Yet there are a whole host of experiments in living 'beyond' or 'outside' the state that are going on all the time, which are very much intentional, and which also amount to a refusal of the state. In that sense, a no borders politics does not just concern people without papers, and is not really just about migration. All kinds of people are seeking escapes from the state. I went on to explore the concept of autonomy in more detail, then, as a means of drawing a connection between the escapes of people without papers and others.

Yet despite the fact that I argued that escape is not reliant on a relation to an external dominant force for its existence, it is the case that contemporary practices of escape are almost entirely in relation to that which we oppose. Coming back to Richard Thompson, '[t]he second they're consequential is the second they'll be noticed [by the state]. At that point, it becomes impossible to break the cycle of antagonism by will alone. *They will come after us*' (Thompson n.d., emphasis added). As such, I went on to argue that demands for rights and recognition also play a part in a no borders politics. Concepts such as disagreement and acts of citizenship draw out what is potentially escaping and transformative about such practices. In the case of acts of citizenship, when non-status migrants come together in protest and act as if they were already rights-bearing, this can transform the logics of political membership. Yet there is a fundamental tension there, between autonomous practices that seek to escape the state, and representational practices that seek to transform it. This for me is the fundamental dilemma at the core of a no borders politics.

In the next chapter I add to this theory of a no borders politics by looking at the spectrum of perspectives and practices held by different groups in the no borders movement. When people come together in groups (either to express collective demands explicitly, or to seek out autonomy together) this is perhaps when the no borders movement appears most like a movement. Here the focus moves on from looking at no borders in theory, to looking at how groups express this theory in their practice.

2 | NO BORDERS POLITICS IN PRACTICE: THE NO BORDERS MOVEMENT AS A SPECTRUM OF ACTION

Introduction

In the previous chapter I talked about what a no borders politics is, largely in theory, and described it as a refusal of the border and the state, which goes beyond contesting the state, by seeking to remain autonomous from it. I said that a no borders politics also includes demands for rights and recognition and that, when people excluded from the realm of rights and representation take action for these things, this has the potential to transform the boundaries of citizenship. As such, a no borders politics is a negotiation between autonomous practices that seek to escape the state and representational practices that seek to transform it.

A no borders politics is my approximation of the politics of the no borders movement. Numerically this movement is mostly made up of people who move without permission. As such, to a large degree this movement is invisible, imperceptibility being a key strategy in people's efforts at staying free from border controls. It's invisible also because in these individual efforts at imperceptibility there is often no need to think of oneself as, or take action as part of, a wider collective of people who are struggling for the same thing. The struggle for the freedom of movement embodies social movement, in the sense of being a force that brings about systemic change (Papadopoulos et al. 2008; Mezzadra 2011). But the structural forms that we often associate with social movements – collective identity, organization and vision, for example – are often missing, or else are fluid, often temporary and diverse. Yet there are numerous moments when people *have* come together in intentional collective struggle, and the movement is also comprised of a multitude of different groups, campaigns and sub-movements. It is in these groups that there is more of a sense that this movement is a 'thing'.

In this, no borders is a movement of people with many different migration statuses, from many different countries, within and beyond

Europe, with many different experiences of the world. It is diverse, yet in that diversity there is some common ground. What could be said to unite all those who take part is a belief that the freedom of movement is everybody's freedom. Beyond this, there are, I think, two other strands of ideas that weave through this movement. First, there is a sense that the struggle for the freedom of movement concerns more than just the fight against physical borders. The border is not just a 'thing', but a practice (Vaughan-Williams 2009). Taken to its logical extreme, it can mean that borders exist wherever a social border – by which I mean a way of distinguishing between different 'kinds' of people – exists. People who are denied the freedom of movement are overwhelmingly poor, black and young – of an age that's most exploitable to labour. Is all that just a coincidence? Shuddhabrata Sengupta's statement that '[b]orders are layers as well as lines ... spanning the distance from the frontier to your epidermis' (Sengupta 2003) gives a sense of the multiple scales and pervasiveness and intrusiveness of borders. In that sense, the no borders movement is concerned with much more than just the politics of migration. It is also a movement that seeks to refuse borders in the broadest of senses.

Second, there is a shared belief in the importance of solidarity. Political solidarity can loosely be defined as the mutual support between and within struggles for liberation that seek to change unjust or oppressive social structures (Scholz 2007). It denotes a connection, relation or unity between members of a group, or between a social class, say, that is expressed through a practice of mutual support (Cohen and Arato 1992; Scholz 2007). Whereas charity signals relationships based on a presumed hierarchy (I give aid to you), solidarity signals relationships based on a presumed equality (we help each other). It is reciprocal in a way that charity is not. It's partly through solidarity and its practical application in making supportive links between different groups of people that the movement remains as diverse and fluid as it does. Despite this common ground, the no borders movement reads the struggle for the freedom of movement in diverse ways. I hope to draw out those variations in the course of this chapter.

The no borders movement in western Europe clearly reflects that diversity. Groups that might self-identify with the no borders movement would likely include numerous migrant-led groups such as the movement of the Sans Papiers (which itself can be broken down into numerous smaller struggles); groups and campaigns working specifically against detention and deportation, like the Campaign to Close Campsfield in the UK, or the broader No Lager (no camps) Network in Germany; broad but more explicitly partisan activist and campaigning networks such as No-one Is Illegal (which has a particularly large presence in Germany); the different anti-racist networks, some of which also express particular political affiliations, like Stand Up to Racism and Fascism in the UK (which is closely affiliated with the trade union movement), or Afrique–Europe–Interact (a network of European and African groups); different anti-fascist networks from the more mainstream Unite Against Fascism on the one hand to the more 'extreme' Antifa on the other; the anarchistic activist network that actually goes by the name of No Borders; the growing number of City of Sanctuary groups (of which there were fifty-one in the UK at the last count); innumerable faith-based groups; and various scholarly strands that blend into the movement, including the two strands of critical migration studies that I have explored so far. And this is without saying much about the connections that exist between this movement and similar diverse and dynamic movements in North Africa, North America and elsewhere.

This is one huge mesh of different groups, struggles and tendencies that might come together at times under a shared banner of 'freedom of movement', but at others can seem more at odds with each other than anything. What it creates is something of a spectrum: between those who see effective action as bringing about changes to the system, and those who see it as an escape from the system. To shed more light on all this, I turn now to look at those groups that I have chosen to feature in this book. One of these groups is active in Calais and the others are active in Athens. Despite the obvious issues that are thrown up by their geographical difference, they tell us a lot about the diversity of perspectives and hence practices that are held within the no borders movement in Europe. I start with the groups in Athens.

The no borders movement in Athens

In this book I focus on three parts of the no borders movement that were active in Athens during the time I was there: the anti-racist left, the anti-authoritarian movement, and the migrant-led struggle for regularization (known as 'The 300'). In a way, labelling them as part of the no borders movement seems a little inaccurate, since previous attempts to establish a No Border Network in Greece had failed. Nonetheless, I still think these struggles and this movement reflect the ethos of a no borders politics. I focus only on three parts of this movement, despite the fact that it was much more diverse than this (including, for example, many other migrant-led groups), because they are the ones I think have a practice that most resonates with a no borders politics. In the case of the anti-racist left and 'The 300', migration issues are a specific focus. In the case of the anti-authoritarian movement (or 'the movement' for short), migration is sometimes included within a broader activism. These three parts of the no borders movement think about and practise activism in very different ways. Yet to a large degree they have a shared radical history rooted in the broad grassroots left in Greece, and this history is a good place to start in exploring their perspectives and practices of resistance.

This contemporary history is heavy with extremes. As a friend pointed out, 'Greece is a very – brutally – politicized country that had been under a totalitarian regime until quite recently and the only answer to totalitarianism is to demand everything, it's almost like a flip side to that … As strong as the dictatorships have been, the left has had an equally strong tradition and an equally strong perspective of what the world should look like' (interview, Anon. 2). This history of extremes begins with the military dictatorship of the Metaxas regime (1936–40), which was replaced by Nazi occupation (1941–44) and a civil war (1944–49) that pitched the Communist Party – the KKE – against the Greek army. All these conflicts reflected a highly confrontational and violent political culture within which communism existed as the dominant alternative to the various forms of right-wing totalitarianism (Schwarz et al. 2010). Seventeen years of monarchy (1950–67) followed by seven years of military rule (the junta of 1967–74) effectively forced any radical left opposition underground. But despite this, radical left political tendencies were incubated, if not publicly visible, and have remained extreme (Vatikiotis 2011).

The incubation period ended in 1974 with the beginning of a period of transition to democratic liberal government known as Metapolitefsi. Metapolitefsi changed the political terrain and brought with it waves of political unrest as the boundaries of Greek political space were redefined. There began to be differentiation among the grassroots left, exposing two divergent tendencies. On the one side were those groups that had wanted the overthrow of the junta and saw Metapolitefsi as a positive if flawed transition to civil democracy. On the other side were those groups that saw the struggle against the junta as part of a wider struggle for social liberation and Metapolitefsi simply as another phase of this (Alkis 2010). The anti-racist left emerged from the former, the anti-authoritarian movement from the latter. More on that later.

Metapolitefsi also brought with it the beginnings of more openness in Greece's international relations. From the early 1990s people began to migrate to Greece from countries with which Greece had special relationships. People from Egypt and the Philippines came to Greece on special worker programmes (Kiprianos et al. 2003). In the late 1980s, the dissolution of the Soviet Union and unrest in other European communist regimes saw people from those countries come to Greece too (Kasimis and Kassimi 2004; Kipiranos et al. 2003; Triandafyllidou and Gropas 2007). Many came to Greece on various worker programmes and often stayed. From the early 1990s, as more settled communities started to form, so a few migrant groups started to emerge. These were organized mainly along national or ethnic lines. For example, the Kurdish student community, the Greek Muslim community, the Social Centre [Haunt] of Albanian Migrants. These groups provided practical support to their communities; helping with immigration, work or housing matters, for example, as well as cultural support, including maintaining links with their countries of origin (Kasimis et al. 2010).

Despite the ad hoc nature of the Greek governmental response to migration that created precarity for many migrants to the country, diaspora communities started to emerge, particularly in the capital, Athens. The response to these communities was largely an outpouring of negative discourses about immigrants that became more prevalent from the mid-1990s. Out of that part of the left that remained separate from, but in dialogue with, parliamentary politics, the anti-racist movement came together in response to these increasingly vocal racist and xenophobic discourses. In its inception, then, Greek anti-racism was a response to anti-immigrant sentiment. Since then, the movement has grown out of a series of collaborations within the left and with migrant-led groups, particularly around the issue of regularization; 1996 saw the first mobilizations in Greece that made this demand. Following a state regularization programme the following year, two similar mass-legalization campaigns were initiated (in 2000/01 and

2005–06) (Syndicate of Anti-racist and Immigrant Organizations n.d), and two further mass-regularization programmes (in 2001 and 2005) (Kasimis et al. 2010). In the present day, the anti-racist movement forms a network of collectives across the country, some organized specifically around the issue of anti-racism, others taking on this issue at specific times.

Migrant-led struggles have not only been demands for regularization. In many cases people have taken more direct forms of action. In 2008 people (mainly from East Asia) employed to pick strawberries staged a strike over pay and conditions that resulted in a pay rise (to 25 euros a day). In September of that year, after the makeshift migrant settlement in Patras was once again raided by police, the Afghan community responded with violent clashes with police that resulted in the hospitalization of twelve police officers. Similar clashes happened again in March 2009, with police using tear gas in an effort to disperse them (Clandestina 2011). Between 2009 and 2015 there were more than twenty reported cases of hunger strikes by organized groups of migrants in Greece.[1]

Returning to the native Greek radical political scene, out of that part of the left that rejected and remained outside of parliamentary political culture, the anti-authoritarian movement came to self-define in terms of its opposition to what was seen as the authoritarian politics of the democratic process (Papadimitropoulos 2010). What was labelled as a movement of 'angry youths' was initially characterized by a number of student-led mobilizations and occupations, as well as the use of new, horizontal forms of organizing and insurrectionist tactics. Partly emblematic of the influence of different strands of anarchism and Marxism (like Situationism and German and Italian autonomism), as well as punk and DIY culture, and partly because of the maturation of the movement over previous decades, from the early 1990s it started to take on more structural dimensions, creating autonomous spaces such as squats, social centres and free parties.

Unlike the left, groups associated with this movement have tended to focus on those issues that are within their direct experience only. When they *have* taken on a specific issue, it has often been in ways that situate that issue against the totality of capitalism and the state, and in relation to their own experience. So, at that time we also see a number of groups emerge that, for example, focused on anti-fascist action (rather than, say, anti-racism or migrant solidarity, fascism being seen as somehow more pervasive or more 'foundational').

What this means is that the movement has generally not sought out solidarity action with migrants, but migrants and people from the movement *have* come together in numerous ways. Connections have formed between migrant communities and communities within the movement during moments of counter-hegemonic protest, for example. These include protests in 2004 in solidarity with migrant workers involved in labour exploitation for the Olympic Games, 2007 riots in Thessaloniki that saw migrants and the movement on the streets in response to the death of Nigerian Tony Onoya in police custody, and a 2008 demonstration in Patras that brought over 1,500 migrants, and parts of the anti-racist and anti-authoritarian movements, together in protest. The involvement of migrants in the 2008 uprising in Athens[2] also went a long way to change the minds of many in the anti-authoritarian movement of who they could think of as allies in the struggle against the state. Neighbourhood assemblies,[3] collective kitchens and unemployed workers' clubs have also brought people from the movement into contact with other locals, including migrants. Anti-fascist action is another factor that has brought people together (more about that later). Having laid out a brief history of these movements, I turn now to look at a specific migrant-led group, 'The 300' hunger strikers.

Introducing 'The 300'[4]

What became known colloquially as 'The 300' was a hunger strike by 300 men from North Africa that took place simultaneously in Athens and Thessaloniki in January 2011. The actions of the strikers themselves were supported by a vast campaign of solidarity that included both of the other two Athens-based groups I talk about in this book. 'The 300' is different from these other two groups in that it came together around a specific action and a specific demand; a hunger strike for mass regularization. In that sense 'The 300' can be thought of more as a campaign than a group. That said, 'The 300' did not emerge out of nowhere. Many of the strikers had been politically active in struggles against the border before, organizing together in a number of migrant-led groups in the city of Chania on the island of Crete. In particular, many had been active within the Forum of Migrants in Chania, a radical left political space that brought together locals and migrants and which had been politicizing migration issues on the island since 2007. Through the Forum, many who came to be active in 'The 300' developed experiences of struggle in this context, as well as a network of people – natives and migrants – to struggle with. One of the first actions of Forum members was a hunger strike of fifteen men from North Africa, which took place in the autumn of 2008. This strike had been brief and successful, resulting in the regularization of those who took part.

Many of 'The 300' had been living and working semi-legally on the island of Crete for many years (some as long as a decade). With the economic crisis, as work dried up, they increasingly found themselves excluded from any legal status, something dependent on demonstrating continuous employment. Faced with this, they took action, broadly demanding regularization for all migrants in Greece.[5] The strike lasted forty-four days. Although this broad demand was not successful, 'The 300' did win a number of concessions, in particular indefinite leave to remain in Greece for themselves, the freedom to travel outside of Greece, including to their countries of origin, and positive changes in the connection between employment and legality for all migrants in the country.[6] By the end of the strike, over one hundred of the strikers were hospitalized.

Introducing the Network for Support to Migrants and Refugees

The Network for Support to Migrants and Refugees (*Diktyo Kinonikis Ypostirixis Prosfigon kai Metanaston*, hereafter the Network) was active in the solidarity campaign that built up around the hunger strike of 'The 300'. Beyond that, the Network plays a fundamental and to some extent coordinating role in the anti-racist movement in Greece. Established in 1995, the Network's primary aim is to show solidarity with migrants and refugees (Syndicate of Anti-racist and Immigrant Organizations n.d). Over the course of its history it has taken on specific campaigns around migration issues (such as actions against detention prisons and mass regularization, as well as numerous solidarity actions, such as support to migrant-led hunger strikes, or struggles for better pay), and has been part of non-migration-specific campaigns too (such as various anti-fascist actions and campaigns against militarism and police violence). These actions have seen the movement acting alongside other parts of the radical left and migrant-led groups.

'The 300' and the Network share a lot in terms of the perspectives that shape their activism. Having laid out a brief history of both of these groups, I now want to look at the two main perspectives that give shape to the kind of resistance tactics they practise.

Perspectives on resistance in 'The 300' and the Network

Anti-racism as part of a struggle against capitalism Although there is diversity of perspectives within each group, both the network and 'The 300' express a collective 'position' in their statements and actions. Both groups emerged from the cross-fertilization between the Greek radical left and specific migrant-led struggles. For them, anti-racism is a fundamental part of a wider struggle against capitalism. Their anti-racism resonates with what Alistair Bonnett (2000) describes as radical anti-racism in that it combines certain anti-racist and Marxist ideological concepts. 'The 300' express their thinking regarding migration in terms of labour relations when they say, '[w]e ask for the legalization of all migrant men and women, we ask for the same political and social rights and obligations as Greek workers. We ask our Greek fellow workers, everyone suffering exploitation, to stand with us' ('The 300', 2011). Similarly, for the Network, anti-racism expresses a radical critique of the state and capitalism and sees racism as an effect of nationalism and labour subordination. 'Race' and racism are produced by the demands of class and capital, with migrant workers exploited as are workers under capitalism, if in some specific and more extreme ways. In the following excerpt from a text of the Network, the link between 'race', labour and 'nation' as structures of domination of the state is made in relation to how migrants are presented as economic and sociocultural threats. The struggle against the border is therefore seen as part of a transnational struggle against capital.

> The local precarious labour force of capitalist cities is not threatened by immigrants to the extent that nationalists claim. They are threatened not by foreign immigrants but because of the changes that capitalists and states make. They are also threatened because employers seek to reduce the cost of production. Instead of asking for protection of borders it is more realistic and right to fight for the increase of labour positions and respectful wages. (Syndicate of Anti-racist and Immigrant Organizations n.d.)

The perspective that natives and migrants, as workers, share the same source of oppression – capitalism – is the foundation for solidarity for 'The 300' and the Network. Rather than resting on shared experiences, identities or social locations, solidarity here rests on shared aims, goals and ideas. 'The 300' and the Network identify a shared source of oppression in nationalism, racism and capitalism that connects the struggle of migrants, as workers, with Greeks, as workers. It's on this basis that these groups express and receive solidarity.

Within this context, collaboration between migrants and natives is important. For 'The 300' the support from native groups 'turned up the volume' on their struggle (Johnson 2012: 121). Sharing this view, the Network has prioritized offering support to migrants' self-organized struggles. This has seen the Network involved in the fight by workers from the Filipino community for decent rates of pay, to the struggle of people from Kurdistan for recognition as refugees, to solidarity with individuals and groups on hunger strike in and outside of detention (Syndicate of Anti-racist and Immigrant Organizations n.d.). The Network was also involved in setting up Steki Metanaston (the Migrants Social Centre, hereafter the Steki), a self-funded, autonomous social centre in Athens for migrants and those in solidarity with them. The Steki runs a nightly bar, once weekly collective kitchen and crèche, an immigration info shop, and free Greek language lessons.

Within and against the state The second logic is a relationship to the state that can be described as within but against it. Both 'The 300' and the Network emerged from a wider political left that expresses a radical critique of the state and capitalism. At the same time, however, state engagement appears as a necessary and realistic stage in the move towards radical social change. In relation to migration struggles, it is seen as a means of achieving immediate and important gains. A radical critique of the state, therefore, comes up against a perspective that sees emancipation through (engagement with) the state. Engaging with the state is seen as a pragmatic decision:

> There is no fantasy world. Even if I was in another country – I can only think of to have a country on this earth – there would still be exploitation, the state, the system, and I would struggle against it and have different problems. So, I don't want to fantasize. Whatever I fantasize, there is still exploitation and injustice. (Interview, Iradz, member of the Network for Support to Migrants and Refugees)

Constantly negotiating between the dilemma of working with/in whilst also opposing the state was one that was particularly alive for Nasim. As a refugee from Afghanistan, Nasim felt that the vast distance between current existing reality and the ideal of a borderless world of equality meant that engagement was a necessary part of that journey:

I can talk about no borders, rights for all and stuff. But I also remember what it was like when I didn't have these rights ... We [the Network] work between the dilemma of state or being counter to the state. You first have to think: what is the state and its role? What is demanding and what is conflicting? If you're not thinking of these things you act with no meaning or purpose ... You also need to distinguish between being practical and bringing about rights and reforms which help now, and being radical and keeping the conflict alive. It's full of contradictions. (Interview, Nasim)

A stance that's 'in and against' the state shapes these groups' practice in a number of ways. First, it prioritizes transformation of, rather than an escape from, the state. Second, with transformation seen as involving strategic engagement with the state, it creates a practice that prioritizes influencing public political discourse on 'race' and migration. The Network has its own website, and regularly releases texts, press releases and position statements on different aspects of migration issues. Awareness-raising forms an important part of its work too. Since 1995 the Network has organized an anti-racist festival in Athens, featuring a weekend of workshops, cultural events and music, in collaboration with a wide range of native, political and migrant groups. Media engagement was an important part of the strategy of 'The 300' during the strike. They released numerous statements to the press, as well as created their own media.

Being 'in and against' the state also creates a discourse heavily laden with the language of rights. Yet the discourse of rights has different effects when it's expressed by those largely excluded from them compared to when it's expressed by the already included. For 'The 300', as a group largely excluded from citizenship, expressing demands for rights challenges the sense that rights are only for citizens and can only be expressed within the context of the state. To demand rights from this position is in some sense a radical act.

For the Network, speaking as a group largely seen as (but far from only) comprised of citizens, the demand for rights is far more conservative, placing the demand within the existing logics of the state. The following excerpt, which refers to the first mass regularization campaign in Greece, attests to the view that the law can act as a tool to bring about greater freedoms: 'What we wanted to show was that firstly certain rights should be established through law, but at the same time to support the saying that "no man is contraband" [illegal]' (Syndicate of Anti-racist and Immigrant

Organizations n.d.). Elektra (member of the Network for Support to Migrants and Refugees) expressed the centrality of rights as a means of achieving equality as what got her involved in the Network: 'Do they have rights? Do they not? Will they ever be Greek citizens or not? Will they ever be as equal as we are in the eyes of the law I guess?' (interview, Elektra). What these two logics shape are practices that prioritize transforming the state, through solidarity between migrants and natives, as workers. For 'The 300', this has led to actions have been migrant-led. For the Network, it has led to self-organized activism too, but also to actions that at times amount to speaking on behalf of migrants.

Having laid out the broad perspectives of these two groups, I now turn to the anti-authoritarian movement, which has a different perspective on activism.

Introducing the anti-authoritarian movement

What I refer to as the anti-authoritarian movement is an umbrella term used by those within it to describe a constellation of collectives and groups that coalesce around a broad range of fluid anarchist principles such as autonomy, non-domination, mutual aid, direct action and direct democracy, where anti-authoritarianism forms something of a baseline (Graeber 2009; Katsiaficas 2007). 'Anarchist space' is a specific part of this movement, as are libertarian, autonomist and non-parliamentary radical left tendencies. These tendencies are organized into numerous assemblies, spaces, collectives and groups, each with a multitude of varying, sometimes overlapping, sometimes contested perspectives. For certain collectives, for people who believe strongly in one tendency and for sections of the activist scene in particular places and times, the identification with a particular tendency can be extremely strong to the point of mutual exclusion. This reflects the fluidity of the movement, as well as the difficulty in trying to pin it down, which is, effectively, against its logic anyway. What could ultimately be described just as well as a series of movements nonetheless coalesces around some core perspectives and practices. Few parts of this political community have focused on struggles against the border specifically, but there have been moments when this has happened, and it is becoming more common. The solidarity campaign with 'The 300' was one such example.

Perspectives on activism in the movement

Above I described 'The 300' and the Network's perspective on activism as leading them to adopt positions 'in and against' the state.

The anti-authoritarian movement also draws on a radical critique of the state, yet reaches distinctly different conclusions. I think there are two main logics that underpin their practice, and both stem from the centrality of autonomy.

In Chapter 1 I explored a particular meaning of autonomy from within the intersection of anarchism, post-anarchism, post-Marxism and post-structuralism. To recap here, I said that autonomy is a collective practice that starts from valuing and acting upon our individual desires, and from there prefiguring communities of equality. I said that experiments in autonomy go beyond the autonomy of migration and are things that the 'newest social movements' are doing all the time. I think this movement shares this conceptualization of autonomy, and that an orientation towards autonomy is a key thing that defines it and shapes its relationship to others in their struggles.

Solidarity as affinity The movement expresses an orientation towards autonomy in many different ways, but at the basis of all of them, I think, is the idea that autonomy begins with individual freedom. In practising a form of autonomy as total, individual freedom, George Katsiaficas suggests that '[m]ore than anything else, the new radicals are distinguished from the New Left by their orientation to themselves – to a "politics of the first person" – not to the "proletariat" or the "wretched of the earth"' (Katsiaficas 2007: 15). That said, autonomy is a concept that negotiates the dilemma of how to bring about such individual freedom while also building relationships and communities without hierarchy or domination (Firth 2010). Affinity describes the way people form connections with others, mindful of individual autonomy. So, I think the first key logic of the movement in relation to this struggle is that of affinity.

Affinity represents a crucial way by which the movement forms connections with others while maintaining the value of autonomy. It describes a way of making connections that's not based on a foundational ethic that might imply duty or obligation, but on mutual aid through free association (Day 2005; Kropotkin 2006 [1902]). As such, it rests on the recognition of resonance, attraction or complementarity between individuals' desires, perspectives and experiences. It's about creating 'configurations of desire' rather than common ground (Anon. 1999; see also Karatzogiani and Robinson 2010; Graeber 2009; Invisible Committee 2009).

Like solidarity, affinity is about ways of making connections to others in struggle, as a means of building and strengthening those struggles. Solidarity and affinity are slightly different, though, even though the terms are sometimes used interchangeably. Solidarity implies a reaching out beyond our experience, whereas affinity implies a connectivity that's far more intimate. Affinity can be thought of as something like a tribal solidarity – making bands, gangs or extended families of people who come together around shared desires and friendship (Gordon 2008). It's not a practice of representing or acting on behalf of anyone, which is often how solidarity is put to use, and how movements or societies organize (ibid.). That's not to say that solidarity isn't also a practice of the movement, but rather that it tends to be practised specifically, as solidarity with other comrades in the struggle against the state (Anon. 2001; Landstreicher/Feral Faun 2003; Porcu 2005).[7]

Being 'outside' the state Affinity is a form of solidarity and a way of building communities of autonomy. It's a way of creating relationships and ways of being that are free from domination and that, in being so, effectively construct 'outsides' to the state (Grubačić 2004). Here 'outside' refers less to a physical 'space' beyond the world system, and more to autonomous 'spaces' or moments within its totalizing logic. Such spaces or moments are autonomous from that state by being (potentially) non-dominating/equal, and render it redundant in the process. 'To seek to empower and maximise autonomy, it is necessary to always look for outsides, however partial, and seek to bring them together into a complete outside, another way of being, another world' (Robinson 2010b). This makes the practice of autonomy an inherently prefigurative one.

Prefigurative practices bloom within the movement. We see it in the proliferation of autonomous spaces and moments; from squats and social centres to collective kitchens and gardens, open libraries and free parties. In a district such as Exarcheia in downtown Athens, which feels a bit like the anarchist 'homeland' in the density of such spaces and moments, it's possible to spend most if not all of your time in such spaces, or engaging in moments that represent 'outsides' to the state. The district contains virtually no chain stores (when I was there it contained one, the goods of which were routinely 'reappropriated'), and there have been times in Exarcheia's recent history when the district was effectively a no-go zone for police. It can lead to a feeling that being outside is more than just a metaphor. Where it feels as if there is no need for the state, or where the only relationship to it is one that seeks to undermine or attack it, it is as if we have really managed to escape it already.

Connections across difference through shared space In practising a 'politics of the first person' that rejects any notion of acting on behalf of others, the movement has often held back from mobilizing with/in migrant communities, reflecting the notion that 'they must do it for themselves, and then we can support them'. In Athens, it has led to a sense among many that the struggle of migrants is not the same as the struggle of the movement; that the difference is too big to be 'bridged' through affinity. In this sense, the movement has largely rejected the sense that real affinity with this struggle is possible, at least in any overarching way. Yet as I mentioned above, there have been some interesting partnerships and connections, often when people have come together to deal with the specific issues that they face in their locale.

Anti-fascist action has, at times, been one of those things to bring these communities together. One example of this is in the response to the pogrom of people of colour that took place in May 2011. On 10 May, the stabbing of Manolis Kantaris in a neighbourhood in down-town Athens resulted in an escalation of violence directed towards people of colour that led to the death of Alim Adbul Mana, originally from Bangladesh, and the hospitalization of over one hundred people, many suffering from stab wounds. During this time, people from a number of long-standing and prominent anarchist squats, who were also coming under attack by police and the same armed gangs, came into the streets to defend the neighbourhoods from the attackers, and be together with others who were under attack. Victoria Square was quickly 'occupied' by people from the movement, which brought them into contact with other residents. In addition to the occupation, there were numerous street confrontations between anarchists and fascists, and a number of statements making the connection between the attacks on migrants and the attacks on the movement.[8]

The connections formed during the uprising in Athens and December 2008 were reaffirmed during this time. Indeed, in the times when the movement has engaged in migrant-led protest, it has often introduced an important and effective antagonistic dimension to such struggles. For example, a quote from one of the protesters in an occupation of

Athens University by Afghan refugees recalled the involvement of anti-fascists in their struggle: 'He made a lot of friends from the anarchist groups. They were the most helpful in defending Propyleia [university building] from fascists. After the stabbing in May, attacks happened often and the anarchists helped defend our occupation. The Afghan protesters couldn't get involved in confrontations. But the anarchists could do that' (field diary, 6 May 2011).

Most of the ways that the movement has mobilized with migrants have been largely incidental, because of the fact that people have been sharing the same space. Yet they have been important, because in these moments people have come together to collaborate in ways of being that potentially escape the state. However, the movement's complete rejection of the state has meant that it has largely stayed away from the legal and rights-based dimensions of migration issues, which has limited the development of ongoing and concerted projects against border controls. This has led some within the movement to question whether their involvement lacks a consistent 'position' or an informed and reliable response to the oppression of migrants. This is an issue for many anarchistic movements. Migration appears as an issue so infused with complex legal and policy-based information and language that many simply feel incapable of taking informed action or even voicing an opinion. For many within the movement, this lack of a coherent or consistent 'stance' on or engagement with migration issues has amounted to a failure to stand alongside migrants in their struggle for their rights. That said, the Assembly for Solidarity with Street Vendors (hereafter ASSV) represented a particular (and virtually unique) example of a group within the movement that specifically organized around the issue of migration at that time.

The Assembly for Solidarity with Street Vendors The ASSV is a loose-knit open assembly of people that grew out of the events of December 2008. The assembly aims to show solidarity with migrants, as workers. As such they draw on largely post-Marxist ideological concepts. However, they're also somewhat connected to the Autonomous social centre (Steki). This Steki reflects a politics influenced by Autonomia, but also queer theory, which subverts understanding identities as fixed and stable markers of subjectivity, and of representation as a means of extending human freedom (cf. Braidotti 1994; Butler 1990; Spurlin 2001). Members of the ASSV are involved in other groups within the movement, but focus more on migration issues in this one. They seek to build their actions collaboratively with those who experience the oppression of the state through being the subject of border controls, and by creating spaces and moments of shared experience. The collective organizes Greek-language classes for street vendors, holding classes in places and at times easily accessible to them. From this connection they organize an assembly, which brings together people with and without papers. From the assembly, they create and distribute texts about relevant issues in the languages most commonly spoken by migrants in the city. An excerpt from one of their pamphlets states:

> For a long time past, we get together with immigrants street vendors and coordinate our reactions: we realise common reunions, we organise Greek lessons, we make interventions of counter-information and gatherings of solidarity, we intervene with dynamism at the streets, the police stations the courts. The permanent struggle of the immigrants for a dignified and free life feeds and inspires the continuous resistance of the people in solidarity against repression, humiliation and exploitation. (People in Solidarity with Migrants 2010)

The no border movement in Calais

> We're not quite organised criminals and we're not quite a charity
> We're a group of disorganised charitable criminals
> We're not here to help
> We're just here
> We don't believe in God. We don't have any particular political agenda
> We're not humanitarians. We don't even typically like people
> We're nihilistic, anti-humanitarians simply doing what we thought needed to be done
> And we really hate cops. (Anon. 8, 2015)

The above quote is a description of Calais Migrant Solidarity (sometimes colloquially called No Borders in Calais and often known as 'No Borders' by people trying to cross) from some people involved in the struggle in Calais. It's totally tongue-in-cheek, yet for me, I don't think I have ever heard a better definition of this particular part of the No Border Network. Calais Migrant Solidarity (hereafter CMS) is explicitly part of the No Border Network, but hopefully by now it's clear that the no borders movement is much broader that just the No Border Network. There are many other groups active in the struggle for the freedom of movement in Calais too. At times, some of these groups have been directly antagonistic towards the state. However, I am focusing on CMS only, because I think it represents a clear and *current* example of a group whose practice resonates with a no borders politics.

Introducing the No Border Network

The No Border Network emerged in the late 1990s following the first No Border camp held in Germany in 1998. The aim was to generate a network of solidarity with the growing movements of people without papers that were also emerging around that time (such as the Sans Papiers movement in France). There have been something like thirty camps since that first one. They have varied in size – from a few hundred to nearly a thousand – as well as in aims and targets – from transit/border zones such as Calais, Lesvos and Patras, to locations at the heart of systems of control such as Brussels and Strasbourg. The camps have brought together people who share an affinity with the broad notion of 'no borders' and the freedom of movement and have been spaces in which to talk and take action. To the extent that the camps have been organized non-hierarchically and through mutual aid and direct action, they have also been experiments in prefiguring societies organized according to these values; in creating temporary autonomous zones (Bey 2003 [1991]). Arguably the most successful camps have been those that have brought people with and without papers together. For example, the No Border camp in Lesvos in 2009 saw a great deal of communication between people held in the Pagani detention prison and people attending the camp, and contributed to the closure of the prison. The No Border camp in Calais that same year saw collaboration between camp participants and people from the 'jungles' which led to a number of collaborative actions at the time (several protests, as well as participating together in camp life and decision-making), and to the establishment of CMS afterwards.

Beyond the camps, there have been No Border blocs at numerous alter-/anti-globalization and anti-summit demonstrations, and a number of No Border convergences and gatherings. Such mass actions are where the Network appears most like a cohesive and homogeneous group, because it's there that collective perspectives are debated and collective demands expressed. Yet No Borders is decentralized in structure. There are no leaders or party lines and a great deal of differentiation. There may be local groups, but their primary focus is often in responding to the way the border affects people in their locality, rather than expressing a network collective demand. What defines No Borders is not its structure, but the approach that people take in their struggle for freedom and against the border. No Border activists visit detainees in detention, provide safer spaces for people on their journeys, put out counter-information to that of the mainstream media's racist account of the 'migrant crisis', help out at refugee advice centres, resist people's deportations, live in refugee camps ... It is the way people engage in these struggles that's crucial and defining, something I shall return to shortly.

No Borders in Calais – Calais Migrant Solidarity In 2009 a group of activists from north-western Europe came together to hold a No Border camp in Calais. At the time, Calais was coming to represent a major site of struggle against the European border regime, yet it had been something of a border 'hot spot' for more than fifteen years, with the first makeshift camps appearing in the city in the mid-1990s (something I elaborate upon in Chapter 4). Over the course of that period, a number of groups had been set up to support the people stuck in Calais. Groups such as Salam and La Belle Etoile set up food and clothes distributions in the city, and some people began visiting the places where people were living. Initially these groups also adopted quite an antagonistic stance towards the local government. However, over time, because of infighting and splits, and the recuperation of such activities through the collaboration of some groups with the local authorities, these groups largely came to focus only on humanitarian aid distribution, which was to some degree condoned by the state, somewhat losing whatever 'radical edge' they once had. In 2009, then, when a No Border camp was held in Calais, there was a major opportunity to radicalize/ politicize the struggle for the freedom of movement, and a chance to build links between activists with and without papers.

The camp brought together local people with people from all over north and west Europe, and people from Afghanistan, Iraq, Sudan, Eritrea, and elsewhere. Out of these connections came a desire to create a continuous No Border presence in the city, under the name of Calais Migrant Solidarity. CMS has been in Calais ever since. A number of local people have been the backbone of CMS, but generally Calais sees a steady flow of people – largely with papers or who are not trying to cross – passing through, some staying for months, others for days, many returning again and again.

Since 2009 CMS has documented the situation in Calais and its perspective on it online.[9] CMS activists have opened numerous squats and autonomous social spaces with and for people with and without papers in the city (the authorities, rightly seeing such spaces as subversive, have gone to great lengths to close them down, often manipulating legal routes to do this). They have helped people without papers occupy land; witnessed and documented police violence;[10] gathered the testimonies of hundreds of people about their journeys and the violence they have faced; and provided practical support in the form of ad hoc immigration advice, clothes, food and bike repairs. Perhaps most importantly they have built up relationships with people, and with the different migrant communities present in Calais. In that sense CMS activists have provided some continuity – of knowledge and relationships – within the mobile commons. They are a part of those 'diverse forms of transnational communities of justice' that are an important part of the mobile commons (Papadopoulos and Tsianos 2013: 190).

Having given a brief and partial account of the No Border Network and CMS, I want to focus on some of the core perspectives on action that is expressed by No Borders/CMS, and then look at what kinds of practice I think that perspective leads to.

No Border perspective on activism

The No Border Network has a lot in common with the anti-authoritarian movement in that it also fits the description of being one of the 'newest social movements' that Richard Day (2005) talked about. The No Border Network practises a form of activism that potentially escapes the state, in seeking other ways of being to it. What defines networks like this is their orientation towards autonomy and against domination, and in the way they combine direct forms of resistance to the state with prefigurative practices that seek to escape it (returning to John Holloway, we can describe this as the combination of the scream against and the movement of power-to). The No Border Network operates largely according to this, and in places like Calais forms a distinct part of the no borders movement that's often *intentionally* seeking to create a different social reality.

Like the anti-authoritarian movement too, the No Border Network is a broadly anarchist one, interpreting the affirmation of the freedom to move and to stay as a distinctly anarchist demand: for the end to all borders and states.[11]

> No borders for me is a totally anarchist position. I don't think it's possible to start thinking about no borders without first thinking about no state. These people who maintain a position of open borders or whatever; even on a theoretical level for me it makes absolutely no sense. For me it's totally inconsistent on even a theoretical level. I know that no borders is kind of a pipe dream, but at least it's consistent! At least it's consistently utopian! I think it's ridiculous to think that any state could possibly tolerate any kind of threat to its existence, which is what no borders entails. (Interview, Anon. 5)

Being anti-state is slightly different from refusing the state. It carries far more political intent. In the quote above, Anon. 5 raises the point that is often used to dismiss no borders: that it's a utopian position and hence totally unrealistic. How are we supposed to create a situation where there are no borders? But as Anon. 4 states, 'It's also important to acknowledge that we're not gonna have no borders any time soon. *We're always on a walk towards no borders.* I don't think it's a realistic demand, just in the same way I don't think we're gonna have a revolution in the next ten years. *It's a constant aspiration and tension*' (interview, Anon. 4, emphasis added). And yet (as I mentioned in the Introduction), No Borders is not a future project but something happening now; diverse experiments in living freely that are often part failure and part success.

What these two interpretations of No Borders have in common is a sense of the importance of prefiguration; of taking action in the present to undermine borders in practical – perhaps partial, perhaps temporary – ways. So, although No Border activists have participated in numerous demos, marches, strikes, sit-ins, occupations and blockades, activity is much more rooted in the everyday; in the largely mundane and unspectacular practices that undermine the ways that borders, as manifestations of domination and inequality, weave into our social world and our relationships with each other. More about that later.

So far, so similar to the anti-authoritarian movement. However, No Borders departs from movements like this in the way it prioritizes taking action in collaboration with people who move without permission. It basically exists for this very reason. In this, No Border becomes a collaboration between people with broadly anarchist views and people who practise autonomy by moving without permission. This creates something new in anarchism.

> It doesn't necessarily have to be different [from anarchism] at all. Maybe traditionally there's some strong anarchist tendencies that seem to somehow lock people into their own circles ... It doesn't have to be that way but it seems to happen a lot. Whereas if you take an approach that somehow also involves migration struggles it kind of automatically starts looking for affinities from all kinds of places and also accepting the fact that because everything is so complicated and everything is in such a mess around the world, that even if you find some small affinities you can still start from that ... Otherwise I would just put a barrier between me and people who are active, if I was to pre-set what it was. (Interview, Anon. 7)

> I think that the anarchism in Calais is something you don't find in many other places, because of the confrontation with the racism of state-based politics. The no borders politics that happens in Calais and its relationship with anarchism is different to other parts of the world. It's more orientated towards the material conditions of the people who are there. It has a more decentralized character. It's less strict about the way it's organized. It doesn't have a programme. It's more open. It's less dense, and the politics is related directly to action. (Interview, Anon. 5)

Radical anti-racism and the problematic of being an ally A practice that takes seriously the need to collaborate with people who move without permission is underpinned by a perspective that I would describe as radical anti-racism. Such a perspective has its roots in the concept of intersectionality. Intersectionality developed primarily out of debates among black women in feminism's second wave (from the early 1970s), and their interventions into feminist standpoint theory of the time. To backtrack a little, standpoint theory argued in essence that all knowledge is situated and hence partial (cf. Alcoff 2008; England 1994; Harraway 1988; Rose 1997).[12] Scholar activists like bell hooks (1982), Kimberlé Williams Crenshaw (1989) and Audre Lorde (2007 [1984]) argued that despite standpoint theory, mainstream feminism (i.e. white and Western feminism) made it impossible to talk about black women's experience in any complete or meaningful way. It was always fragmented, by focusing *either* on gender *or* on race. In not offering/generating the tools for thinking about both (and more), black women's experience was effectively written out of feminist narratives, reinforcing their oppression (Crenshaw 1989). An open letter to fellow radical feminist Mary Daley from Audre Lorde illustrates this problem starkly: 'Within the community of women, racism is a reality force in my life as it is not in yours. The white women with hoods on in Ohio handing out KKK literature on the street may not like what you have to say, but they will shoot me on sight' (Lorde 2007 [1984]: 70).

This intervention led to the main tenet of intersectionality: that our selves are comprised of multiple dimensions of identity (I am not only my gender, or my race, or my sex, or my ...) *and* that these *interact with each other* (Crenshaw 1991; Yuval-Davis 2012). As such, intersectionality engages with power as it flows – unequally – through multiple axes of identity.

Intersectionality has had a big influence over debates around identity politics, particularly the issue of privilege. Indeed, the idea of dealing with privilege has perhaps been one of the biggest debates within radical activist communities in recent years. What this debate has brought out is how being aware of our privileges means taking responsibility for how we are all implicated in reproducing inequality, regardless of the fact that we never signed up to having these privileges in the first place. The issue of responsibility is present in how Chris Crass talks about racism, in the context of anti-racist organizing (Crass n.d. a).[13] Racism functions through a dual process. On the one hand it renders people of colour inferior. On the other hand it renders white people superior (see also Braidotti 2006). White supremacy both conceals and perpetuates racism, because it means that white people effectively don't have to think about racism (Allen 1994; Braidotti 2006). They can choose to be colour blind.

Tackling structured inequalities like racism involves more than just acknowledging our privileges, though. Liza McKenzie, in her thoughtful and powerful posts on the blog 'Black Girl and Dangerous', raises the importance of going beyond recognition and taking action.

> The truth is that acknowledging your privilege means a whole lot of nothing much if you don't do anything to actively push back against it ... The bottom line here is that if you acknowledge your privilege

and then just go ahead and do the same things anyhow, you have done absolutely zéro things differently from people who don't acknowledge their privilege at all. Because the outcome is exactly the same. The impact is exactly the same. (McKenzie 2014)

What does 'pushing back against' privilege look like? For McKenzie, it involves relinquishing the power we get through our privilege: actively making space for people of colour to speak and be heard, being together with people of colour in the struggle against racism and together taking action in ways that value their experiences and are based on *that* knowledge and experience (ibid.; Crass n.d. c). Chris Crass describes this as abandoning 'whiteness' (Allen 1994; Crass n.d. a; Roediger 1994).

The idea of pushing back against privilege as the abandonment of a dominant identity is mirrored in the concept of 'becoming minor' as developed in the work of Gilles Deleuze and Felix Guattari (2004 [1987]; see also Braidotti 2006; Kaplan 1987: 188). Becoming minor isn't the same as 'minority', which is defined oppositionally to a (superior) majority (Braidotti 2006). To put it in the terminology of Deleuze and Guattari, becoming minor is a 'de-territorialisation' of identity; a decoupling of identity from fixed markers. It's a becoming and not a being; a movement *between* locations that does not express one, fixed subject that has 'become' (Deleuze and Guattari 2004 [1987]: 262). It prioritizes learning and change over knowing and stasis.

Becoming minor is a process. It's a journey to the margins. In making this journey we develop the potential for greater oppositional consciousness; a perspective of radical otherness and resistance (hooks 1984, 1991; Sandoval 1991). In practice, then, becoming minor involves being in ways that are generally devalued or considered deviant, unacceptable or abnormal by dominant social reality, or being with people considered as such. Put another way, it is the experience of alienation, exile and disassociation from dominant social reality, and the positive valuation of that experience (Kaplan 1987; Robinson 2010a).

I think it can be seen as a practice that identifies with and positively values exclusion, and then, through opening up to others who share that space, and who are excluded in different ways, creates something else (Janz 2002; Robinson 2010a). I'm not suggesting that such otherness is some kind of heroic state of being. I think instead it comes from recognizing that our own struggle to push back against privilege is about becoming 'other', or being from some kind of position 'outside'.

In CMS I think people push against privilege in many different ways. Conversations about privilege and intersectionality happen often, and people often take action based on these reflections. For example, recent incarnations of the CMS space in Calais have set aside a specific women, queer and trans sleeping space as a way of practically addressing how people who express these identities are often more vulnerable in Calais than cis men.[14] In 2015 people involved in the group also released the zine 'Some thoughts on gender in the Calais No Border context', which reflected on issues of race and gender within the context of activism in Calais. Intersectionality and reflecting on privilege have had further consequences for the way people associated with CMS think about activism. Activism is approached as something that has different effects and meanings for different people. For example, a risk worth taking for one may be a risk too far for another. It means that a form of activism that's perceived as regressive or conservative for some may actually have the potential to be transformative, depending on who it is that performs it. Because of this, CMS uses a diversity of tactics that have often seen people associated with the group together with people without papers in a range of activities, from actions that express autonomy to those that demand rights and recognition. Within all this, the group prioritizes building relationships with people trying to cross and being together in everyday ways. This is what Ella Baker (key organizer in the civil rights movement in the USA) called 'spade work' (Crass n.d. b). This spade work often leads to building community collaboratively.

Collaborative community-building isn't easy. Gloria Anzaldua sees it as a daily practice of bringing different perspectives into contact, and conflict. It's the process of building bridges, of challenging our views, which takes us away from the safe spaces of the normal, familiar and nameable; our 'home'. More than that, it's about reaching a point where 'home' doesn't have to be always a safe space.

'Home' can be unsafe and dangerous because it bears the likelihood of intimacy and thus thinner boundaries ... To bridge means loosening our borders, not closing off to others. Bridging is the work of opening the gates to the stranger, within and without. To step across the threshold is to be stripped of the illusion of safety because it moves us into unfamiliar territory and does not grant safe passage. To bridge is to attempt community, and for that we must risk being wounded (Anzaldua 2002: 3).

Struggling collaboratively in this way also questions the idea of what it means to make distinctions between 'the oppressed' and 'those in solidarity with them'. For 'A few of the many anarchists in St. Louis' (who talk about the term 'white ally' in their article 'Another word for white ally is coward'), such distinctions can be seen as reinforcing the sense of what's different between us.

> To be a White Ally is to stop thinking for one's self, to blindly follow a leader based on no other criteria than their identity. At least this is what is demanded of us by those who would make us into Allies ... One cannot be an ally to a category of people ... There is no singular black voice that can be listened to, no authentic community leadership to follow. There are only many different people with different ideas, life experiences and perspectives. To think otherwise, to think that all black people share a common opinion is extremely problematic, one might even say racist. One can be an ally to individuals though there are other words in the English language which describe this relationship with more grace: friend, lover, partner and sometimes cellmate or co-defendant.

From this perspective, asking a question such as 'who is the most oppressed?' is meaningless. This is a rejection of the kind of identity politics that ranks privileges and oppressions. Yet ultimately I think these differences in opinion highlight a fundamental tension in how we struggle together, and how we bring about a world of equality while navigating a path through inequality. I see this struggle played out in groups like CMS, and I think it points to the presence of a perspective that thinks critically about solidarity, what it means in relation to equality, where it reaches its useful borders and what's on the other side of those borders. Ultimately, what it leads to is a practice that prioritizes being together with people trying to cross and building community together. But I also don't think it is a perspective that blindly subordinates what's most personal and important to us either. It is, in my view, a perspective that bleeds affinity and solidarity together. CrimethInk (n.d.) see such activity as something creative that enables us and others to live a life full of meaning. 'Building friendships and alliances with people whose experience of oppression is different from our own is much more than a strategy for working towards specific political ends; it is also a way to live life more fully and do our part to make it possible for others to do the same.' In this book, I call this practice collaborative community-building. This practice seeks to undermine 'the rupture in the separation [of what she terms citizens and refugees]' that the police order institutes (Doppler 2015). 'It's a form of solidarity, not a paternalistic charity. Not something where people treat the subjects of the solidarity activism as people who need to be mollycoddled and controlled and stuff. It's about spending time with people, migrants, refugees, asylum seekers. Working with them, organizing with them, living with them' (interview, Anon. 6).

A focus on collaborative community-building doesn't only express a perspective of radical anti-racism. It also expresses a perspective that takes seriously the idea that the autonomy of migration is a political practice. With this in mind, CMS seeks to overcome what Angela Mitropoulos and Brett Neilson (2006) call the separation between movement as politics and movement in a kinetic sense that is instituted within dominant social reality. Drawing on this and the work of Jacques Rancière, Joe Rigby and Raphael Schlembach describe this as a 'division in the account given of what constitutes a political movement. The separation of "movement as politics" from "movement as motion" consistently presents the acts of undocumented migrants, their movements as "bereft of political decision and action", thereby suturing politics to sovereignty and territoriality' (Rigby and Schlembach 2013: 163). 'Activism' is the other side of what remains after the separation of movement as motion from movement as politics. What this often means is that 'properly political' activities such as protests often fail to overcome this division. CMS has sought to overcome the division between movement as protest and movement as action by continually questioning what collective action could look like. In doing this, their interventions 'reflect a call for a continuous "recount" of the situation, over an affirmation of a particular framing of the situation' (Millner 2011).

Conclusion

In this chapter I have explored the more structured parts of the no borders movement; the parts where people have come together largely in organized, visible and intentionally political ways. It's in groups like these that we see the clearest articulation of certain ideologies and beliefs. Despite their sharing some important common ground, the struggle for the freedom of movement is read in different ways within this movement; ways that resonate with a variety of different ideologies (from anarchist to left perspectives) and none. A group that reads it first and foremost as a struggle to escape the state will reach very different conclusions as to what effective action is from a group that reads it primarily as a struggle to transform the state through demands for rights and recognition. Within this, concepts like equality and solidarity are also open to differing interpretations, valued to differing degrees and expressed in different ways.

For groups like 'The 300' or the Network, whose practice is shaped by perspectives that see racism as an effect of capitalism, where taking action expresses a stance of being in and against the state, solidarity is built on the basis of our shared struggle against capitalism, where equality means equal rights for all, as workers. Despite sharing similar perspectives on activism, the practices of 'The 300' and the Network diverge, though. By virtue of their being excluded from citizenship yet making demands on the state for rights, the activism of 'The 300' potentially challenges/undermines the idea that rights are somehow tied to the state. Here, equality takes on a different meaning from that of citizenship; as something broader and less qualified. For the Network, which is primarily seen as a group of citizens (even if in reality a number of its members are not), their involvement has the potential to 'turn up the volume' on migrant-led demands for rights and representation. However, a politics of representation remains more bounded by a relationship to the state here. Equality here generally means equality as citizens, and solidarity is often expressed as a form of empowerment to migrants.

For the anti-authoritarian movement, whose practice is shaped by affinity, where taking action expresses a stance of being outside the state, their activism largely prioritizes creating other ways of being to the state, or else actively antagonizing it. People from the movement have created community with people without papers in moments when they have shared space. They have become friends, built affinities. But generally solidarity has extended only as far as to those who share similar means and ends in their activism.

For groups like CMS, whose practice is shaped by a radical anti-racism that is about becoming minor, their activism prioritizes creating other ways of being to the state, through building collaborative communities with people without papers. An activism like this is also about seeking to undermine the border that exists between movement as motion and movement as politics. Here solidarity involves subverting the idea of what being an ally means; seeking affinity whilst also being aware that structural differences make that difficult.

By laying out these different perspectives and what they tell us about practice, my aim has been to give a sense of the spectrum of activism that makes up the no borders movement. In doing so I have sought to add to what a no borders politics is, as laid out in the previous chapter. What this spectrum points to is ambivalence in what constitutes effective action to refuse the border and why we might take that action in the first place. It raises a second fundamental dilemma for a no borders politics: how to navigate between being together with others in their struggle for liberation while also staying faithful to what is our own struggle. Put another way, it navigates between different conceptualizations of what effective action is. The following two chapters take these ideas and look at how these groups play them out in practice. First I look at Athens, then I look at Calais.

3 | THE STRUGGLE FOR MOBILITY IN ATHENS

Some history to this struggle

Athens is not a border zone, but by 2011, when I lived there for a year, it had very much become a flashpoint on the map of European migration. Recent years had seen many people travelling through Athens on their journeys farther into Europe, from the Middle East and North Africa, via Turkey. Few planned to stay in Athens, but many had become stuck there. By 2012, the Greek authorities estimated there to be around a million people without papers in the country (Human Rights Watch 2013) and Greece was demanding that the European Union step in and help.

How did this situation come about? Partly what was painted as a 'migration crisis' was the result of a national history that had long either ignored immigration (Greece having been a country primarily of emigration until the 1970s), or that engaged with the issue retroactively, to prevent or else restrict it, with little effect.[1] Indeed, located along historic transit and trade routes between western Europe, North Africa and the Middle East, for most of its history Greece had been a place of transit, or else departure[2] (Cavounidis 2002; Kiprianos et al. 2003). Despite these things, from the early 1980s, as Greece became wealthier, relationships with its neighbours friendlier, and as visa restrictions with certain countries started to relax, various diaspora communities built up (in particular Albanian and Egyptian communities), transforming Greece from a country people left, to one people wanted to get to (or at least pass through).

The national response combined legal measures to deter new arrivals with periodic attempts at 'cleaning the slate'. In 1991 the first legislation to directly deal with immigration focused on remedial (e.g. deportation procedures), punitive (e.g. enhanced border controls[3] and detention facilities) and preventive measures (e.g. visas as a requirement for entry of third-country nationals) (Konsta and Lazaridis 2010).[4] In 1998, following the lead of other southern

European states, Greece carried out the first of four mass legalization 'amnesties' to date (the others taking place in 2001, 2005 and a smaller one in 2007) (Kasimis and Papadopoulos 2005; Konsta and Lazaridis 2010). In each case, large numbers of applicants were not successful, and legalization temporary[5] (Konsta and Lazaridis 2010). Nonetheless, this has been one of the few means by which undocumented people could gain legal (if temporary) status.[6] Despite such 'amnesties', by 2012 the population of people without papers in the country had reached that estimated one million.

Greece's position in, and relationship with, the European Union has also played a huge part in shaping the situation. In 1992 Greece became a signatory to the Schengen Agreement (fully implementing it by 2000), and as such a participant in the creation of an area of free movement for the citizens of those states signatory to it. With accession to Schengen, Greece's external border became the frontier of the EU and the Schengen zone. As such, Greece became responsible not only for 'protecting' and 'defending' its own sovereign borders, but for doing so on behalf of all those member states in the Schengen zone. In theory this meant enhanced border controls. In practice, Greece's increased importance as an access route to the rest of the EU for those travelling clandestinely meant a huge increase in clandestine travel into and through Greece (Konsta and Lazaridis 2010; Triandafyllidou 2012). Despite the laws and border controls, becoming a part of the Schengen zone changed the nature of migration to Greece, because arriving in Greece meant arriving in Europe.

Whether intending to come to Greece or continue into other EU states, people from the Near and Middle East and North Africa navigated Greece's still relatively leaky borders (the complex coastline and myriad tiny islands make border controls particularly difficult to enforce here) to come to Europe, often crossing from Turkey to the nearest Greek islands of Samos or Lesvos and from there to the mainland. Greece (largely financed by the EU) continued efforts to reinforce the country's external borders.[7] The efforts of various enhanced border control missions did have an effect. With attention focused on the islands, journeys increasingly shifted to the land border between Turkey and Greece, across the River Evros. By 2010 it was estimated that 90 per cent of all clandestine entries into the EU came via Greece (Frontex 2010).

At the external border, then, measures to stem the flow of 'illegal migration' largely failed, within a migration regime that created an increasingly large category of 'illegal immigrants'. At the same time, Schengen saw the removal of internal state borders and the implementation of a range of measures within countries to compensate for their perceived loss of sovereignty. What are called compensatory measures included what were effectively 'soft' internal border controls, in the sense of being more discreet, supposedly ad hoc[8] and carried out by domestic security agencies such as the police (Bigo 2011). As a part of this, in 2011 Greece introduced a 30-kilometre zone of 'enhanced border monitoring' in the sea between Igoumenitsa on the north-western mainland and the island of Corfu, from where people take ferries to Italy (Welcome to Europe 2011).[9] Exiting Greece became harder, and the cost to smugglers of securing false documents for this part of the journey went sky high (field diary, 2012). The following year Greece completed the construction of a 12.5-kilometre wall between itself and Turkey in the eastern region of Evros. Those people who had come to Greece seeking to pass through it now found themselves increasingly penned in, and Greece found itself in the role of European incarcerator.[10] At the same time, for those who had left Greece and claimed asylum elsewhere, the Dublin Regulation[11] meant that some were returned to Greece, adding to the 'migration problem' there.

These policies resulted in Greece becoming a giant prison for many people without papers. But factors beyond those directly related to migration turned Athens into a particular site of struggle. The economic crisis that started to bite deep into Greece in 2008 saw work dry up in many industries, including those employing large numbers of people without papers, such as tourism or agriculture. As work dried up, more and more people came to the capital, either to find work, or to better access networks that could facilitate their onward travel. As this took place within the trap of Greece's borders, many found themselves stuck, with Athens representing the most populated part of the 'national jail'.

By 2011, hundreds of thousands of people without papers were living in the capital, trying to survive while also seeking ways to make their exit from Greece. It was common for people to be living ten to an apartment, and people who were unable to cover rent had started camping in the city's parks. These camps were ethnically separate, as were many of the ways that people found to make a living at that time. People from Afghanistan were those to be found at most traffic lights, washing car windscreens; people from the Indian subcontinent were selling pirate DVDs in the city's squares; people from Africa were forming expansive street markets, selling bags, shoes, sunglasses, clothes and electrical goods. Roma families were begging in the streets, squares and metro stations, and everybody, including many Greeks, were looking through the rubbish bins for food. All of these ways of survival formed part of the growing black market, with most people without papers excluded from legal forms of employment.

There was a tangible feeling of growing insecurity and desperation in downtown Athens at that time, as these inner-city neighbourhoods became populated by ever-growing numbers of people without papers, increasingly existing beneath the breadline. That summer, the Muslim Association of Greece estimated they fed 6,000 people every day during Ramadan and housed many hundreds too (interview, 12 November 2011).

Practising the autonomy of migration – the apartment

I started spending time in an apartment in Athens after being invited to celebrate Persian New Year there by a mutual friend. The apartment appeared nothing out of the ordinary, but squeezed twelve people into a living space ordinarily designed for a single family. This extraordinary situation had become increasingly commonplace in recent years, as an ever-growing number of people without papers sought ways to live in a city they could barely afford to be in. Acharnon was now a neighbourhood full to bursting. It had changed unrecognizably in less than a decade: from a prosperous neighbourhood of ethnic Greeks (as was most of the city and indeed country at that time), to one of cheap rental accommodation taken up by those most desperate for it (which was often people from other countries). This slide into a slum had taken hold of many of Athens' downtown districts. Many native locals felt it had become disreputable and dangerous – a no-go zone. It was chaotic, but also beautiful in the chaos that comes when cultures mix together in a place that has too little space to go around.

All of the residents of the apartment were from Afghanistan and had come to be living there through family or friendship connections. The apartment was largely a staging post for people on their journeys farther out of Greece, and many had passed through over previous months. Some were new arrivals destined not to stay for long, but others had been there months. You could say there was some kind of social hierarchy in the apartment as a result. Some of the long-termers' knowledge about the local area, means of travel and connections to smuggling networks made them particularly able to help in the onward movement of others. Despite this form of hierarchy, ultimately the apartment did not function because it was 'owned' by anyone. People came and went and helped each other out, and the apartment remained. That's not to say the apartment was for everybody. Access was limited through friendship and kinship.

The apartment was a hub in a network of support for those living there, and for their friends and relatives. It provided a place to gather energy before moving on, to return to if things didn't work out, or to send friends to if they needed a contact. It was a little like a transit zone; a place of friendship, but also where journeys could be arranged and plans formulated. It was a place of mutual support within a society people were outside of. A way of sharing limited material resources and of keeping each other safer in a city where racially motivated street and state violence was commonplace. Ultimately, the apartment was an important node in the mobile commons.

I doubt that this place is still rented by this group now, but I thought the apartment was remarkable while it lasted. Yet from the point of view of an outsider looking in it was totally the opposite. Indeed, being unremarkable was part of what made it subversive. The fact that Athens is a huge and sprawling city of millions has meant that travellers have to a large extent been able to 'blend in'. This is part of the reason why so many travellers to Greece come here. In a city like Athens it's possible to 'become imperceptible'; to get lost, and to link into a network of others who are also moving by getting lost.

The fact that it's not supposed to be there is part of what makes it subversive. This 'being out of place' can be interpreted as a little practice of escape, because it creates a small community of those denied equality, but in some way make it among themselves. It's a space for people who are not supposed to be there, and refuse that fact by being there anyway. It makes no proclamations, but in its presence it says 'we are here, and we will make our way regardless'. This is what makes the apartment remarkable to me, because in these ways people escape, through particular expressions of autonomy (even if that escape is temporary). The apartment is a very small example of autonomy – specifically the autonomy of migration. These little 'outsides' are replicated thousands of times all over Europe, and in that replication force a response in the regime of control.

How the state responded to the 'migration crisis'

After I visited the apartment, in 2012 Greece began construction of thirty new detention prisons across the country, largely financed by the EU (Clandestina 2012). This expansion was accompanied by a ramping up of coordinated 'sweep operations' of people without papers in the country; the practice whereby police would suddenly appear in a neighbourhood and carry out supposedly random ID checks on people of colour. Under these conditions, people increasingly went out of sight as a means of remaining under the radar and more able to stay on the move. The specific sweep operation 'Xenios Zeus' (ironically meaning 'hospitable god') resulted in an estimated 85,000 people being detained in the country between August 2012 and February 2013[12] (Cossé 2013). For those who were imprisoned, there has been an ongoing wave of protests, unrest and hunger strikes against their detention.[13]

Ahmed,[14] who had come to Greece from Bangladesh, talked about how, in the time he had been in the country, he felt the situation for migrants had radically changed. Whereas before you could perhaps find a way to gather money for the next part of your journey, or even to make a life in Greece, now the options were very slim. In particular he talked about how, whereas a few years ago people had been able to make money selling some goods on the street, these days it was becoming increasingly risky to do so, because now the police were simply in the habit of confiscating all the goods, rather than arresting them. People were losing all their money in the loss of their stock and were unable to start again.

That people without papers had to hide from the police was not unusual. However, as Ahmed's account points out, the police represented more than just a risk of detention at that time (which often resulted in release rather than deportation); they were undermining people's ability to exist in the city at all. Indeed, a Human Rights Watch report of 2012 documented evidence that explicitly made the link between the Athens police and racist practices towards migrants (Human Rights Watch 2012: 12). There have been numerous other accounts of abuse by police towards migrants (see Clandestina 2011). Between 1998 and 2008, it was estimated that of the fifteen fatal shootings of civilians carried out by the police, most were of migrants (Sakellaropoulos 2012).

'Xenios Zeus' and the building of thirty new detention prisons were part of the growing use of detention as a technology of control across Europe, particularly around the European frontier, in places like Greece (Fekete 2011). In Athens, the operation severely undermined diaspora support networks by making many public places where communities previously gathered even more risky to spend time in. People were forced out of public spaces, behind closed doors. More chose to bypass the city and continue their journeys out of Greece in other ways, if they could. One interviewee reflected on the change they had witnessed from 2011 to 2015. 'It's quite stunning and very depressing because Athens has changed from a very buzzing kind of crazy city to quite empty compared to what it used to be. Many migrants are still there, but in private homes, and a lot of them are detained' (interview, Anon. 2). An excerpt from my field diary further illustrates this point: 'X said how a few years ago, coming to Athens and not being already connected wasn't so much of a problem, because there were certain places where you could count on finding people, such as various squares. But that's changed now. There are so few spaces where people can hang out visibly' (field diary, 22 March 2012).

Some people arriving in Europe took other routes that avoided Greece (via Bulgaria or Serbia, for example; a 'jungle' subsequently built up outside the town of Subotica, on the Serbian side of its border with Hungary). Others changed their routes into Greece, reverting back to those that landed on Greece's easternmost islands by boat, rather than approaching the now heavily militarized land border with Turkey (a reversal of what had happened before). For those already in Athens, Operation Xenios Zeus made it a very risky city to be in.

Control measures such as Xenios Zeus were underwritten by a generally racist response from many native Greeks and older-generation migrants too. Indeed, in Greece the connection between migration and racism is quite explicit, such that the recent history of immigration to Greece is seen as a unique and negative phenomenon that brought race and racism with it. Race and migration are deeply intertwined, such that any person of colour in the country is also an immigrant, both in the minds of citizens and in legal terms (naturalization is based on ethnic kinship and no non-Greek has the means to become naturalized, for example).

Dominant civic and political discourses around migration have fermented a culture of hostility towards migrants that has made it easy to scapegoat them, particularly during times of social crisis. The control measures described above came at a time when the economic crisis was really starting to bite deep into Greece. This generalized anti-migrant sentiment helped create the right conditions for such anti-immigration policies, because the economic crisis justified the scapegoating of migrants. Parties across the political spectrum regularly made explicit links between migration and the country's ills (Sunderland and Cossé 2012; Human Rights Watch 2012). The sentiment that 'nobody who comes to Greece in their right mind wants to stay here' was common.

At that time, the far right were well positioned to work within the already accepted racist discourse of danger, crisis and blame to manipulate the connections between migration and crisis. The neo-Nazi group Golden Dawn won eighteen seats in the 2012 parliamentary elections, making them the third-most popular party in the country (Sunderland and Cossé 2012). They campaigned heavily on an anti-immigrant platform under the slogan 'So we can rid this land of filth' (Rabinowitz 2012).[15] Investigations (such as those by the newspapers *Ta Nea* and *Eleftheropea*) demonstrated a connection between the Golden Dawn and the police too.[16]

Within this context came the rise of organized street violence towards people of colour, connected to 'citizens' committees': self-appointed neighbourhood watch groups with the agenda of making their neighbourhoods 'Greek only' (Sunderland and Cossé 2012). As a result, central Athens became the site of numerous public, racially motivated attacks. Doctors of the World, which in 2011 opened a polyclinic in downtown Athens, estimated that they treated 300 people for attacks during the first half of that year.[17]

Despite this racism, and controls like Xenios Zeus, people without papers have nonetheless made an indelible imprint on the city by weaving the mobile commons through Athens in many ways. Neighbourhoods like Acharnon have become 'migrant neighbourhoods', themselves important hubs of information and support. Over time, certain neighbourhoods have become ethnically distinct. Victoria is primarily an Afghan neighbourhood, Kypseli home to many people from West Africa, Ambelokipi to people from Albania. Private spaces – shops, restaurants, cafés and internet cafés, for example – have become important places in which to meet others and share information.

Having laid out some of the struggle over mobility that was expressed through practices of the autonomy of migration and control of it, I now want to turn to look at how people also took collective action in the struggle for the freedom of movement in more visible ways. Returning to the specific example of the hunger strike of 'The 300', I look now at engagement in a politics of rights and representation, through protest that also took place at this time.

The struggle for visibility – the hunger strike of 'The 300'

> We are migrant men and women, refugees from all over Greece. We came here to escape poverty, unemployment, wars and dicta- torships. The multinational companies and their political servants left us no choice but to repeatedly risk our lives to journey towards Europe's door. The West that is exploiting our countries while ben- efiting from much better living conditions is our only chance to live decent lives, to live as human beings. Whether by regular or irregular entry, we came to Greece and are working to support ourselves and our families ... On issues of migration, the propaganda of fascist and racist parties and groups has become the formal language of the State while their 'proposals' have already become government policy: the wall in Evros, floating detention centres and a European army in the Aegean, repression in the cities, massive deportations. They are trying to make Greek workers believe that we are suddenly a threat to them, that we are to blame for the unprecedented attack from their own governments. The response to the lies and the cruelty must be provided now and it will come from us, from migrant men and women. ('The 300', 2011)

So far I have looked at those struggles against the border regime that essentially went on 'beneath the radar' of public attention. Yet at that time, with increased numbers of migrants in the country and increased measures to control them, there was a growing underclass of people existing in Greece with few or no rights, including the right to stay.

This system of differential inclusion – by which I mean the inclusion of people as inferiors, or as those who fall outside of any category and get labelled as 'illegal' – wasn't new. Lauretta, one of the main organizers of the United Women's African Association, had been in

Greece for twenty-nine years with a status of semi-legality; a short-term residency paper that was dependent on continuous employment, and which she had to renew every six months. Another member of the group had been in the country for twenty-five years and in the same situation. Their situation wasn't unusual either. As a process of the 'inclusion of migrant labour by means of its criminalization', border controls in Greece created an underclass (Mezzadra 2004b). But not all inferior statuses are the same and few, if any, are permanent (Düvell 2006). For example, a person may arrive in Greece legally on a working visa. They might be able to maintain this visa if they can uphold the conditions of its application (continuous employment, for example), but they might also lose this legal status if they can't (they may then apply for legalization if a regularization campaign is in operation, but as I said before, such amnesties have been limited and temporary).

The presence of an underclass of the differentially included wasn't new, then. What was, was its size. The number of people categorized as 'illegal' was high and on the up. Partly, this was because at the same time the number of people losing some kind of semi-legal/permanent status and falling into illegality was also on the rise. An increasingly large number of people, increasingly denied any rights, were having to find ways to assert their right to be in Greece.

A background to the strike In Chapter 2 I introduced the hunger strike of 'The 300'. I return to it now, as an example of a key event in the struggle for the freedom of movement that was highly visible, and made a demand for rights and representation. Indeed, the hunger strike of 'The 300' was an event that persistently reappeared in the discussions and stories of activists from across the political spectrum, from migrant hang-outs to anarchist social centres. Any discussion that touched on migration would eventually come round to 'The 300' without prompting. It affected the trajectory of the field of activism in the city, opening up and closing down certain possibilities.

As I mentioned in Chapter 2, many who were involved in this strike had memories of a previous successful strike that had taken place in Chania two years before. The political climate was a lot bleaker two years later, though. Work was becoming more scarce, applicability for legal residency more restrictive,[18] and workplace raids more common. After so many years of precarity, many who had been living in Chania with some kind of temporary or semi-legal immigration status were starting to talk about the need to fight what was increasingly looking like their collective slide into illegality.

In the autumn of 2010 people from the North African community started to hold public meetings to discuss this issue. The meetings were really well attended; hundreds of people at times (interview, Anon.). After a number of public meetings it was decided that the course of action would be a hunger strike. Although there were many more hundreds of people who wanted to strike, it was decided that 300 people would participate and represent all migrant workers with precarious status in Greece.[19] It was also agreed that in order to demonstrate the seriousness of their demands, to maximize the spectacular nature of their action and to demonstrate that their struggle was Greece-wide, they would carry out their strike at the source of decision-making, Athens, and the second city, Thessaloniki. I will focus on the strike in Athens.

In Chapter 1 I talked about how migrant-led acts of protest can at times transform the logics of belonging and also potentially escape the state insofar as they represent a practice of equality. I talked about the concept of disagreement as about mobilizing an obligation of the state to recognize the excluded as political subjects (Rancière 2006). But the state seeks to deny the existence of the excluded part; to undermine and delegitimize it. Indeed, Rancière argues that the role of the police order 'consists, before all else, in recalling the obviousness of what there is, or rather of what there is not, and its slogan is: "Move along! There is nothing to see here!"' (Rancière 2010: 37). Within the mainstream media, reports of the strike sought to undermine its validity by regurgitating and feeding anti-immigrant public sentiment. The strikers had chosen to base themselves in the Law School of Athens University (the Nomiki), a space chosen first because of a rule of asylum that prevented the entry of police or military into such spaces, and second because of its historical link with radical left protest. Vitriolic commentaries sought to undermine and belittle this choice, lambasting the strikers and their supporters for what they saw as an abuse of the asylum rule by foreigners. Other commentaries questioned the strikers' hygiene and sanity. In these ways the government, via the mainstream media, presented the strike not as a political act, but an administrative abuse and a health risk.

Parliament debated suspending the asylum rule, which was already under attack. In response to this threat, on day three of the strike 'The

300' released a statement refusing to move, but on the fourth day the government successfully sought a suspension of the university asylum rule and surrounded the building with armed riot police. At three that morning the strikers, along with around five hundred supporters, left the university and moved to a private building a few kilometres away (called Ypateia). After the move, the strikers released another statement saying, '[w]e are committed and we continue the hunger strike; despite all the pressure and the bad conditions of the place that, by force, we accepted to move' ('The 300', 29 January 2011). The strike continued for a further thirty-nine days.

Despite the government's denial of the legitimacy of the strikers and their demands, as the strike persisted the government was forced to engage. Very public images of emaciated activists being wheeled out of Ypataeia and taken to hospital, along with a continual flow of demonstrations and other actions by supporters, placed the strike firmly in the public domain. The resulting image was of a state losing the moral war in a very public way. Negotiations (which took place behind closed doors with a team of lawyers and negotiators) continued for forty-four days. By that time over one hundred of the strikers had been hospitalized and, in an effort to ramp up the pressure, many were refusing water. At this point, the government made a number of concessions which the strikers were willing to accept. The strike ended.

Beyond the practical concessions, the strikers created something that transformed the political terrain; that brought new possibilities into being. Nasim, who was involved in the strike as a supporter, felt that it changed the terms of the debate:

> The strike changed the agendas of discussion. Before: mass deportations. After: new ideas entered the public sphere … The strike brought the struggle of people who were invisible and without rights into the public consciousness. There were some discussions for new asylum rights and abilities to renew work permits and stuff, free doctors, etc. A new agenda in the public sphere. (Interview, Nasim)

In making these concessions, the government had been forced to recognize the strikers as legitimate political actors. This is something that the strikers already knew about themselves. The extended quote that opened this part of the chapter came from the initial statement released by them. It is resolute, unapologetic, scholarly and thoughtful.

In it, they refer to themselves in many ways; as family members, refugees, workers ... They explode any definition that reduces them down to one category. This is the statement of people who are not asking to be recognized as capable of political speech and action, because it is a clear demonstration that they already are. The statement reflects what was also present in their actions: a presupposition of equality. In making a protest of this kind, protest being something normally the reserve of citizens with rights, they acted as though they *were* citizens (Butler and Spivak 2007).

The strike was a demonstration of the presupposition of equality. But it emerged from a pre-existing collective practice of equality in their organization. The meetings that took place in Chania in the summer of 2010 were self-organized by those who went on to strike. They created a form of direct democracy that sought to allow everybody to express their views and reach decisions collectively. They also demonstrated an important degree of autonomy over the participants' actions. Direct democracy continued in the self-organized assembly held daily during the strike. Their ability to organize autonomously and through non-hierarchy was very important to the legitimacy of their actions. 'We take our decisions by ourselves during the assemblies we hold, and we do not get influenced by external factors ... We, 300, took the initiative for that kind of struggle, without the intervention of political parties, organizations and individuals' ('The 300', 29 January 2011). John Holloway suggests this is perhaps the key outcome of such actions. 'The most important outcome of the struggles is often not the realisation of the immediate demands, but the development of *a community of struggle*, a collective doing characterised by its opposition to capitalist forms of social relation' (Holloway 2002: 208). It was in the creation of this 'community of struggle' – temporary but strong – where I think the strike made the raising of what Rancière calls disagreement even possible, and that represented some kind of escape from the state.

The strike politicized a vast number of people, both the strikers and their supporters, many of whom had not been involved in migration struggles before. It also made connections between migrant and native activist communities that previously didn't exist. Indeed, through the very process of participation, the strikers acted themselves into a position of political agency. Youssef expressed the importance of this 'doing it for ourselves':

I was glad. I know that it's not too much organisations. Not too organised, but I was glad. Because they other immigrants start to act. I don't want it to be just me and these three and these other two. I want others … I know that if I can do it in a week, the Greek he can do it in three days, OK? But no, let the others work. And now, they are working. They are working politically. (Interview, Youssef)

Solidarity and 'The 300'

The struggle of 'The 300' comprised more than just the actions of the strikers. The strikers were supported by a solidarity campaign that brought together a large and diverse array of groups and individuals. I focus here on two of those groups, previously introduced in Chapter 2: the Network, and the anti-authoritarian movement.

As is the tradition of almost all forms of collaborative radical political action in the country, assemblies formed the main decision-making structures of the solidarity campaign. Because of the diversity of the groups involved, several assemblies were formed, rather than one. The assembly of 'The 300' made decisions over their actions, and fed into an assembly of anti-racists and the left (of which the Network was a part), an assembly of radical left, anti-authoritarian, libertarian and anarchist groups, and a semi-organized assembly of specifically defined anti-fascist (Antifa) groups.

Within this fragmented structure, the Network came to be one of the largest and most influential groups in the campaign.[20] It made sense that it would be this way. The politics of the Network resonated with those of the strike: it was migrant-led, and so created a clear role for the Network in showing solidarity with the strikers, and the strikers' demands for rights resonated with an approach that sought to challenge the structures of domination through demands for recognition. In addition to providing practical support and participating in organizing mass protests, the Network was heavily involved with media and legal work. They supported the strikers in releasing their press statements and held a number of press conferences. They also released their own statements and were involved in establishing a dedicated strike website.

The relationship between the movement and the strike was less straightforward. The main reasons for this were threefold. First, the movement felt that the involvement of the left raised concerns that people were signing up to an essentially leftist and therefore reformist struggle. But second, people from the movement felt that they didn't have the expertise, or a clear position on such issues, to be able to decisively engage without the involvement of the 'expert' left anyway. Finally, there was the fundamental ideological difference: despite the idea of diversity of tactics, was the movement prepared to overcome its refusal to engage with the state in this case, and show solidarity with a struggle for rights and recognition? As a result of these doubts, some felt that the movement failed to support this struggle. But such a criticism isn't equally applicable across this movement, and the assembly of anarchists and libertarians formed a clear presence in the campaign. Still, responses to several call-outs for participation in this assembly were largely weak and non-committal. Collectives were poorly represented, turnout poor and decision-making slow. Despite all this, the anarchist and libertarian assembly continued. Over the course of the strike, the assembly organized several demonstrations, occupied a government building, distributed statements from the strikers in different languages, and provided practical support to the strikers.

These different perspectives on political action created tensions between the assemblies. Media engagement was one of them. The strikers wanted to engage the mainstream media, and this was supported by the assembly of anti-racists and the left. It was based on the rationale that boosting the voice of the strikers would generate mass support and create leverage on the government through public pressure. These aims were not shared by the other solidarity assemblies, which saw the mass media as a tool of statist and capitalist propaganda, reinforcing dominant, oppressive and alienating perspectives on the racialized, classed and gendered dimensions of the strike. The move of the strike from the Law School was also controversial. On the one hand there were those who saw the move as beyond the control of the strikers and supporters; as an essential means of ensuring the continuity of the strike in the face of the threat of violence. On the other hand there were those who saw the decision to move as an unacceptable lack of solidarity with wider radical social struggles, which included sustaining the university asylum law.

After they left Nomiki, mainly the people who went to Ypateia were leftists and the anarchists kept their distance, trying to protect

people, but kept their distance, because they started to feel that this
thing didn't express them, that too much was going on behind the
scenes that they were excluded from. The media was a problem.
They were there from the beginning because the immigrants
were convinced to give interviews every day. The media was
misrepresenting the message the immigrants were trying to get across.
(Interview, Sami)

After the move, then, some from the assembly of anarchists and
libertarians left the struggle, and there were a number of denunciations
of the strike from various parts of that movement that saw the strike as
'too reformist'.

It's a different movement because they don't want to discuss with the
state and in this struggle someone had to go to the ministers and say
how things will go on and push the government and something like
this and the anarchists say OK, our frame is totally against the state
and we will not transform it now. I think this is the main reason and
also they don't trust Diktyo, they don't trust AK and they don't trust
the Greek left. They don't have good relations. They did have some
good relations during the revolt of 2008, some of them. Let's say the
base, people from the grass roots. But in 2011 you didn't have good
relations with them ... After what happened in Nomiki the anarchists
felt that the migrants could have stayed in Nomiki and the state
wouldn't do anything. So they said loudly that the Forum, AK and left
were cowards who didn't support the asylum status of the university.
(Ibid.)

Animosity between the different assemblies meant that paths
of communication started to break down. Laurence, who had been
involved in the solidarity movement (but who had stayed away from
the assemblies), illustrates this issue in recounting her attempts at
participating in the various demos organized by the different assemblies.
'She told me how she remembered at that time it was not unusual to go
to one march called by one group at say, 4 o'clock, then have to rush
to another, going on simultaneously in another location by a different
group, and then go to a third, held at a different time by a different
group!' (field diary, 4 December 2011).

Activists from the ASSV also talked about how their choice to stay
involved left them feeling isolated. As large parts of the movement
chose not to participate directly, they felt that their decision to

persevere was frowned upon by others. Stuck in the middle, they were labelled as leftist traitors by the movement and unpredictable radicals by the left.

These tensions put a strain on the decision-making structure of the campaign. The assemblies still acted as the official structures through which decisions were made, but differences *within* assemblies were exacerbated by the animosity between assemblies. It meant that many 'unofficial' actions ended up taking place, as people lost patience with the assembly structure. Beyond the assemblies there were many cases where people *were* cooperating, independent of any political group or label. People from across the political spectrum were going together into inner-city neighbourhoods to distribute texts written by the strikers. They were spending time with the strikers, in the buildings where the strike was happening and also in the hospital. It was in these acts that some different dimensions of political praxis were expressed and bonds created. Certainly it is these acts, when people organized beyond the decisions of the assemblies, that people recounted, with good feeling and warmth, a sense of success in their solidarity:

> But then there were so many good people in the base of these groups doing such good things ... I think this was the real solidarity movement, the people that were not only talking in assemblies but the people that did work and there were people from both assemblies and people who were not going to the assemblies because they didn't like the political civilization there because it was so problematic in both these assemblies ... But it was different, for example me, I did different work inside the anarchist assembly. Different work in Ypateia. Different work in the base with other people doing occupations and stuff like this. And different work with communicating with people. This is how a lot of people worked these days. (Interview, Sami)

The proliferation of different organized and autonomous actions that took place points to how the solidarity movement of 'The 300' proved partly successful in creating a resistance that connected different modes of struggle. However, there were limits to this connectivity. As people reflected on the solidarity movement after the strike had succeeded, a common feeling was that effectiveness had been limited by how groups had felt compelled to protect and promote their own ideas and practices of resistance. Sami highlights a number of these issues:

For the Greek left in Athens it [the strike] was something that was
going very well, by doing a different kind of, you know, having a
different social movement repertoire. And it was the anarchists
that were saying this hunger strike is doomed to fail and it's totally
controlled from people that are bureaucrats or the Greek left ... I
think in Athens there were not the preconditions so that we could
have a bridge in between the different solidarity groups because
everybody wanted to do it his way without communicating ... It's
impossible for them [the anti-authoritarian movement] to concede
things, such as use of the media. That's why most of the actions
happened outside of the collective organization. But all these
different pressures were communicating. And some time we were
together.

Me: 'X' and 'X' were disappointed in the anarchist response

Yes, for me too ... I'm also disappointed with the left. They couldn't
even find a way to work between them. They were like crazy kids.
(Ibid.)

Youssef, a member of the Forum who was an advocate for the
strikers, also recognized how partisanship inhibited collaboration.

We [the solidarity movement] were talking about 'I' and 'my', so it
was obvious we had a problem with Greek solidarity. OK. Then 'The
300' was here, left from here, anarchists from here. The left came
to talk with 'The 300' to put them next to them. Anarchists came to
try to put them. OK? And who will lose? 'The 300' will lose at the
end. Who will win? The government will win ... For that reason I say
nobody can act from himself. If someone acts for himself he will pay
for this OK. (Interview, Youssef)

The excerpts above tell us a lot about the problems that arise
when different ideologically driven perspectives come into contact
with each other. The strikers felt that solidarity was crucial in
order to make their campaign successful. They felt that without the
support of native groups to amplify their message, the likelihood
of their struggle being heard might be minimal. At the same time,
native groups' compulsion towards partisanship meant that solidarity
became a practice of patronage used by them to further their political
perspective and goals. The effect of this was to lead to splits between
the strikers:

We find that if they [the solidarity movement] have the same demand like us, we could win; like fifteen day like that. But everybody had different ideas. We broke. Half go with Kontra [a radical left group] and half go with the Forum and later with Steki Metanaston [the Network] in Athen. We have problem. We want to make assembly but we have problem, because the Kontra is make problem. (Interview, 'The 300')

The support of solidarity groups in this campaign created problems. In ways like these, native groups can actually undermine the effectiveness of such struggles and the ability of migrant-led groups to remain in control of them (Lentin 2004). Struggles for liberation are not exempt from hierarchies and inequalities that create boundaries between who gets to speak/act and who doesn't (Sajed 2012). Lauretta (United African Women's Association of Greece) reflected on how this seems prevalent throughout struggles for the freedom of movement. '[T]here are almost no migrants' groups who are autonomous. Most have Greek political groups behind them, pulling the string. Why will Greece not let us to do our own thing?!' (interview, Lauretta).

The strike put the issue of legalization and migrant rights back on the political agenda. The Network kept in contact with many of the strikers and after the strike there was a lot of energy for developing the struggle into a new mass regularization campaign. Over time, though, momentum for the campaign dissipated. The difficulty of transforming the strike in this way partly reflected the political climate at the time. In the months after the strike, as the economic crisis in Greece deepened, there was a growing feeling that to articulate discourses of rights, particularly the rights of foreigners, was impossible in an environment of domestic economic and social crisis. In the political chaos and new possibilities of that summer and autumn,[21] with regular strikes and protests that called the democratic system into question, the issue of migrant rights slowly disappeared from public political discourse. Among the parliamentary left, talking of migrant rights was seen as political suicide.

As a migration-focused anti-racist group, the Network struggled to respond to this change. On the one hand some felt that the struggle of migrants was increasingly looking like the struggle of everyone in Greece. Now was a time when the connections between natives and migrants in their exploitation under capitalism were more apparent than ever and a *universalist* class struggle could be best pursued. Others felt that using a generalizing class-based discourse obscured the *particular* oppressions migrants faced, which were becoming more acute in the crisis. Now it was more necessary to address these oppressions specifically.

There was also the sense that migrant communities themselves were not mobilizing. At a loss as to how to articulate the oppression of migrants with migrants, the situation was described by one Network activist in this way: 'We are at risk of becoming like a lawyer without a client to represent' (field diary, 17 October 2011). It hadn't always been this way. There had been numerous times in the past when the Network had mobilized with particular communities over different issues. Now, however, they were struggling to see where this was happening, or possible:

> Many communities are inactive. Migrant community groups are less and less representative of their communities because the system is making these communities more dispersed, more transient and more precarious. People are less willing and able to build community structures. There are huge migrant populations, but less and less politically active migrant groups. A few years ago we went to Omonia and the focus was on Somali refugees who had many needs. The situation there is very different today. It's very difficult to find people to work with. We need to search for migrant communities we can work with and support. (Field diary, summarized contributions from members at a Diktyo meeting, 15 June 2011)

The low participation of migrants and migrant communities in the Network has been a contentious issue and debated since the Network's inception. For some, low participation was the fault of the Network for failing to prioritize the everyday experience of oppression, particularly racism, and subsequently not prioritizing building relationships with migrant communities as the basis for their anti-racism. For others, it was the problem or even the 'fault' of migrants: 'Migrants won't participate. I don't want to fight for the migrants; I want to fight with them! The communities of them they're not really strong and everything. When people have difficulties surviving they cannot do it collectively. They can't, I think. For me that's the main difficulty' (interview, Marina).

Conclusion

This chapter is an account of the struggle for mobility as I saw it during my year in Athens in 2011. This struggle pitched different expressions of the freedom of movement against expressions for its control. Part of this struggle played out in the realm of rights and representation, as was largely the case with the hunger strike of 'The 300'. The strikers and their supporters mobilized to force the state to recognize them as political actors. In doing so, they won important concessions for themselves and for many migrants in Greece. But they also went beyond this relationship of control and resistance in creating a community of struggle that was not dependent on or in reference to the state. Places like the apartment also created moments of autonomy and creativity, if in different ways. For me, both these examples amount to different ways of making 'outsides' to or 'escapes' from the state, however temporary or partial.

However, all of these practices came with practical dilemmas for those who took part. For those practising the autonomy of migration, there was the constant need to respond to the actions of the state, which sought to discipline their mobility. Here the struggle to remain free from control becomes something of a temporal game, of remaining ahead of controls. This 'game' forces people without papers to live in a perpetual present. It undermines their ability to plan, to anticipate and take risks, and to imagine a future with them in it (Nyers 2003; Anderson 2000; Anderson et al. 2012). Living in this perpetual present is difficult and traumatizing.

For 'The 300', who engaged in a politics of representation, despite achieving some of their aims, it took several months before the strikers benefited from some of the concessions they had won, and some of them are still fighting for the government to honour their demands. For example, many of the strikers made visits back to their country of origin and struggled to gain entry back into Greece. Beyond this, they wanted, needed and largely got the support of native groups, but felt constrained and at times led by them, which undermined the effectiveness of their campaign.

This issue of paternalism spills over into the dilemmas faced by solidarity groups such as the Network. The hunger strike of 'The 300' was a struggle that rejuvenated groups like the Network. However, over time, the Network struggled to see its place in this struggle, feeling increasingly that migrant communities weren't organizing, and that they were unable to be together with those who were.

The anti-authoritarian movement, which had found itself struggling alongside migrants in moments of antagonistic protest and in numerous neighbourhood-based community projects, struggled to show solidarity with 'The 300'. The strike raised a lot of conflict within this movement over how to show solidarity with migrants when their struggle made demands on the state. For some it raised the question as to whether their struggles are compatible at all.

Having laid out parts of the struggle for the freedom of movement in Athens as I saw it, in the next chapter I turn to look at this corresponding struggle in Calais.

4 | THE STRUGGLE FOR MOBILITY IN CALAIS

Some history to this struggle

Calais, like Athens, is a 'flashpoint' on the map of European migration. Both France and Greece are under the remit of harmonized EU immigration and asylum policies and both form part of the external border of the Schengen free-travel zone. In Calais, as in Athens, controls have forced people to be immobile, blocking the freedom of movement. But unlike border-zone Athens, Calais is a physical borderline, and this gives the struggle for mobility a particular quality or intensity.

Located on the north-east coast of France, the city of Calais is port to one of the busiest sea routes in the world. The 22-mile crossing between France and the UK sees more than four hundred commercial ships and ferries cross the Straits of Dover each day (Maritime and Coastguard Agency 2014). To some extent, the fact that Calais is a border point at all is almost irrelevant to those who arrive there hoping to cross. More importantly to them, it is a crucial point in the routes of thousands of trucks crossing Europe on their way to the UK.[1] This is what brings travellers to Calais. It still offers one of the best means of crossing to the UK clandestinely, without documents and without money.[2]

France was one of the five original signatories to the Schengen Agreement, and has been an external border of the Schengen Area since 1985. Despite being a member of the EU, the UK is only a partial signatory to the Schengen Agreement and has not given up sovereignty over its borders. France's accession to Schengen didn't remove the border between the UK and France, then, but it did radically change the struggle for mobility at the border between the two. How did this happen?

Schengen made redundant those borders between other participating countries. Once people were in the Schengen free-travel area, the next time they might be asked for papers could very likely be the next time they crossed its external border.[3] So although border controls between the UK and France remained, in effect, Schengen made the UK more accessible, because once people entered the area, there might be no further border controls until they reached Calais.[4] From the perspective of the UK government, in the interests of protecting its own sovereignty, enhancing border controls in Calais became more pressing (something you could say was a conflict of interests with France). Establishing the border between France and the UK as an external border of the Schengen zone led to enhanced border control technologies there.

Following the advent of Schengen and the beginnings of enhanced border controls in Calais (such as tighter entry visa requirements and better technologies for detecting false documents or finding stowaways), from the mid-1980s it began to be commonplace to see people who had been refused entry at the border living rough on the streets of the city. Beyond the intervention of a few charities, the focus for the French and British governments continued to be on procedures to prevent the 'illegal' entry of travellers without leave to enter the UK. In 1994 the UK and France began implementing juxtaposed controls (UK border checks on French territory and vice versa), in the Eurotunnel entrance at Coquelles outside Calais. Juxtaposed controls meant that people were subject to British immigration control before leaving French territory (Clayton 2006). These measures were extended in 2003 when the UK and France signed the Treaty of le Touquet, which introduced juxtaposed controls to all ferry ports on the north-west coast of France and Belgium.

Juxtaposed controls increased the number of people refused entry to the UK. They also came at the height of the exodus of people fleeing the wars in the Balkans. By the late 1990s camps of those people who had been refused at the border, largely from places like Croatia and Bosnia, started to appear in Calais. In response to this, in 1999 the French government opened a hangar on the outskirts of Calais to house those living homeless in the city. The Red Cross-run centre (so often referred to as the 'infamous' centre at Sangatte) was closed in December 2002 at the behest of the British government, which believed it to be a pull-factor for people trying to reach the UK. In the years that it was open, an estimated 75,000 people passed through the camp (Courau 2003; Walters 2008). After the camp closed, people once again sought whatever ways they could to meet their own needs while waiting in Calais to try to cross clandestinely (the most common method of which has been to get into lorries, either before or after they enter the port).

Making the border as difficult to cross as possible has been a major part of the strategy of the British and French governments in Calais.[5] People trying to cross have responded to these controls in many different ways. Over time, people have spread across the north-west coast of France, Belgium and the Netherlands, accessing different truck parking areas and different ferry routes. This has also led to some national and ethnic differentiation in the routes people take to cross. For instance, Calais has become a place to cross for people mainly from Afghanistan, Eritrea, Ethiopia and Sudan; Dunkirk for people from Kurdistan and Iran, and so on. Over time also, certain districts of Paris have become something like suburbs of Calais, increasingly important staging posts for people trying to cross at Calais, and a network of resting places to return to in between attempts. In each case the authorities have responded differently. For instance, in Norrent-Fontes people have generally been allowed to build their own camps with little interference from the police, whereas the police in Calais have always sought to destroy such spaces (interview, Wennesson).

Operations against people trying to cross (or live) in Calais have involved a number of different types of police, including the national police, the Gendarmerie (similar to military police), frontier police (La Police aux Frontières) and the CRS (Compagnies Republicaines de Securité, otherwise known as the riot police). At any one time there are between four and six platoons of CRS in the city. The involvement of the CRS in particular gives a sense of how the authorities have approached this issue in Calais. Collectively they have gone above and beyond the usual tasks of internal border control (such as checking documents), by routinely using physical violence against people without papers,[6] destroying their settlements and belongings, contaminating their water supplies, detaining them without charge and then dropping them miles from the city, and criminalizing the work of those who seek to help them.[7]

Making life at the border as difficult as possible has been another part of the authorities' strategy in Calais. This has often played out as a struggle over space, as people have needed to find ways to live while they continue to attempt to cross. For most this has meant living rough or squatting, and when numbers have been great enough, coming together in self-organized camps, known as jungles. Because Calais is a relatively small city, such spaces have often become very visible. In this visibility, they have been vulnerable to attack by police.

Jungles are an effect of the struggle for mobility and are not unique to Calais. They build up wherever the struggle for the freedom of movement results in the forced immobilization of travellers, from Patras in Greece, to the Serbian/Hungarian border, to the Spanish enclave of Melilla, to sites along the US/Mexico border. They exist because people are being held back from crossing, but in their immobility still need to meet their basic everyday needs. The term jungle is also a confusing one. In Calais it is used both by the authorities and the people who live there. On the one hand it has racist overtones: that the people living there are animals in a state of nature. On the other hand the term jungle (which is also the term given to the self-organized hobo camps you find around major train junctions in the USA among other places) is given to such places by the inhabitants. Rumour has it in the case of Calais that the name derived from the Pashtu word for forest, *dzhangal*, the first jungles being in local woodland.

In Calais, whenever people have come together to make a settlement, this has often built up into something bigger and more structured – a jungle – before becoming a threat to the authorities, who have moved in to destroy it. It takes time to build a critical mass of people such that a jungle emerges, but they have always reappeared in Calais. Jungles are, ultimately, the safest and most efficient way that people can meet their needs in resource-limited situations. Jungles have built up in all kinds of places, mostly out of sight and in locations accessible for travel: in the dunes or woodlands around the port, on wasteland by the motorway that surrounds it, in parks or on wasteland in the city. In the time that jungles have been a regular feature of Calais life, the number of people stuck in Calais has varied a lot, from tens of people to thousands. Generally the number of people in Calais has been lower in the winter than in the spring/summer, which are the best times for people to begin their journeys into Europe. However, the last decade has seen the appearance of huge jungles of several hundred people or more at times, and it could be said that, over time, as measures to prevent illegal entry into the UK have increased, so the number of people stuck in Calais has generally risen. In the summer of 2009, for example, when the No Border camp was held in Calais, it took place alongside a huge jungle of an estimated two thousand people, one of the first of the huge jungles to appear in the city.

The struggle over (the right to) space in Calais has generally played out as a continued cycle of jungle or squat creation, followed by their violent destruction, and their emergence somewhere else. In most cases, jungles have been treated as squats and served with eviction notices. Faced with no alternative, many have stayed in the jungles and suffered ongoing harassment, followed by early morning raids by the CRS, violent mass eviction, destruction of housing and belongings, and arrest and incarceration. But, still facing the need to live, people have often resettled in other places, often hidden at first until such spaces become so populated as to be visible.

Making life at the border as difficult as possible for people trying to cross in Calais has been a central part of the state (national, regional and local) strategy towards irregular migration. But social factors particular to Calais have exacerbated this too. The city of Calais grew around port trade and heavy industry. The decline of both of these things has left Calais one of the economically poorest cities in one of the economically poorest regions in France (Cunningham-Sabot and Fol 2007). Calais has among the highest rates of unemployment, housing eviction, inequality, mortality and depopulation in France (ibid.; Jany-Catrice 2009; Walsh et al. 2009). Within this context, people trying to cross have often been used as a political football by parties from across the political spectrum. In this context, the far right have pushed this theme further. In Calais, support for the Front National (National Front) is high, and has fostered the emergence of grassroots anti-migrant groups such as Sauvons Calais (Save Calais), Calais Libre (Free Calais) and Calaisiens en Colère (Enraged Calaisiens), some of which are overtly far right and racist and others of which position themselves as movements of concerned citizens. Such groups have organized extensively online, and held numerous demonstrations in the city. Within this context racist/fascist violence against people of colour in Calais is a regular occurrence.

Practising the autonomy of migration – the church in Tioxide jungle

Jungles are an effect of controls that enforce immobility. Indeed, it has been argued that camps (of which the jungles are a form) are the ultimate sovereign spaces of exception; spaces where state power has reached its zenith and where the camp occupants become completely both the subjects and objects of the state (cf. Agamben, 1995, 2005; Rajaram and Grundy-Warr 2004; Rigby and Schlembach 2013). As Rigby and Schlembach suggest, '[t]he camps are in a sense outside Calais since for those living there the normal civil protections and rights of redress do not apply. And yet precisely because of this, life in the camps is much more closely subject to the scrutiny of the law and the rule of the police' (2013: 160). Despite this, indeed perhaps because of it, they represent spaces where autonomy from the state is equally possible. The jungles are spaces of exception, but they are also self-organized spaces of autonomy. In that sense they are important hubs in the mobile commons; key points that people from Afghanistan to Sudan know to head for; points for the sharing out of limited resources and information, of support and care.

I have been a regular visitor to Calais since 2009. At the end of 2014 I started to spend a lot more time in Calais and, for the first time, chose to live in the jungle. At that time there were around two thousand people without papers in Calais, living in two large jungles, one squatted factory and a number of other places. I stayed in a jungle in the eastern part of the city close to the port. It was known as Tioxide because it was next to a major chemicals factory of that name. At its peak, Tioxide was home to something like one thousand people (my estimate), roughly organized into four sub-camps along nationality lines. There were Eritrean, Sudanese, Afghan and Ethiopian parts. In the eleven months or so that this jungle existed (from April 2014 to March 2015), it grew from a small collection of dwellings largely hidden in the trees to a sprawling tent city. For six weeks in 2015 I lived in the Afghan part.

When I first heard about the idea of the mobile commons, it sounded so beautiful and utopian. Imagine a social world based on equality, care and cooperation! I couldn't see how it could describe somewhere like Tioxide; a squalid place, temporary in everybody's mind, where nobody wanted to be. But even in situations of exclusion and squalor, people need to live, and are often creative about it. Aware of the huge privilege I experienced in being able to come and go from the jungle as I wished, aware of how much this shaped my perspective, I still feel that, beyond the squalor, Tioxide was also a beautiful place in some way, because of it being a place of life and creativity too. The reason for this is that it was primarily a community of care, and necessarily so. Having been travelling for so long, many people in the camps were highly experienced in meeting their needs collectively and cooperatively in situations of conflict and limited resources. It was fundamental to building a commons in a community as transient as the Calais crossing community is. This structure or this habit of care was a resource that anyone who arrived could access. As such it outlasted the presence of any one individual. People took care of each other in ways that made me ashamed of how we take care of each other back in the UK. With extremely limited resources, people cooked and ate together, worshipped together, sang songs and made music together, helped each other get into trucks to try to cross. This was the extreme dependability that Papadopoulos and Tsianos (2013: 190) talk of when they describe the mobile commons. One interviewee described this as a constant prefiguration of community. 'So it's not even the question of trying to build a community, but to build those tools that enable us to always start again' (interview, Anon. 7).

Tioxide was there long enough that people started to build less temporary spaces, to diversify spatial use beyond just accommodation, and to find other ways of organizing or multiplying their resources. There were spaces of trade – a barber shop, a tobacconist, a shisha lounge, two restaurants/cafés and a few general stores. There were spaces of religious worship, numerous mosques and a church.[8]

The church was erected in the jungle around six months before its destruction. It was built and used mainly by the Eritrean Catholic Orthodox community. On the outside it was nothing more than a large tent with a cross on top. Step inside and you entered another world. The space was suffused in candlelight and incense, kept warm and intimate-feeling with rugs and wall hangings, and made beautiful with religious icons. It was a gentle, peaceful and deeply sacred-feeling space. It was made that way by the effort of making it, using it and caring for it under such adverse conditions. Being there took you away from the jungle completely, and yet it was so of that space (the artificial factory sounds, the chemical tang from the factory, and the smells of burning rubbish and wood smoke reminded you where you were). The church was a minor miracle because it represented the persistence of autonomy and humanity; things that people forced to live in the jungles were denied or presented as incapable of being or having. The church (and the mosques and all the other sacred spaces in the jungle) screamed of humanity. In this way they were a demand for equality.

I don't want to romanticize the jungle. I'm not saying that the people living there are more benevolent or caring than anyone else. The extreme nature of the situation seems to warrant people's investment in structures of care which comprise the mobile commons. People are compelled to, because to do all of this alone would be so much harder. Equally I'm not saying that what goes on in the jungle is beautiful. It's a violent, exploitative and degrading place for some. There is a lot of poor physical and mental health, which makes it volatile. And finally, nobody wants to be there. Even for those who had come from refugee camps in Africa and the Middle East, the jungles were a disgrace. But the mobile commons existed there *despite all this*. There are any number of accounts of the suffering of people trying to cross in Calais, and of the terrible living conditions they have to endure. But I also think it is important to recognize that, *despite all this*, such places are still also places of humanity, equality and autonomy, and I think this makes them also amazing and hopeful and beautiful, because people make their lives there, despite controls.

Connecting escapes – collaborative community-building

I wanted to begin with an account of Calais that focused on the struggle between people trying to cross and the state in shaping the regime of mobility, because this is, fundamentally, the most direct part of this struggle in the sense that it really comprises people exercising their freedom of movement (rather than, say, people demanding that they or others have the right to it). Owing to the numbers of people practising the freedom of movement, I would also argue it is the most significant or influential part of this struggle. The control regime is forced to respond to people's autonomous mobility. Thus it is in the largely imperceptible, unnoticed and somewhat mundane everyday activities of survival and life-making that people play out their autonomy. But the recent history of struggle in Calais includes numerous examples of collaborations in expressing the autonomy of migration. A few people, primarily those who were connected to the no borders movement/Calais Migrant Solidarity, who were not trying to cross but who wanted to show solidarity with those who were, had for a long time also been living in places like the jungles (to a lesser extent as a means of finding accommodation solutions for themselves too) and participating in the mobile commons in that way. Indeed, my decision to live in the jungle was largely based on the perspective that being in such a place of outsiders and making my own life in that place – participating in what was a micro-struggle of the everyday – was about the most political thing I could do to resist the border regime. But being in the jungle was not the only way that people connected to CMS had participated in the mobile commons. There had been numerous cases where people had collaboratively made smaller, more intimate living spaces that created a different kind of community from the large and anonymous jungles. Squatting by people trying to cross in the city goes back much farther than 2009. But squatting from that time has been documented much more prolifically because it was something that people connected to CMS often prioritized, concerning themselves wholeheartedly with documenting and intervening in police raids and evictions of squatted spaces, and opening and defending such spaces (Calais Migrant Solidarity, forthcoming). I want to go back in time from the church in the Tioxide jungle to talk about a particular example of such a collaborative community: the squat on rue Victor Hugo.

Collaborative community-building – the squat on rue Victor Hugo[9]

The squat on rue Victor Hugo (known generally as Victor Hugo) existed from September 2013 to May 2014 in a house in the centre of Calais. The house was originally occupied by a group of CMS activists, and went through the channels of becoming a legal squat.[10] The aim was to create a shared space for organizing and a sleeping space for vulnerable people and people active in CMS. At the time, it was the only legal indoor space with running water and electricity that people trying to cross had access to. Being one house open to a population of homeless people in excess of four hundred – a population that was growing and increasingly containing families, women and children – it was hugely over-extended and unsafe as people vied to access it and to assert control over it. Over time, in response to this pressure and to the increase in women in the city, people invested in the space decided to make it specifically for women, children and the most vulnerable trying to cross, and for CMS activists. The boundaries between who could and could not have access to the space were complicated and often blurred. The struggle over access never really resolved itself and took many forms.[11] But essentially, the space became one that was limited to these groups for the remainder of its existence.

In Chapter 2, I argued that collaborative community-building has the potential to generate communities that bridge difference, where the autonomy of migration is connected to intentional practices of autonomy that prefigure alternative, egalitarian ways of being. It is here that I think the possibility for escaping the state is most alive. I find Victor Hugo an exciting example of this because it represented a moment when autonomy and equality were carved out collaboratively, within a situation of extreme oppression and inequality. I think that Victor Hugo represented something bigger than just a mutually beneficial space that met the needs of a minority. It was, I think, an active example of prefiguring a different kind of community based on equality. In Chapter 1 I talked about what I mean by equality. To recap, I mean a way of being with each other where everyone is valued simply by being there. This isn't created by treating everyone as the same. Conversely it's not created by weighing up everybody's privileges and oppressions and dividing tasks strictly according to our differences (Rose 1997). I think it's created by *negotiating between* these two extremes. Indeed, despite the decision to restrict the space to particular groups (a decision made together, among the residents at that time), Victor Hugo was something of an experiment in equality for its residents. It was an entirely autonomous space. It existed in a squatted building that actively put it in conflict with the local authorities who tried to evict it. It was maintained and run by those who lived there, and decisions were largely made collectively. For example, decisions over the access of certain men to the space were taken collectively, and tasks was allocated according to the different capabilities of residents.[12] These more structured ways of egalitarian organizing were underpinned by numerous informal expressions of equality. People cooked and ate together, shared stories, hung out, and built strong bonds of friendship in the process.

These bonds took time and were not easy to create. There were language barriers to overcome, cultural barriers, barriers created because of different everyday experiences (people without papers having to try to cross and people with papers not having to do so being probably the biggest one). These were intensely personal experiences, and I wasn't present in Victor Hugo long enough to build any really meaningful relationships myself. But being in similar spaces long enough for relationships to take hold makes me think that they were built here tentatively and delicately and were, essentially, the foundation of the place. In her extremely personal and deeply raw account of her time at Victor Hugo, Amy Non describes the cautious building of relationships, how they came out of everyday shared experience and how they then shaped that everyday experience:

> The women live upstairs, spread across the rooms. I speak neither Amharic nor Arabic. I can speak haltingly in English with some and with some not at all. Eyes, expression, hands, that has to be enough. And laughter, lots of uncomprehending laughter. I begin to clean the house, to get paint, to spruce up the chaos. Sometimes the women ask me if I would like to eat with them. Slowly we become friends. I move into the first floor. Together with four young women from Ethiopia, I live in at most seven square meters. (Non, n.d.)

What I think is conveyed in this text is the centrality of sharing; of trying to find ways to care for each other and, through this, understand each other. People talked about how carrying out the tasks of meeting each other's basic needs meant that everybody involved had to re-evaluate their prejudices and agendas. They talked about how there was something powerful in the normality of just going about the general tasks of living and caring for each other together. It created space for developing the kind of intimacy you make with people when you undertake the mundane tasks of care together. Making a meal together or cleaning the kitchen reinforces a sense that you are the same, or not the same but equal. It reinforces the sense that, in the end, you have the same needs: to be safe, warm, fed, rested, loved. It suggests to me that these mundane tasks are not mundane, but essential to making equality. Indeed, many people have told me that the most meaningful moments in Calais for them are those when people carry out the tasks of caring for each other together, making and drinking tea, making and eating a meal together, just hanging out. This is certainly my experience too.

Victor Hugo was built around a process of sharing, because it aimed to be a space of collaboration (between people crossing and CMS activists). My deeper involvement in similar projects to this leads me to suggest that it compels us to create something different to some kind of theoretically perfect anarchist project. People had to compromise. Crucially, being open to other perspectives and different voices was a key part of the process. Working together changed people's perspectives and disrupted their agendas. People often engaged with rather than dismissed the discomfort that arises when your views are challenged by a different way of doing and seeing things. The result was something different, not perfect, and more complicated and hard to manage perhaps, but also possibly more equal.

> These [meetings] were particularly interesting because it was a time where our particular views about the space and how it should operate were brought into contact and sometimes conflict with the other residents. Suddenly things which we took for granted, like the fact that males who had been abusive should no longer be allowed near the house or that no men could be allowed inside, were brought into contact with the reality of the situation and also the wishes of those we wanted to be in solidarity with. It was very difficult to apply some rules wholesale and we had to constantly feel out situations and make decisions that were sometimes contradictory to our rules but in the end best for the residents of the house. This was a skill that took time to develop but also primarily trust with the other residents. (Interview, Anon. 10)

Victor Hugo had other successes. Over time it became a space that the neighbours, as well as other migrant solidarity groups in Calais, came to support. In the long term, it nurtured some new connections between these groups, migrant communities and CMS activists. It challenged the view that 'CMS were just the scary anarchist squatters who would steal your house while you went on vacation' (interview, Anon. 10).

As a space of equality, Victor Hugo was a far from perfect example, though. It aimed to be a space of equality, but inadvertently gave room for other inequalities to take root. Maintaining it as a safer space for women, children, vulnerable people trying to cross and CMS activists was difficult. CMS activists took on the role of doorkeepers twenty-four hours a day. Being on the door involved 'policing' access to the house. Although this meant that access was denied to anyone who was a threat (a nationalistic French neighbour would be prevented from entering, as would the police or journalists), it also meant turning away people who wanted a warm drink or to charge their phones, and facing people who were drunk and sometimes physically violent. There was continual pressure to turn a blind eye compounded by recognition of some glaring inequalities. Running the door was often about people with papers stopping men without papers from coming in. It was largely white Europeans with papers denying access to largely black Africans with so little. At other times it involved cis male CMS activists turning away cis male people trying to cross.[13] In seeking to undermine forms of domination based on gender, it reaffirmed forms of domination based on race. The situation brought the intersection of race and gender into stark focus in a way that made these differences feel huge, and the means of not being complicit in their reinforcement impossible. Carrying out this policy of exclusion was difficult, made more strenuous by having to do it twenty-four hours a day. Often this role was performed by just a few people, who became increasingly burnt out by it.

Living day to day in Victor Hugo, turning down people at the door, seeing friends leave night after night to try to cross and failing, it's easy to succumb to feelings of anger and guilt over our privileges and easy to feel responsible for solving this problem. People often responded by working day and night without breaks, seeing basic self-care (eating, sleeping, washing and taking time out) as something lavish. Not only did this lead to burn-out for some, it also put people in some kind of aid-worker position, which undermined their ability to build something collaborative and non-hierarchical.

Then there were complex power dynamics *between* residents. Not everybody had an equal voice in the house. Meetings were often dominated by those with the most social capital, or the most dominating meeting style, or who shouted the loudest. Many power dynamics CMS activists didn't see at the time, but have recognized in retrospect. Those women connected to smuggling networks had greater power in the house and gave privileged treatment to some women (those also accessing these smuggling networks), while bullying others (those trying to remain free of them). Some CMS activists felt that, rather than creating a space of relative safety, they had unwittingly become complicit in a structure that was being used to further exploit women trying to cross.

After months of living together, with CMS activists essentially still taking responsibility (or feeling responsible) for the space, many were suffering from burn-out. The group were approached by the city prefecture, which proposed to give the space to another charity which would take over its running, while another women's space was established somewhere else. On the one hand this was a proposal; on the other it was a threat: hand over Victor Hugo or we will evict it. People were conflicted over what to do. Some saw the project itself as the most important thing, and having the authorities recognize the need for it, and having a charity run it, could be a positive step. Others saw this as reformism and recuperation, considering how Victor

Hugo was run, the ethos behind it, the most important part. For them, attempting to resist eviction and failing was a better outcome than handing the project over to the state.

After Victor Hugo

Owing partly to lack of agreement over the response, partly to the burn-out of those involved in Victor Hugo and a lack of capacity to continue to 'bottom-line' this project, in March 2014 Victor Hugo was taken over by another charity, and CMS activists forbidden access to the house. The policy of exclusion had shifted. Victor Hugo was closed a few months later, when a state-funded, charity-run women's space of a series of Portakabins outside the city was opened. This centre was also closed down in February 2015, when its occupants, around eighty women and children, were moved, largely against their wishes, to a new day centre some seven kilometres from Calais (which became known as Salam, after a charity that used to distribute food in the city).[14] The area around the day centre was to become what was the only jungle in Calais (at the time of publication).

In January that year the existing jungles and squats again faced eviction and had been issued with eviction notices. But the authorities' strategy was different this time. People were given the 'option' of moving somewhere else; to a piece of wasteland around this new day centre. Faced with the 'option' of violent eviction or relocation, most chose to relocate. This 'silent eviction' began in February 2015 with the move of the people from the women and children's centre. Despite the efforts of people in the jungle and those in solidarity with them to come up with a collective resistance to the eviction, for a period of about seven days in the spring of 2015 around two thousand people dismantled their homes and moved all their belongings to the new site, largely under their own steam. In a matter of days a new jungle emerged from the sand dunes of the 'tolerated' area. The Tioxide jungle was empty, the church gone.[15]

The forced and silent eviction of around two thousand people and their relocation to this new 'tolerated' area added an additional barrier to people's attempts to cross. As securitization at Calais port had increased,[16] recent months had seen more people trying to cross from the Eurotunnel at Coquelles. Now more than 10 kilometres from the new jungle, people faced a 20-kilometre round trip just to reach the Eurotunnel line and come back. But the new jungle also created opportunities. As it was located next to the highway that leads trucks into Calais port, people had direct access to trucks on the highway when traffic jams formed. The image of people swarming across the highway and gaining access to trucks was something of a mainstream media motif of Calais at that time.

The new jungle became home to the two thousand or so people who had been forced to move from other jungles and squats in the city. Over the spring it swelled to also house thousands of new arrivals who had travelled up from Libya through Italy, or Turkey through Greece, and come for their chance to cross too. By the middle of the summer, estimates placed the size of the jungle at between three and five thousand people (Fjellberg 2015). This growth was unprecedented in the history of Calais; the result of a combination of ongoing long-standing and large-scale conflicts (in Syria, Afghanistan and Iraq in particular), instability in previously stable states,[17] and access to well-established smuggler networks and routes. At the same time, people still came to Calais because, despite increased securitization, it was still a place where people had a 'chance'.

In a lot of ways, the situation in Calais was the same, just on a totally different scale. However, this new scale did change the struggle in a number of ways. First, Calais became part of a transnational discourse of the European migration crisis that pitched European states against 'illegal immigrants' rather than a localized discourse of a 'Calais crisis' that made it the problem of Calais mayor Natacha Bouchart (who had been mayor since 2008). With attention focused on Calais, the French and British governments threw more money and more resources at Calais. Two new fences were erected around the Eurotunnel, CCTV installed along its perimeter; the land around the tunnel cleared of vegetation and flooded. A fence was erected along the highway leading to the port (part of pre-existing plans for port expansion) and efforts made to reduce traffic jams. More CRS, gendarme and private security guards were brought to Calais, and border officers from the UK were at times employed around the tunnel too. As a result of these measures, the numbers of people crossing went down, and people started to take ever greater risks to cross. People also took collective action, organizing themselves to swarm across the highway and create traffic jams (the jams having diminished after new traffic measures were introduced in the port). In a number of cases people stormed the port and the Eurotunnel in attempts to cross. The result of this has been an increase in injuries and deaths at the border. For instance, between January and October 2015 there were twenty-one known border-related deaths (Calais Migrant Solidarity 2015; Doctors of the World 2015).

These direct control measures were accompanied by a range of secondary deterrent measures. Some of these measures reflected European states' attempts at reimposing sovereignty over their borders. For instance, several countries re-established border controls at their external border, which undermined the central tenet of Schengen as a free-travel zone. Of most significance for people trying to reach Calais was the re-establishment of border checks between Italy and France. The result was the emergence of a jungle on the Italian side of the border in Ventimiglia. Some of these measures reflected attempts to reimpose EU-level agreements on the control of 'irregular migration'. For instance, France increased compensatory measures within its territory in an effort to undermine the ability of people without papers to travel freely in France. Police presence at train stations went up and the experiences of many living in the jungle suggest that on some lines at some times people were able to purchase train tickets only if they could also show proof of identity. In an effort to enforce the Dublin III Regulation, the OFFII (l'Office Français de l'Immigration et de l'Intégration) started more regular visits to the jungle to persuade people to claim asylum in France (with Dublin deportations to places like Italy and Greece still taking place), or to take time out from Calais in what the authorities called respite centres across the country.

Under these circumstances, many who saw all this as further limiting their chances to cross took the decision to claim asylum in France.[18] Of these, some were rehoused relatively quickly, but many remained stuck in the jungle, waiting to be housed. Others took buses to the various respite centres across the country, and others sought different routes to try to cross to the UK.[19] People left in these ways, and new people kept on arriving. Measure for measure, the jungle continued to grow. By the autumn it had reached a population of around six thousand people (Gentleman 2015).

Second, as Calais grabbed the headlines, there was a massive humanitarian response, not from the state or even from most of the NGOs (the French state refused to recognize the jungle as a refugee camp), but from people from across Europe who had seen the news and wanted to help. Many people simply turned up in the jungle with a vehicle loaded with goods for distribution. There was an undeniable lack of even the most basic resources in the jungle and people were suffering from living in squalor. Responding through bringing aid was one of the most obvious and accessible ways that people could get involved. As such, much of this new attention on Calais manifested as an aid effort to the jungle. Groups started to appear on social media through which people began to coordinate their efforts. Groups such as 'Calais – people to people – solidarity action from the UK' on Facebook provided a basic infrastructure that facilitated the emergence of a more collectivized UK aid effort to the jungle. Some people set up online donations pages dedicated to Calais which, given the scale of public attention at the time, brought in thousands of pounds' worth of donations and goods for distribution. UK-based groups such as Care for Calais, London to Calais, Calaid and Help Calais grew out of these fund-raising missions. At the same time, a number of Calais-based organizations took advantage of the new attention on Calais and suddenly found themselves managing massive budgets. The organization Auberge des Migrants, for example, which had been active in Calais since 2008, providing humanitarian aid to people without papers with a skeleton staff and a handful of volunteers, now found itself inundated with money and donations. In a matter of months it was overseeing a huge warehouse receiving donations every day, managing many volunteers, and leading a project to build housing for everyone in the jungle.

Over the course of the summer the jungle grew from a gaggle of tents to an increasingly structured shanty town. People who had been forced to move to the new site took the opportunity to rebuild stronger homes, and bigger and more impressive churches and mosques. Many saw the jungle as a business opportunity or a means to sustain themselves while living there. Numerous restaurants, shops, cafés and nightclubs sprang up as a result. Groups such as Care for Calais and Auberge des Migrants constructed wooden homes for people in the jungle. Larger NGOs such as Médecins sans Frontières and ActEd installed basic sanitation. Médecins du Monde opened a tent clinic. Many independent projects responded in different ways, with a well-being centre, a women and children's centre, a theatre and several schools among the infrastructure.

People connected to Calais Migrant Solidarity struggled to find their place within this new situation. Until that point one of the things that had made CMS effective had been the relationships that existed between CMS activists and people trying to cross. This was the result of a continued presence in Calais for the previous six years, and a focus on spending time with people in the places they found for themselves (often making places together), such that many people trying to cross before that point knew who 'No Borders' was and what they were about. It was possible to maintain the reputation 'No Borders' had among people trying to cross because the community of people crossing was generally small enough, or at least spatially dispersed enough, for them to see each other. The size of the new jungle, and the fact that it brought all communities into the same space, made for a much more anonymous place, one in which it was difficult to maintain any reputation. Furthermore, to a certain extent the activities of the group also changed. With the arrival of so many new aid groups, CMS stopped undertaking distribution of material itself, feeling relieved of this task by all the newly arrived aid groups.[20] To some extent, this changed the group's reputation. And this was within the context of an ever-expanding number of solidarity and volunteer aid groups, each with their own particular take on the situation and their own agenda. Equally, many felt that the struggle for the freedom of movement was not really about the jungle at all, and that attention should be placed more on trying to make other, more autonomous spaces back in the city. In a situation that seemed to be becoming more and more of a spectacle, some connected to CMS questioned whether the group still had a purpose in Calais at all.

Despite all that, CMS continued, and people focused their attention on maintaining a continuous presence in the jungle, building a living space there. Work continued to document police violence, focusing mainly on tear gas attacks in the jungle. In October that year the group opened an information point in the jungle which shared information on things such as claiming asylum and travel to different countries in Europe, as well as goings-on in the jungle and texts written by people trying to cross.[21] The principle behind the info point was that sharing knowledge was one way of sharing power, enabling people to make informed decisions. The project was also started with the aim of being a space of sharing, where people trying to cross could bring information and use the space to organize from. These were seen as key ways to facilitate the freedom of movement. As one person connected to CMS put it, 'we distribute information, not trousers, or blankets or tents' (email exchange, December 2015).

Few had wanted to move to the new jungle, seeing it as a ghetto created by the state to assert greater control and undermine the self-determination of people trying to cross. However, the new jungle did not extinguish that autonomy completely, and continued to reflect the mobile commons. In a way the mobile commons flowed more intensely through this new jungle because, given that it was a place with a greater level of infrastructure, people were more easily able to meet their daily needs (being able to sit in a café all day, whether you purchased something or not, was better than sitting in your tent, for instance). Equally, this infrastructure provided numerous social spaces. The jungle grew organically, the direct result of people trying to meet their needs and live as best they could. Being effectively abandoned in a place that was seen as a ghetto and of no value, people were free to make it whatever they wanted. Of course, that freedom was so severely constrained by the lack of resources, the squalor, the need to keep trying to cross, the trauma of many living there, and their recognition that they were living in abject conditions, that it was virtually unrecognizable. But it was still there and present in all the ways that people experimented with living together in that place.[22] To me, this jungle felt a lot like I imagine a frontier town in the American Wild West might have felt; a place filled with experiments in exploitation but also in cooperation, where it was not clear what kind of place it would turn out to be, or which 'force' would 'win'. I think the persistence of autonomy of the people living there was most apparent in these experiments.

The authorities responded with attempts to undermine this autonomy. From October, the CRS started daily patrols inside the jungle (under the pretence of providing 'security' to jungle 'volunteers'), and ad hoc roadblocks at the jungle's entrances which sometimes prevented people from leaving or entering. At around the same time, work began on the construction of a state-controlled and walled-in container camp within the jungle space, built on land previously occupied by around four hundred people, who were forced to move once more. The camp opened in January 2016 with space for 1,500 people (more about that in the concluding chapter).

The struggle for visibility – protests and the new jungle

In the face of life in a ghetto, with opportunities to cross becoming rarer, the autonomy of migration appeared increasingly difficult to practise in Calais. People looked to other means of action; which often involved adopting visible, protest-based forms to express certain messages or demands in public ways. From April to October there were numerous demonstrations from the jungle to the city of Calais, or the port. Some were organized by groups in solidarity with people in the jungle, and some by jungle residents. These protests opposed life in the jungle and demanded that the border be opened.[23] None of these demands, or this kind of action, was unusual in Calais, but the number of actions like this in such a short space of time was. The demonstrations aimed to be peaceful, and most of the time this was the case, but in a number of cases protesters met resistance from police which resulted in clashes (often with tear gas) and sometimes further repression back in the jungle.

By the autumn, this wave of protests had tailed off. I think the main reason for this was that people did not see any tangible positive change as a result of their actions. People living in the camp generally felt that if they upheld the rule of law and protested peacefully, they would demonstrate their civility and their demands would be taken seriously. Sadly, this never happened. If anything, the protests brought more repression by the police. People became tired and disillusioned. The strategy of visible protest was not working. Why was that?

Fundamentally, the protesters did not assert enough pressure on the state, which found it relatively easy to deny their legitimacy, ignore their demands and quash their actions. Mainstream public political discourse framed the self-organized actions of the people living in the jungle as administrative problems that needed eradicating (through more controls over the jungle, forbidding marches, etc.), not as political expressions. The actions of those who stood in solidarity with protesters were presented as those of a crazy, irrational and possibly violent minority which should also be silenced.[24] Rather than being presented as expressions of self-determination, these protests were largely dismissed as threats to democracy. These securitized discourses were not challenged by the protests that took place that summer/autumn.

I think the tactic of protest also did not work because it was a confusing means of articulating demands. In a sense, calls to open the border fitted within a politics of rights and recognition, as ultimately they were demands by people to be recognized and treated as human (and were potentially transformative in the sense that they were actions taken by people excluded from the realm of the political). Yet in their universality they could be ignored. In some respects the French government *had* to ignore them; opening the border effectively meant the end of the state. The UK government could ignore them because, taking place on French soil, they could be dismissed as France's business. These were effectively universal demands for freedom of movement and to be seen as human – directed at a state that by its very function puts provisos on who has access to rights, including the right to be human (in other words, rights granted by the state are not for everybody, but for citizens). Paradoxically these were demands for autonomy directed at the state.

Furthermore, there were a number of things that undermined the build-up of these protests into a mass movement; something that seems essential for effectively articulating collective demands on the state. First, there was the volatile structure within which this struggle was taking place. People were trying to mobilize in a diverse community that was constantly changing. People crossed, or got burnt out by the work of organizing their communities, or left, meaning that the population was never stable. This constant change limited the build-up of knowledge and trust that seems essential to making a community of resistance, and a prerequisite for thinking beyond pre-existing ways of resistance. Thinking of other ways to take action beyond that of tried and tested protest seemed impossible with trust and collective knowledge missing. Second, there were so many different perspectives on what effective and visible collective action should look like. A number of solidarity groups came to the jungle with pre-planned demos in which the jungle inhabitants could participate if they wanted. Some found this helpful whereas others found it paternalistic and disrespectful to the jungle residents, and boycotted them. A number of solidarity groups were of the view that if the energy for protest was coming from people in the jungle, then it was their role to support and nurture that energy and make something collaboratively. This led to a different mode of organizing and different protest models. Despite the idea that a diversity of tactics could strengthen the struggle, the competing messages and alliances that the protests expressed also undermined the building of a collective movement, or a collective 'faith' in protest as a good strategy.

CMS largely held this latter view. As I mentioned in Chapter 2, CMS has a difficult and critical relationship with discourses of rights and recognition, yet prioritizes being with people without papers who at times see their struggle as one for rights. The group emphasizes the importance of taking action together, rather than being led or leading. At that time CMS worked with a number of different groups in the jungle to organize protests. Often this meant a lot of what American civil rights activist Ella Baker called spade work (Crass n.d. b): spending time talking to people, sharing information, putting different groups in contact with each other and facilitating people coming together to talk.

In some cases it led to large-scale protests. In others, it came to nothing. For me, it was difficult to stay enthusiastic about a course of action that I did not think would achieve any meaningful outcome, practically (for the people in Calais now) or ideologically (for the struggle for the freedom of movement). I think this was something that a number of people connected to CMS felt at the time. Certainly we talked about it a lot; about the difficulties of being somehow neutral or objective when we all had strong ideas about effective political action. It raised uncomfortable feelings around who was leading and who was being led, when what we were trying to nurture was horizontally organized collaboration. We continued to justify our involvement on the basis that we were standing with, rather than leading, the people living in the jungle. But in an effort not to lead, I think the group often adopted an attitude of non-responsibility (of taking on merely logistical roles, for instance), which undermined such collaborations.

Yet I want to emphasize that there were many demos, protests and attempts to collectively storm the border which CMS were simply invited to, which had no organization outside of the community of demonstrators from the jungle. For every 'top-down' attempt at a protest there was a demo or march that was totally autonomously organized by people in the jungle and CMS had to just turn up.

Then there were those who thought that visible collective action could only fail. Many people in the jungle were unconvinced of the tactic and saw their own experience in Calais not as part of a bigger political struggle, but as an individual experience of mobility. They were in Calais to cross, not to score political points. Consequently, their focus was on that struggle to cross. This in itself was not seen as political, and it also left no space for participation in collective visible action. Equally, people *were* participating in collective action, just not of the visible and obviously 'political' kind. There were numerous organized actions that were focused on crossing rather than protesting at that time (such as storming the tunnel or the port, or organizing traffic jams).

Many of the volunteers involved in the aid effort also directly or indirectly undermined the protests. Many felt too overwhelmed with the job of distribution to take part in demonstrations. Others actively opposed the demos, arguing that such actions were not safe, and only brought more violence upon the people in the jungle. They saw No Borders as naïve and reckless; playing games with the safety of people trying to cross. On the other hand, No Borders, although not always convinced by protest, wanted to come together with anyone who wanted to resist in any way collectively, feeling that to not resist was surely going to leave state control unchecked (or at least unnoted). They saw 'the humanitarians' as collaborators with the state, depoliticizing the situation,[25] equally naïve in seeing protest as what made people unsafe rather than the border, and deeply arrogant in the idea that it was their role to keep people safe somehow. There was judgement and resentment on both sides. As people became rooted in their positions, the possibilities of collaboration closed down.

There was the feeling that 'the humanitarians' were allies in the struggle for the freedom of movement up to a certain point. Many of them were there, day in, day out, and in undertaking their distributions they spent a lot of time with people living in the camp (indeed, some of the volunteers lived in the jungle too, and as such also faced the tear gas and police repression). But they were also one of the biggest obstacles to it. Only a minority of 'the humanitarians' were involved in any of the discussions around collective action, or in the actions themselves. Furthermore, given that their presence in the jungle was largely focused on distributing materials reinforced the idea that Europeans were the ones with ownership over 'the stuff'. Most people in the jungle made the assumption that every European there had things to hand out, and this really undermined the sense of any possibility of making the jungle a site of shared struggle with some degree of equality between Europeans and foreigners.[26]

Conclusion

This chapter is an account of the struggle for mobility as I witnessed and participated in it during various times in Calais. I have sought to create something of a timeline that stretches from the autumn of 2013 to the autumn of 2015. Like the struggle in Athens, this struggle pitched different expressions of the freedom of movement against expressions for its control. Also, as in the struggle in Athens, places like the church in the Tioxide jungle went beyond this relationship and created moments of autonomy and creativity that amounted to an outside to the state, however temporary or partial.

Calais also highlights how actions for autonomy are often collective. For example, there are the various times people from the jungle organized collectively to storm the Eurotunnel or highway. Then there are examples of actions for autonomy that were collective and collaborations between people with and without papers. The squat on rue Victor Hugo is one example of people with and without papers making a community together. Such spaces emerge out of need, but equally out of a desire among people with papers to take responsibility for the structural inequalities that they are implicated in and push back against privilege. However problematic Victor Hugo was, it nonetheless built bridges between people with and without papers. In this, it amounted to an experiment in equality that was also another way of being outside the state. All these examples are ways that people have taken action together, but do not amount to any kind of demand on the state. They are examples of people expressing autonomy, and in this way posing a problem for the regime of control.

Victor Hugo raised numerous practical dilemmas for those involved. The reality of trying to push against privilege brought into stark focus how collaborations like this are far from easy. For many people involved in CMS this pushing back against privilege – what I described in Chapter 2 as a process of 'becoming minor' – was a deeply uncomfortable, incomplete and frustrating process. Ultimately many who were involved in Victor Hugo were burnt out by it. And this raises numerous issues around the sustainability of actions such as this. Furthermore there is the issue of recuperation by the state. Like so many other experiments in autonomous community-building, Victor Hugo was eventually taken over by the local authorities.

Calais also highlights how there is an interconnection between autonomy and representation. People made demands on the state for the right to the freedom of movement. In a sense this was a demand for autonomy made in the realm of representation. Here we also see ambivalence between autonomy and representation. Making this demand to the state was to some degree paradoxical and was, in my opinion, one of the main reasons that these protests didn't bring about any positive change. The fact that the energy for protests tailed off after a summer and autumn when there were so many of them tells me that people living in the jungle also recognized this.

And organising for collective visible action in places like Calais is beset with other difficulties. Not only are the structures necessary for building communities of resistance constantly undermined by movement, within whatever that community is, there are differences of opinion on what constitutes effective action, which makes taking collective action really difficult. In groups like CMS, people wanted such actions to be led by people trying to cross. Crossing was what people came to Calais to do. Yet this also undermined the ability of those who remained to mount a collective visible resistance.

CONCLUSIONS: SO WHAT IS A NO BORDERS POLITICS?

These days are for the hundreds of migrants and refugees murdered at the borders, in police stations, and workplaces. They are for those murdered by cops or 'concerned citizens'. They are for those murdered for daring to cross the border, worked to death, for not bowing their head, or for nothing ... They are for the humiliations at the border and at the migrant detention centers, which continue to date. They are for the crying injustice of the Greek courts, the migrants and refugees unjustly in prison, the justice we are denied. (Social Centre of Albanian Migrants 2010).

The action to bring about the end of borders implies not separation, but inclusion ... What we want is democracy and inclusion of all – not in a nation, a state or an identity that always presupposes exclusion – but in a life in common. (Fernandez et al. 2006: 480)

Introduction

This book was driven by a problem: that the freedom of movement is encouraged for some and denied to others. In this way, the border regime instils a fundamental inequality in our social world. The border control regime makes the notion of 'illegal immigration' seem normal. But the control of movement is man-made, not innate, and human illegality is *produced* through its logics (Anderson et al. 2012). In opposition to such a logic, I argued that a world of equality would be a world of free movement. It would be a world that rendered borders meaningless.

This problem led me to a question: How do we refuse borders, in a current existent reality in which they proliferate?

This question in turn led me to propose a no borders politics. I laid out what I think are the main characteristics of this politics in theory in Chapter 1, and in practice in Chapter 2, which I recap once more here. In summary, I argued that a no borders politics is first and foremost a refusal of the border and the state. It goes beyond contesting the state, by seeking to remain autonomous from it. However, demands for rights and recognition also play a part in a no borders politics, because such acts can transform the logics of political membership. Yet there is a fundamental tension there: how to navigate between autonomous practices that seek to escape the state, and representational practices that seek to transform it? A no borders politics negotiates this dilemma. As people negotiate this dilemma in different ways, I argued that this creates a spectrum of activism that makes up the no borders movement. This raises a second fundamental tension in a no borders politics: how to navigate between being together with others in their struggle for liberation and staying faithful to what we see as our own struggle. Put another way, it negotiates the dilemma of dealing with different conceptualizations of what freedom is, or what effective action is.

Chapters 3 and 4 each looked in detail at the struggle over mobility in Athens and Calais. I looked at those practices that I think most closely express a no borders politics: the autonomy of migration, collaborative community-building and migrant-led protest. I also looked at some of the different expressions of solidarity that run through these practices and that to some degree constitute a practice in and of itself. In each case I wanted to draw out how people practise the freedom of movement, and the relationship between these practices and the mechanisms of control. As such I looked at some of the practical dilemmas that people face when taking action in these ways.

These practical dilemmas point to theoretically deeper dilemmas for a no borders politics, and tensions between what a no borders politics is (in practice) and what it could be (in theory). In this chapter I begin by reflecting on these deeper, theoretical dilemmas, before turning to look at what more this tells us about a no borders politics.

In Chapter 1 I introduced the idea of the autonomy of migration. To recap I defined it as the largely mundane and everyday strategies that people who move without permission use as a way of continuing to practise the freedom of movement. From sharing information on the best routes of travel, to maintaining safer houses or jungles, such practices can be a refusal of the border in the way that they inherently disobey the border regime. At the same time they force a constant transformation in the operation of that regime, and demonstrate that border controls are far from free of constraint (Bojadžijev and Karakayali 2010). As expressions of autonomy, they have the potential to escape the state in being moments of autonomy and equality, no matter how temporary.

Through the example of an apartment in Athens and the church in a Calais jungle I showed why I think such places represent this other way of being to the state. For me, such spaces carve out moments or possibility for autonomy; spaces that are equal by being open to anyone who needs to use them, who are those largely excluded by the state. Though they are generally written off as something like 'the undersides of capitalism', I think such spaces are also beautiful in the way that they are another way of being to the state. In situations of rawness and violence, they nonetheless function through a logic of deep interconnectedness that compels people to take care of each other. But the autonomy of migration poses dilemmas for a no borders politics.

First, there is the dilemma of how the autonomy of migration relies on remaining invisible and is undermined when it becomes visible. This is a bigger problem in a small city like Calais than it is in a big one like Athens. In Athens, a lot of people without papers have been able to remain imperceptible to control in this huge, dense and sprawling city. Equally, large diaspora networks and a large black market economy provide more opportunities for people to blend in (knowledge about the area, money to pay rent). In Calais, not only does being at the border make controls far more intense, in such a relatively small city it's hard for people without papers to blend in. People often live exposed, and although jungles are a way of collectivizing resources and provide safety in numbers, they are also visible and, as such, vulnerable. People respond with new expressions of autonomy (making new spaces, finding new ways to cross), but constantly changing your strategy is tiring. Because of this, I think practising the autonomy of migration in Calais is harder than in Athens.

Although the practices of autonomy in Athens and Calais are different, conceptually the autonomy of migration raises many similar dilemmas for a no borders politics. People without papers find different ways to evade controls. Control responds with new strategies of capture. People respond. And so the process continues. In Athens, people live in places like the apartment and remain relatively anonymous. The state responded to the massive increase in people without papers in the city with a series of crackdowns. People were forced farther out of public space as a means of remaining invisible. In Calais, people built the Tioxide jungle of which the church was a part. The state intervened and forced those living there to move. People did, and built a new jungle (with a much bigger church), which contained new possibilities for autonomy. The state responded by undermining the structure of that jungle. To what extent are these acts of autonomy something other than just a response to control that elicits an ever tighter control response? A large part of the autonomy of migration is always recuperated by control, because the autonomy of migration is largely defined by the relation to that which it seeks to escape from. Doesn't the autonomy of migration just get recuperated by the state?

And beyond this, perhaps control is transforming in ways that are shrinking the possibilities for escape altogether. Stephan Scheel (2012) suggests that people's ability to practise the autonomy of migration is increasingly undermined by how biometrics and virtual controls make people who move without permission increasingly traceable, and enables the authorities to predict and then seek to account for future escapes. The ability of virtual controls to predict future escapes has had a big effect on people in places like Calais and Athens, where having your fingerprints recorded on Eurodac[1] means that you are liable to be returned to the first 'safe' country you travelled through. Many people with such records have been deported back to those countries, particularly Greece, Spain and Italy. In this way, administrative tools like Eurodac and the Dublin Regulation undermine the ability of people to have agency over their mobility. People respond by ignoring these policies and hoping to fall through the gaps in their administration (such policies only functioning as well as the state's ability to administer them), or by claiming asylum, for example. But as the control regime becomes more sophisticated, do the gaps within control get smaller?

But then there's that part of autonomy that's *not* in relationship to control, that's self-referencing, entirely creative and independent from that which it opposes. This is the part of autonomy that's created in the moment – immanently. These are the moments that demonstrate another way of being, that are an important dimension to how autonomy functions, or what it creates. These moments continue to emerge wherever there is a gap in control. And all the while the number of people defined as 'illegal' and hence excluded by the border increases, as does the number of people forced to move. The movement of those excluded by the border but nonetheless moving – the movement of autonomy of migration – continues to grow.

What all this means, I think, is that the dilemma of recuperation is less a problem of the autonomy of migration, and more a problem of how autonomy is viewed. In practical terms it might mean that people trying to cross in Calais might one day find that the border is really closed, or that organizing in jungles there is impossible. If this happens it won't mean that the border regime has somehow 'won', but that the autonomy of migration will have shifted. The struggle will take place in some other realm, in some other way or space.

Taking these things into consideration means ditching the idea that autonomy has failed if it's neither total nor permanent. It also means seeing the struggle against the border as not limited to places like Athens or Calais, or even limited to the realm of movement per se, but as existing anywhere that autonomy comes up against control (which probably includes the place you come from too). As one interviewee suggested, 'basically this movement of people around the world is such a large scale at the moment that it's pretty much happening everywhere. There are some specifics to do with Calais, but actually these tendencies are happening everywhere, especially places on the route' (interview, Anon. 7).

How we view autonomy raises other dilemmas. In many cases the kind of autonomy I have described in this book is not seen as a practice of politics. Generally people think of politics as an intentional and collective power play in the public realm. But the autonomy of migration is rarely collective or public. It does not rest on intent, so much as on the practice of escape, regardless of intent (Mitropoulos 2007; Papadopoulos et al. 2008).

People move without permission and these practices amount to a refusal of the border. But people don't come to Calais or Athens to make a political statement. They come to keep moving. Refusal is, to a large degree, an unintended effect – a political activity by people who have no intention of behaving politically – and this makes it hard to think of it as political, if what we think of as political is intentional activity. But I don't think this makes it directionless. The autonomy of migration is a movement that's created and reproduced because of need, and compels those who take part to create relationships based on deep interdependence. It's replicated over and over again, and in this repetition creates a movement that expresses the freedom of movement. This is not the same as a collective demand; neither does it often express a collective identity. I think this is because the autonomy of migration is essentially only 'faithful' to itself in all its diversity, and to the possibilities of an equality that's created immanently, through practice, use and necessity.

Not being 'faithful' to any political agenda, not amounting to a self-identifying mass movement, consisting largely of activities that have unintended effects, the autonomy of migration lacks many of the characteristics that we commonly identify politics by. I think these practices are *intensely* political. But not being seen in this way makes these practices *isolated* because they are often ignored and devalued. In the places where the struggle over mobility is intense (such as Calais or Athens) there are many groups in solidarity with those trying to move. Yet in my time in both these places, few of these groups spent much of their time in the places where people trying to move often were. In other settings, many of these individuals or groups invest in autonomous practices and spaces (making social centres, squats or other land occupations), but the living spaces of people without papers often seem to be left off this list. There is a gap between how politically conscious activists organize and this everyday practice of 'the migrants' that weakens this form of autonomy.

Escape from the state is in most cases an unintended, unpleasant and temporary side effect of/for people on the move and rarely seen as valuable. This is another dilemma that the autonomy of migration raises for a no borders politics. People without papers access and reproduce the mobile commons as a way of escaping controls, but they're trying to escape the mobile commons too. Few people want to be in the jungles, or squashed ten to an apartment.[2] They see such places only as spaces of exclusion and as such these places are disinvested of the possibility of being anything else. Andrew Robinson describes this dilemma in the following way: 'the problem with identifying with the excluded is also a problem for the excluded' (Robinson 2010a: 227). Put another way, the excluded don't value their exclusion. Why should they? Such spaces are no one's idea of 'making it'.

And yet, I am not advocating for a situation where anybody has to value exclusion, but more a situation where the division between inclusion and exclusion is no longer there. For me, the erosion of this boundary begins with autonomy, which is also a valuing of another way of being, a form of equality that rejects the distinction between inside and outside, but which for now can be thought of as a kind of 'being from the outside'. What I argued in Chapter 2 is that the autonomy of migration is not (and cannot be) a practice only of people without papers, because 'being from the outside' is not the task of the excluded, but of everybody. As such, the question is not how the excluded can come to value being from the outside, but how people, regardless of what oppressions or privileges they carry, can come to make a life from the outside together (ibid.). Actually there are numerous examples – like squats, social centres or land occupations to name but a few – where being 'from the outside' is not an unintended effect but very much the central aim. I talked about the importance of going beyond recognition of our privileges and taking action, collaboratively and meaningfully, with people who experience oppressions that we do not. That's why I argued that the most powerful expressions of the autonomy of migration are when different kinds of people participate together in the mobile commons. It is for that reason that I have made collaborative community-building such an important part of this book (and why I also include it as a form of autonomy of migration).

Reflecting on the autonomy of migration

As a part of the autonomy of migration, many of the dilemmas that I have explored so far also apply to collaborative communities of people with and without papers, but such communities face particular dilemmas too. In Chapter 4 I drew out some of the practical dilemmas for people practising collaborative community-building in the case of the squat on rue Victor Hugo. I focused on those that people with papers face in this endeavour, because this is the position that I can talk from. As such, the issues I raise here are dilemmas of autonomy but also of solidarity.

Victor Hugo was eventually taken over by the state, and in that sense was recuperated by it. It points again to another variation of the dilemma of how we navigate existing power relations while also attempting to escape them. I was not there when people connected to CMS debated whether to continue their involvement in the house and how to respond to the threat from the local authorities. To be honest, I don't know what the resolution of this dilemma is, or if there even is one. Such situations are struggles of power, but they are also struggles between differing perspectives and experiences within one group. In such situations our responses are limited by a power bigger than us, but also by differentiation within the collectives we identify with. We continue to engage with this dilemma and the risk that what we do is recuperated by the state, which is different in each and every case.

Victor Hugo had the potential to create another way of being to the state, by being an experiment in equality. Yet in bringing different people together, many different variations of struggles over issues of privilege and oppression (of race, class and gender) played out in the house. Dealing with these issues raised uncomfortable feelings of guilt, contributed to burn-out among many, and undermined the sustainability of CMS involvement in the long term. As such, Victor Hugo raises what I think is the main dilemma of solidarity: that of creating equality in a highly unequal existing social reality.

In places like Calais, the inequalities between people are thrown into stark relief. You witness the material ways that these inequalities affect people every day. It can feel as if every interaction you have and everything you do brings recognition of the unearned advantages you have over others. We try to push against these inequalities that we didn't initiate but are nonetheless complicit in, but this often feels like plugging holes in a dam that is failing faster than we can repair it. You try to build on the assumption of equality, yet inequalities constantly come up. For Amy Non,

> this equality doesn't exist. Plain and simple. We can express solidarity, yes, that's OK. We can show that we're not willing to stand by silently and leave all these people by themselves, we can duke it out with the police and the fascists, play little games, squat houses, do media work, throw soli-parties. But we won't manage it, not totally, we will start to get a clue and then fall back on ourselves and our own histories. (Non n.d.)

And here the idea that we can really be together with people trying to cross in their struggle weakens. Within a situation of such deep violence on the part of the border regime, people not directly experiencing this violence (such as people not trying to cross) are outside of the realities that many find to survive. It can raise uncomfortable feelings over differences that seem too big to overcome. It can raise doubts over whether this is really our struggle at all or one we are simply playing at being involved in. At times it seems that people without papers share these doubts too and ask you, either in words or through actions, 'what is this to do with you?' They have a point.

I think the dilemma of equality has another part to it too. On the one hand it plays out in the way we – as white people, and/or Europeans, and/or people with papers ... – try to push against our privilege. On the other hand it plays out in the way we navigate other people's ability to oppress others. In Victor Hugo this issue came up in how those women connected to smuggling networks had greater power in the house and gave privileged treatment to some women while undermining others. It also came up in how, rather than creating a space of relative safety, some felt that they had unwittingly become complicit in a space that was being used to further exploit women trying to cross. It demonstrates the intersectionality of power structures and also how those structures are themselves affected by numerous, less structured advantages and disadvantages. Put more bluntly, we can all oppress, even the oppressed.

This is particularly stark in relation to gender issues in Calais. Women trying to cross have to deal with the risk of sexual violence in addition to the other violences and dehumanizations that affect all people without papers in Calais. Cis female CMS activists also constantly come up against behaviour from other people in CMS, or from people trying to cross, that judges them according to their gender and undermines them.[3] It leads to situations when you say, 'we are all fighting against the border, but I end up fighting against you when I feel you oppress me because of my gender'. Things like this are a huge barrier to creating a collaborative community, further undermined by the way that categories like 'refugee' and 'supporter' fail to capture how these power structures and advantages intersect (Ünsal 2015). How do we negotiate these things without ruling out the possibility of building community together?

I find the concept of groundless solidarity, developed by feminist scholar Diane Elam, a useful way of negotiating these dilemmas. Groundless solidarity involves undecidability, a term borrowed from Jacques Derrida. Undecidability is not an inability to decide between different perspectives and take political action. Rather it's a 'process that always depends on the specific nature of the situation at hand' (Elam 1994: 87). Groundless solidarity is based on decisions that are never made in advance, but are made through continual negotiation. It refuses to close down questions of difference or account for it by merely balancing competing claims to rights.

Groundless solidarity involves making judgements in each case. It therefore rests on the presumed equality of human beings that creates 'a network of responsibilities to others' (ibid.: 105). In practice, it's about working with others, through a process of constant negotiation. It goes beyond thinking and acting around privilege, and to a large degree comes into conflict with the idea, because it works from the principle of dealing with what people bring to the moment, rather than working from any preordained sense of who they are. I don't think it proposes we either engage with or dismiss structured forms of oppression, but rather that we take them into account while also having an orientation towards autonomy and in striking out for that.

I find Elam's notion of groundless solidarity compelling because of the way that shared ethical commitments are based on being together, rather than a pre-formed set of values and principles. This take on a shared ethical commitment does not assume the existence of the same vision or idea, but assumes that we might just come to a shared vision through practice and synthesis. Hence, it opens up to the possibility of creating common ground across difference that neither appropriates nor externalizes the struggle of others. In this way, such a practice appears to abandon the need to create and articulate a collective identity, or to seek representation for it. Groundless solidarity calls on us to put aside fixed ideas about how to do things. It forms part of a politics that's not confined to any particular politics or practice.

The judgements made in each case are based on the situation that faces you. In relation to these dilemmas groundless solidarity is about building community out of valuing and making judgements over individual relationships; of building equality step by step, relationship by relationship. In that sense, groundless solidarity is an intimate process. It operates at a micro level. It's about communication, making a safer space where it's possible to communicate bravely, sharing our feelings on the behaviour of the people around us, being willing to call someone out over racist or sexist behaviour, being willing to be called out yourself over such things. Yet this raises other dilemmas, not least of which is how, if what we're aiming for is radical social change, might we connect so many tiny instances of equality.

These are some of the ways we can reflect on the dilemmas of equality. Yet there are other things that remain out of our control. Indeed, what I think often gets left out of many of the texts on privilege or community-building is how, in places like Calais, all this takes place in a situation that is *simply traumatizing*. Calais overwhelms. Everyone. There are the low-level traumas of living in spaces outside of the state: the anxiety that these places could get raided by police at first light. Add to this the low-level traumas of daily life in a community that's not supposed to exist: the friend who's been stuck in the jungle for two years; all the people who are apart from their families; the ways that people cope with their own traumas (alcoholism, violence); the traumas that people in solidarity bring with them. Add to this the occasional high-level traumas: the actual police violence and incarceration; the deaths, accidents and abuse. This can add to feelings of guilt, which people often deal with through lack of self-care, or attempts at solving the situation by adopting aid-giver roles. It contributes to burn-out. Guilt and burn-out don't only come about because people struggle to process their privilege. They also come about because the situation is *simply traumatizing.*[4]

All of these issues mean that collaborative community-building is unpopular, partly because attempting to make spaces of equality in devalued places is difficult, and partly because it's so difficult to stay mentally well while doing it. This makes sustainability an issue for groups like CMS. Many people who get involved in this kind of activism do so transiently and temporarily. People often pass through, staying for a few weeks. When they leave, the decisions taken and agreements made often leave with them. Knowledge is lost, and with it part of what's needed to build things (community, spaces) is also lost.

Perhaps this lack of continuity is just the price we pay for doing the 'spade work'. But perhaps it's just a matter of expectations. Pushing against privilege is about participating in making experiences that actively undermine inequality. But it never shakes off its association with inequality. In this, we can easily feel that we are always failing, because there is always so much more to do. Equally, the politics I describe doesn't proclaim to be or need to be a politics that's prescriptive, that's driven by the idea of what must happen, or that's of the masses. In fact, it can be considered 'anti-mass' in the sense that it seeks to stay beneath the gaze of the state and therefore benefits from being small and discreet (Red Sunshine Gang 1999 [1971]). It needs a critical mass of people to be able to sustain it, but that's not the same as that mass needing to be identified, organized and collective. That mass, or those masses, are present in places like Athens or Calais already, in the thousands of people moving without permission. So partly this dilemma is about perspective, about feeling that we are a part of the mobile commons, rather than that people trying to cross are a part of our struggle against the state.

Reflecting on migrant-led protest

In Chapter 3 I looked at the hunger strike of 'The 300' as an example of a significant moment of visible protest that was also migrant-led. In

Chapter 4 I talked about a wave of protests – some of which were migrant-led – that took place in Calais in the summer/autumn of 2015. The hunger strike and these protests reflect a no borders politics inasmuch as they were practices that potentially transformed the logics of citizenship and belonging, and that potentially escaped the state through forms of self-determination that prefigured equality. But practices of visible protest by people without papers raise dilemmas for a no borders politics too. To what extent did either of these actions raise a disagreement or amount to an act of citizenship? Let me look at each of these actions in turn.

In Chapter 1 I talked about Rancière's concept of disagreement and the concept of acts of citizenship as two theories that shed more light on how certain acts of protest can potentially bring about radical social change. To recap I said that disagreement is about making visible that part of society that is not counted as equal. It is about disrupting the 'order of the visible and sayable', which is the order of what can be seen as political, or what is seen as counting as something of value. I said that acts of citizenship are acts in which people come to constitute themselves as new political subjects and how recognition of them as new political subjects can transform the logics of citizenship. I argued that both disagreement and acts of citizenship shed light on different aspects of protest by the excluded. To a certain extent disagreement is what comes before (recognition of) representation, whereas acts of citizenship are a possible outcome that comes after representation.

I want to start with the protests in Calais, because I think these actions are the least convincing in terms of generating radical social change in either respect. Certainly I think it's hard to suggest that these protests amounted to an act of citizenship. The protests didn't force any recognition of legitimacy from the state; neither were any of the demands of the protesters met. But did these protests raise a disagreement?

To the extent that the protests brought out into public space large numbers of people from the jungle, who were largely self-organized and expressed a collective demand to be seen as human and heard as properly political beings, these protests did attempt to raise a disagreement. Yet in each case the possibility for disrupting politics – of actually being seen in this way by the state/public political culture – was foreclosed. The involvement of people living in the jungle was seen either as manipulation on the part of No Borders, or as violent outbursts. In either case the activities of 'the migrants' were depoliticized and kept invisible. In contrast, the involvement of supporters was seen as the actions of a radical minority who were 'leading' 'the migrants' and as highly political (by which I mean conforming to a mode of political behaviour that was comprehensible to the state). Rigby and Schlembach raise a similar issue in their account of protests during the No Borders camp in Calais in 2009. 'Invariably in this picture what gets presented as "activism" essentially remains defined by the state … Policing the separation between migrants and activists involved not only denying undocumented migrants the capacity of protest, but also framing protest and "activism" in a particularly statist way' (Rigby and Schlembach 2013: 167–8).

That the people trying to cross were somehow incapable of taking action autonomously, without the help or leadership of European citizens, smuggled in racist assumptions of who was capable of being political. It meant that the state managed to continue to deny the presence of a miscount here. As such, the way that the protests were framed and dealt with failed to break with sovereign conceptions of protest and as such remained impotent to bring about any social change. Such actions fail to disrupt the separation between protest and movement; a distinction I argue groups like CMS try to dismantle by taking autonomous action too (ibid.).

That said, the ways that people came together to organize these protests *was* a form of equality. In the organization, people met together as equals, and formed strategies together that were based on the assumption of already existing political agency. In this, the meetings that took place prior to many of the protests represented a form of equality that was also a form of autonomy that 'abandoned' a relation to the state. But this coming together ended when the protests did (and indeed rarely continued between protests because those organizing such actions often changed too), the protests being seen as the thing that was political, and the process as something else. These potentially escaping practices – these other ways of being – 'remained at the scene' of the protests and were not nurtured afterwards.

I think that the hunger strike of 'The 300' is perhaps more interesting in terms of an expression of a no borders politics that potentially brought about radical social change. The state was forced to give in to some of the demands of the strikers, and in the process recognize them as political actors. In this way, the strikers made visible a disagreement, and brought new political subjects onto the scene. Yet once more, the strike raises dilemmas for a no borders politics. First, in order to be understood, the strikers had to speak to dominant power in 'its' language, using the same terms as those used in 'the mainstream'. Yet using the language of dominant power to speak to dominant power seems to generate conflicting discourses that can undermine our struggle and perpetuate further oppression. Feminist scholarship on migration has drawn attention to how migration regimes reinforce certain constructs of migrant identity – the feminized, helpless refugee, or the dangerous and immoral migrant – that fix people into playing out certain 'scripts' (cf. Andrijasevic 2009; Hyndman 2010; Nolin 2006; Pupavac 2008; Wolfram Cox and Minahan 2004). The strikers challenged certain stereotypes in using themes of courage, defiance and autonomy. But in addressing the government using terms it would understand, certain stereotypes were reinforced too. They used a certain language to demonstrate their legitimacy, but at some expense. Here are some examples, taken from the statements of 'The 300': 'We live by the sweat of our brow and with the dream that one day we will have the same rights as our Greek fellow workers ... We do not have any other way to make our voices heard, to raise awareness of our rights. We risk our lives because, either way, there is no dignity in our living conditions' ('The 300', 23 January 2011); '[w]e are not those piteous, destitute migrants, deprived of housing, work and clothes, that the media are describing. We have houses, families and jobs in the cities we left behind. We are not looking for housing here in Athens, but came to fight, for as long as our bodies will allow us, for our rights and for a life with dignity. ('The 300', 27 January 2011).

In the first quote 'The 300' employ a discourse of victimhood, which stands in contrast to the strong and forceful group, demanding their right to rights and dignity. In the second statement, 'The 300' proclaim their legitimacy against an other, 'those piteous, destitute migrants' that they are not. In the process they align themselves with the already included against the 'scrounging migrant'. They present themselves as the 'ideal workers', playing into discourses of deserving and undeserving that they actually seek to contest (Lara et al. 2009/10: 23). This fits very well with neoliberal priorities that work through divide and rule, and that see rights as privileges and virtues (Bauder 2006; Lara et al. 2009/10).

Second, there is the dilemma – raised already in relation to the protests in Calais – that relates to what the strikers and others saw or counted as political action. Like the protests from the jungle, the hunger strike emerged from a long process of meetings and self-organized assemblies of the strikers. Like the protests in Calais I think this represented a form of equality that was also a form of autonomy that 'abandoned' a relation to the state. Yet also as in Calais, and for similar reasons, the practice largely ended when the strike did. Equally, the strike was often perceived by other activists in one dimension that overlooked these practices of equality; as an appeal for rights that reinforced the status quo, and hence was incompatible with a radically libertarian politics. Youssef comments:

> They [activist groups] say you are asking, begging. No we are not begging. I go to take my right for a simple thing. But tomorrow I fuck him [the state] again. Tomorrow I can go there. Tomorrow I can make *katalypsi* [occupation/squat]. If I need it, OK? As immigrant, my needs, and when I say my I'm talking our, our needs as immigrant is in these things. I *have* to talk. I have to be open with everybody. But not friendship. Not comrades, but open. (Interview, Youssef)

And indeed, to a large degree these practices of equality were undermined by the very practices of recognition, which is another, crucial dilemma. The strikers were seeking and demanding inclusion, which involved appealing to and emulating the social norms of the included group and not seeking to transform or escape those power relations through other ways of being. The strike demonstrated how acts that refuse the border are often *mixed in* with elements that contest and potentially undermine their potential to escape the state. Separating out contesting, transformative and possibly escaping elements of political action can be difficult, because they are so often mixed in together. Seeking to be heard by the state, but also practising something provocative and potentially transformative/escaping, demonstrates the ambivalence and impurity of such struggles by necessary engagement with dominant power.

This leads to questions over the extent to which demands for rights such as this one can be considered as transformative acts at all. As Anne McNevin (2009) suggests, such struggles perhaps better demonstrate the state's *discretionary* power to include, rather than the ability of such struggles to transform the logics of belonging. This dilemma is clear in struggles for regularization, for example, where amnesties are often followed by and indeed justify the introduction of tighter regulations afterwards.

Claims for recognition remain bound to the state; tied to a territory where those rights or recognitions apply. But most people without papers in Greece, or with limited status there, wanted only to leave the country. The right to move, which seems the most urgent of all claims that people without papers want to make, is one that struggles for rights seem incapable of making. For those who can focus only on getting out of Greece, regularization is not what they're in need of; opening the borders is.[5]

> Being here without papers and trying to escape is a totally different situation. It is about having no hope, being in a country that is in a crisis, doesn't give you work, doesn't give you enough opportunities. So, er, this struggle is a different kind of struggle. And if I can understand well, it's two different subjects for discussion. Two different ways of being 'illegal'. (Interview, Iradz)

I disagree with Iradz that the hunger strike of 'The 300' had no bearing on the struggle of people without *any* status in the country. However, I do agree that the tactic of protest seems unlikely to be able to address the desire to keep moving. I think this is a key reason why the protests in Calais failed to bring about any positive change. The primary demand of the protesters was to 'open the border'. Yet who to address this effectively transnational demand for the freedom of movement to? Such a demand doesn't have a place in territorially bounded discourses of rights that are generally expressed through protest, even if acts of citizenship open up possibilities for thinking of political membership differently. This need to escape remains unexpressible within current discourses of rights and visibility. The issue of whether it's possible to articulate a demand that's not connected to territory remains unresolved, and this also acts as a limit on the transformative potential of acts of citizenship (Balibar 2004b).

Reflecting on solidarity in struggles for rights and visibility

Although solidarity is also central to the activism of 'The 300', in this book I have largely focused on solidarity as practised by those who are not directly denied the freedom of movement, but who participate in this struggle through standing with, rather than speaking for, people without papers. My accounts of Athens and Calais both featured different ways that people showed solidarity with this struggle. In some cases solidarity formed part of the mobile commons (as in the case of the collaborative community-building of groups such as Calais Migrant Solidarity); in other cases solidarity formed part of a struggle for rights and visibility. It is the latter I turn to look at now.

Dilemmas for the anti-authoritarian movement From anti-fascist actions in Victoria Square, Athens, to the various community kitchens or assemblies, the anti-authoritarian movement has come together with people without papers largely incidentally, through the fact of sharing space together. In these ways, it can be argued that they participated together in creating community. Yet when it comes to visible action for recognition or rights, the movement has struggled. It faced big doubts over whether to support the hunger strike of 'The 300', for example. These doubts raise important issues about how we resist alongside others when the means and ends of their activism appear at odds with our own. It expresses a particular view on what effective political action is, which here is seen as those things that enable us to achieve a total freedom from the state. Engaging with the state as a means of making demands on it was seen as deeply problematic for those whose politics and political community remained defined by being essentially 'outside' the state. At the level of theory, the struggle for papers was seen as hopelessly contaminated by the state. Within this there was limited scope for recognizing moments where this campaign could be anything else:

> But many of them [migrants] have the point of view that they want to come to Europe to work, make some money and send it back home. And since they have this view it's very hard to show solidarity, because they have totally different aims and goals and perspectives. They don't have the access to radical knowledge, the mental tools to think that we should fight and do something different. (Interview, Anon., anti-authoritarian movement)

Uri Gordon, in the context of anarchist activism in Palestine/Israel and the struggle for Palestinian national liberation, suggests that this theoretically 'correct' response often makes anarchists irrelevant to such struggles: '[t]he tension between anarchists' anti-imperialist commitments on the one hand, and their traditionally wholesale rebuttal of the state and nationalism on the other, would seem to leave them at an impasse ... The lack of fresh thinking on the issue creates a position from which, it would seem, one can only fall back on the one-size-fits-all formulae' (Gordon 2008: 151–2).

The view that there is anti-state activism and then there is 'everything else' that's contaminated by the state draws out something of a paradox. The movement is steeped in anarchistic ideas that are designed to disturb fixed theories, but at times their practice reflects fixed and absolute ideas about resistance. A conversation with an activist involved with the Network *and* the movement raised this issue. 'The anarchists and those who consider themselves radicals actually often adopt more conservative positions ... She said she and her friend often discussed how many who define themselves as radical or anarchist often display very unradical behaviours' (interview, Regina).

This 'one size fits all' perspective towards political action in this case seems to rest on a sense that people have relatively similar abilities to take action, or that they can or even want to do so in the same way, to the same end (Crass n.d. c). The effect of this is that movements like this one often construct anarchist ghettos that effectively (if unintentionally) exclude difference (Martinez 2002). As Hakim Bey points out,

> [t]he anarchist 'movement' today contains virtually no Blacks, Hispanics, Native Americans or children ... even tho *in theory* such genuinely oppressed groups stand to gain the most from any anti-authoritarian revolt. Might it be that anarchism offers no concrete program whereby the truly deprived might fulfil (or at least struggle realistically to fulfil) real needs & desires? (Bey 2003 [1991]: 61)

Bey wrote the above text fifteen years ago, yet it feels as true now as then. Being comprised overwhelmingly of white, straight, young and able-bodied citizens, the movement – like many anarchistic movements – reflects its supposed homogeneity (Graeber 2009). Such homogeneous and powerful subject positions impact the ways that radicals conceive of politics and their place in it (Crass n.d. c). They create situations where their tactics of activism are inaccessible to others. Actions considered as 'anarchist' are largely *not* attended by those most directly affected by the oppression such actions seek to attack (Koopmans 2008; Lamble 2001). Often this is because highly confrontational actions disproportionately place people of colour or people without papers at risk (Graeber 2009; Luu 2004; Martinez 2002). They also create 'a false contrast between "inauthentic" activism and some imagined form of "authenticity"' (Anon n.d.). 'When anarchists talk about not dealing with the state, they are doing that from a position of being a citizen status. When they go to protests and get arrested, they get arrested. An immigrant will get deported' (interview, Nasim).

Another effect of adopting a stance that seeks a total freedom from the state is that issues of difference within the movement appear essentially resolved, because of the assumption that such a struggle is capable of dealing with specific forms of oppression within itself. This can at times silence difference and encourage the proliferation of informal hierarchies where difference, privilege and oppression are not discussed (Freeman 1970). The following quote, where the author reflects on the Greek movement, illustrates this point:

> I prefer to say that I'm an anarchist than to say that I'm a feminist. The problem is very philosophical, between the partial and the total. If I protest for my partial freedom, as a woman, I would focus on being able to get a good job, receiving welfare from the State when I have a baby. That would be my partial freedom, and it would be completely compatible with capitalism. (Iulia 2010: 32)

In the same article, though, Iulia goes on to raise concerns over this position:

> But this umbrella of the anarchist movement, which is a powerful thing, creates a trap of making people suspicious of anyone who doesn't wear the label of anarchist. So it's not easy to get access, and also not easy to introduce new lines of politics. So the subject group can become a bit sexist. And the anarchist movement here excludes aesthetic matters, cultural matters, spiritual matters. (Ibid.: 33)

Not fitting the anarchist image or strict world-view creates exclusion.[6] That they are discussed sometimes shows that such movements are aware of these issues. But I think that intersectionality and all the concomitant issues of difference are effectively shelved so as to keep anarchism somehow 'whole'. Sasha describes this as anarcho-purism (sasha n.d.). 'Anarcho-purism is a morality that tries to keep anarchism pure and separate from certain tactics or from working with certain groups for the sake of purity.' However, such purism is reasserted by effectively reinstating the uncrossable border between engagement and rejection of the state: 'That said, it is also a simple fact of language that those who want to reform the system are called reformists' (ibid.). Again, the dilemma of engagement versus rejection of the state is essentially sidestepped, and purity reinstated.

Dilemmas for the Network   In contrast, the Network had little trouble supporting the hunger strike of 'The 300', but struggled to be with migrants on an everyday level. In practical terms they struggled with what they saw as increasing isolation from migrant communities. Partly they felt this was because they were failing to make connections with such communities, but partly it was because they felt that migrant communities weren't organizing.

I think this problem reflects a deeper tension in understandings of what political action is. For the Network, the problem was that migrants weren't mobilizing. But another way of saying this is that they weren't mobilizing in a particular way. It was a problem for the Network because, ultimately, they saw political action as first and foremost about visibility and recognition. For the Network, which emphasizes influencing discourse, policy and law, recognition is a key part of what it sees as politically relevant. Being publicly visible is an essential prerequisite to being influential, with recognition seen as a first step to greater self-determination (Goldberg 1993). This visibility doesn't implicitly rest on the participation of the oppressed, because expressing universal principles (such as human rights) can be expressed by anyone who wishes to take part (Lentin 2004). It doesn't necessarily require the involvement of those who experience their loss first-hand.

The Network has always been driven by solidarity with the self-organized struggles of migrants. But despite this desire, the involvement of migrants has not always been at the top of the list of priorities for their anti-racist work. In fact, acts of visibility have at times been seen as more effective when carried out by already more visible citizens (ibid.). The actual participation of migrants comes second to the need to make them visible, the task of which may be best carried out by citizens. This issue came up for me in one action to distribute information in migrant neighbourhoods about the first attack on migrants by members of the Golden Dawn to reach trial. 'I felt acutely aware that the poster was entirely in Greek, yet the company of the square was almost entirely not Greek. There was a corresponding leaflet being distributed, but again, only in Greek ... When Ahmed came to see what we were doing, I asked him what he thought of the poster and he said that he couldn't read it, ditto for the flyer' (field diary, 4 December 2010).

The fact that this poster was in Greek only may have been an oversight (posters for the anti-racist festival were always written in multiple languages, for instance). But it was a huge barrier to anyone who didn't read much Greek, such as many migrants (including me).

The valuing of visibility can mean that acts of public protest often appear as more important or 'more political' than building relationships between communities and being together in everyday ways; the 'spade work' I talked about earlier (Crass n.d. b). Spade work is seen as important, but inessential compared to work at the 'rock-face' of politics. The balance between 'spade work' and 'political work' topples in favour of the latter. The result is that many solidarity-based anti-racist groups end up defending migrants rather than nurturing self-organization and collaboration, increasing the space between them (Lentin 2004: 101).

It also means that anti-racist groups can unwillingly find themselves acting as the 'managers of dissent', where migrants have the opportunity to participate, but according to another group's terms (Della Porta 2000; Lentin 2004; Zavos 2008). Pushing back against privilege means not speaking for the movement, but giving space for people without papers to do that. 'In theory this should nurture mutual understanding, political awareness and solidarity, but for our daily self-organization white paternalist behaviour constitutes still a huge obstacle' (Ünsal 2015: 6). In the moments when the rights of migrants are articulated on their behalf by citizens, the possibility of transformative action is closed down, because it remains locked in statist conceptions of what resistance is. As Heather Johnson suggests, when citizens advocate on behalf of non-citizens, activism remains a privileged activity of citizens (Johnson 2012: 119). The result of all this is that at the times when solidarity seems most essential, the connections between communities are often not there to enable it to happen without hierarchy. The reciprocity that is a fundamental aspect of solidarity is assumed to be there, but is missing.

Collective visible action and Calais CMS sought to straddle some kind of position between that of the anti-authoritarian movement and the Network. The group is largely anti-state and seeks to be together with people trying to cross in the everyday, while at the same time being with them if and when people take collective and visible action. Like the movement, CMS is comprised largely of white, native, young and able-bodied people with papers. Yet this is only the case when it comes to the formal structure of the group. When it comes to action, the group is very mixed and remains oriented towards participation in the mobile commons (and perhaps it has to be this way, seeing as people trying to cross are inherently transient, in their own mind if not always in reality). Yet at times CMS also struggles with pre-formed ideas about collective action, and struggles with solidarity too.

In Calais, as in Athens, there were also tensions between different individuals' and groups' approaches to protest. For all those involved in the jungle who had an opinion about visible collective action, the division was largely between those who saw it as dangerous, ineffective or a waste of time, and those who saw no other choice but to resist publicly. Among the groups of supporters specifically, this division existed as one that pitted a realist humanitarianism against an idealist radicalism.

In Chapter 4 I talked about how the material squalor and lack of resources in the jungle meant that responding to people's needs was a clear and urgent one. But faced with this, humanitarian sentiments often overrode more explicitly political ones. The people engaged in the aid effort saw what they were doing simply as the 'obvious' thing to do. Put another way, they generally didn't see what they were doing as political. Seeing the situation in these terms also ruled out the possibility of seeing the people whose suffering they were supposedly relieving as political actors too.

There have been numerous critiques of humanitarianism in the way that it reinforces hierarchies by presenting or dealing with the oppressed as powerless (cf. Kumar Rajaram 2002; Millner 2011). In a place like the jungle, this perspective and practice exacerbates the division between the 'haves' and the 'have-nots', which are at the core of the much more global inequalities that lead to places like the jungle existing in the first place.

But perhaps what is more of a dilemma for a no borders politics is how humanitarianism often closes down the possibility of action that has the potential to transform or escape the state. A standpoint of pity towards people without papers converts expressions of vocal dissent into matters for moral sympathy, closing down the possibility of raising a disagreement (Millner 2011). In adopting an apolitical stance in situations like Calais, humanitarianism often ends up reinforcing exactly the state's control regime, by expressing the same realism as this regime (Rigby and Schlembach 2013). Such 'realism' is part of a 'police logic of order, which asserts, in all circumstances, that it is the only thing possible to do' (Rancière 1999: 132). Protest on 'humanitarian realist' grounds reduces protest to a contest over 'the possible' which can only ever mean, at a fundamental level, a conservative acceptance of the existing framework for grasping problems and their solutions (Rigby and Schlembach 2013: 166).

All that said, I find it hard to simply argue that the humanitarian stance in opposition to many of the protests was right or wrong, given the fact that many people living in the jungle felt that the strategy of protest was ineffective in this case, myself included. Yet faced with such overwhelming oppression and violence, it can often feel that to do nothing (at least to appear to be doing nothing) is also not an option. But the possibility of thinking beyond collective visible action as protest is also not often present. And then there is always the hope that the next action will change the situation somehow. Among many supporters there has always been the notion that if we could just get enough people out onto the streets – people with and without papers – then perhaps something could change for the better. Yet even here, coming up with a collective demand would be difficult, and tends to fall back into the frame of demanding 'realistic change'. How can we say what the 'right' course of action is among all that? Who are we to say it anyway?

There is the famous saying, '[i]f you have come here to help me, you are wasting your time. But if you have come because your liberation is bound up with mine, then let's work together.' This is the beautiful core of collaborative struggle. But there are numerous dilemmas we face in finding the balance between my liberation and yours. I think that all the dilemmas of solidarity I raised here are essentially different shades of this issue: around making equality in an unequal social reality; around identifying who 'we' are, and how far we value or stretch that definition; around valuing autonomy but also visibility. In reflecting on them, I am brought back to the importance of being together in the everyday, and of seeing the ways that people refuse the border as part of a spectrum of activities. At times this bubbles up into visible collective action; at even rarer times this action has the capacity to undermine the separation between protest and movement and bring about radical social change. And numerous invisible actions that are rarely even recognized as political acts continue all the time too.

What does all this tell us about how we create a borderless world?

A no borders politics exceeds any political ideology ... except anarchism? In no case can it be said that one practice has provided 'all the answers' to how we can refuse the border and the state. What I've sought to show instead is how a politics that aims to do this doesn't exist as a 'pure' or complete politics. It's a current that flows through many practices and exceeds each of them. Because ultimately, it's a politics of autonomy first and foremost, and what we seek autonomy from depends so much on who we are and what our experience of the world has been. Autonomy is 'loyal' to desire and not to any pre-formed idea about how we become free. Put another way, autonomy is a practice of immanent experience (Bey 2003 [1991], 2009; Vaneigem 2003 [1967]). It cannot be prescriptive.

Being immanent, particular and not prescriptive means that a no borders politics doesn't rest or rely on expressing a particular collective identity. A politics that's oriented towards autonomy doesn't articulate a 'we' easily. Sometimes we take action together and build community together. The movement of the Sans Papiers in France is an example, the squat on Victor Hugo another. At other times we stand together and express collective demands. The hunger strike of 'The 300' is one such example. These forms of collective action unite us, but they don't homogenize us. They're often responses to specific instances of oppression, to finding solutions to the situations we share because we are in the same place. The social movement of refusal of the border doesn't have one collective identity, but many. It's not the politics of anyone in particular, but a politics of the mobile commons, which is a realm for anyone who wishes to practise the freedom of movement and to refuse the border. A no borders politics demands that we abandon the idea that fixed and stable identities are possible or desirable (Braidotti 2002).

What all this means is that a no borders politics largely slips out of any existing political ideology. Attempting to make the struggle for the freedom of movement leftist, anarchist, Marxist or any other -ist is going to fail and runs counter to what's important about this struggle anyway (Papadopoulos et al. 2008). A no borders politics is about struggling without attempting to organize anyone but ourselves, where who 'we' are is unclear, diverse and changing (Day 2005). Even in movements or groups with some kind of structure, such as CMS or the Network, the idea of a collective identity is deeply contested.

Exceeding any one politics or practice doesn't mean that a no borders politics has no orientation, in my view. As I have said already – and indeed the reason why I'm interested in this politics – it is, above all else, oriented towards autonomy and away from the state. Anarchism, like a no borders politics, could also be said to have an orientation towards autonomy, and I think there's great affinity between refusing the state and certain anarchist expressions of being anti-state. In Chapter 1 I outlined how autonomy is key to an anarchist ethic. We see this coming together particularly in practices such as the collaborative community-building I described in Chapter 4. What I'm talking about here is an anarchism beyond the Eurocentric, orthodox accounts of it; one that confronts anarchism in an anarchist way, as a 'multi-centred, fluid … a fully internationalist, non-linear, global, horizontal, de-centred, geographically and culturally non-hierarchic movement' (Evren 2012: 303–4).

But if a no borders politics exceeds any existing political agenda, why tie it to a named political ideology now? Because I think that anarchism is – or at least can be – fundamentally unideological, and I agree with David Graeber when he calls anarchism an ethic rather than an ideology. 'Marxism has tended to be a theoretical or analytical discourse about revolutionary strategy; anarchism, an ethical discourse about revolutionary practice' (Graeber 2009: 211). I think this is because, like a no borders politics, anarchism has an orientation to autonomy that also makes it exceed its own definitions. Both are becomings.

I also want to make the connection because I think people are often afraid to use the 'a' word (not autonomy, the other one) for fear that it brackets off what they're saying into some category of 'extreme' that can be used to sideline or dismiss it. Anarchism does carry baggage, but making the connection allows us to recognize and pay respect to a long history of revolutionary life-making oriented towards autonomy and equality, which are practices as old as humanity (Graeber 2004), and which ultimately are what anarchism boils down to for me.

It starts with the autonomy of migration A no borders politics has an orientation towards autonomy, expressed through a multitude of practices. For me, it begins by recognizing that the movement of people who travel without permission represents *political* acts. I don't want to heroicize these acts, or set the people who practise them up as some kind of vanguard. I want to say that a no borders politics begins with a perspective that takes mobility as its point of reference, and not control.

People who move without permission articulate a refusal of the border through practising the freedom of movement. Other people articulate a refusal of the border in other ways, or from other motives. In Chapter 2 I talked about how squats and social centres, land occupations, collective gardens, community kitchens, raves, protest camps and open-source communities are all examples of projects which can be said to refuse the border inasmuch as they share an orientation towards autonomy. What these projects also often share is that they prefigure a different way of being to the state that's sometimes also intentionally anti-state. In Chapter 4 I looked at how people connected to the No Border Network practise a refusal of the border that's also often intentionally anti-state. Some take that motive and use it to build collaborative communities with people who practise autonomy from the border. I think that a no borders politics goes on from recognizing that the movement of people who travel without permission is an escape/refusal, to seeking out ways of connecting different kinds of escapes/refusals.

This means that collaboration is an essential part of a no borders politics. Through connecting our escapes/refusals we have the chance to mount a 'Grand Escape/Refusal'. I don't mean the creation of a mass movement – a resistance big enough to topple the state and in doing so bring about a new kind of domination. This would be counter to the logics of autonomy. Rather, returning to Foucault, I mean a multitude of micro-refusals that are connected to each other rhizomatically and in their connections render the state more and more redundant.[7]

Collaboration is important for other reasons. Connecting the escapes of different people – people differently affected by the unequal diffusion of power – creates the potential to make communities of equality that are such because they work counter to the logics of privilege and oppression. Gloria Anzaldua, in reference to the title of her and AnaLouise Keating's book *This Bridge We Call Home*, states that '[a] bridge, such as this book, is not just about one set of people crossing to the other side; it's about those on the other side crossing to this side' (Anzaldua 2002: 4). This is what intersectionality is. It teaches us that that the freedom of others is also my own freedom, but that just as I can't fight for the freedom of others, so others can't fight for mine (Crass n.d. a). Practising equality – refusing the border – *involves all of us, because we all experience inequality and are implicated in bringing it down.* As a collaborative practice, a no borders politics is therefore a demand for a radical equality.

It recognizes that we're all affected by the state differently

Collaboration also involves recognizing that what we escape from – what our autonomy is – is different depending on what our experience of power is. Put another way, it involves recognizing that we're all affected by power/the state differently. What I see as my autonomy, and how I see myself moving towards it, is particular to me. This also means recognizing that different forms of resistance are necessary. As was the case with 'The 300', sometimes a demand for rights can be transformative depending on who acts. Acknowledging this also involves making and respecting a distinction between that resistance which reflects our own positionality and our own sense of what autonomy is for us, and participating in the resistance of others that may reflect a different positionality and a different sense of what autonomy is. Put another way, it involves working within the dilemma of how, if my own resistance involves fighting for a world without borders (and papers), then the resistance I engage in with others might involve fighting with them for their right to have papers. This is an uncomfortable position to negotiate. Yet it illustrates the inherent turmoil in practising a politics that seeks to refuse the border and bring about a borderless world in a present where borders proliferate. Such a politics *is not perfect* and doesn't shy away from the complexities and difficult decisions that are made in reality.

Maurice Stierl has described resistances to the border regime as a politics of discomfort (Stierl 2012). Discomfort is present in how seeking to refuse borders often involves *negotiating* borders even as we aim towards their negation. From the closure of Victor Hugo and the reopening of a women's centre outside of Calais, to the hunger strike of 'The 300' as a way of claiming rights while immobile, there's this discomfort. Negotiating borders even as we aim towards their negation is an always ongoing process of overcoming; of being attentive to the presence of borders while also trying to render them redundant

(Mohanty 2003). A no borders politics is not just a naïve demand to bring down all borders. It's a constant, *deeply realistic* practice that undermines their logic; that makes other worlds in the gaps.

The negotiation of borders as part of a strategy of their negation even means that the strategic *construction* of borders is sometimes necessary too. Many communities that seek to prefigure an alternative to the state restrict access to those who share their vision and/or put it into practice. I would say that the No Border Network is open to anyone who's motive is to refuse the border and oppose the state. This is definitely not everybody. As Diane Elam suggests in relation to the construction of communities organized on the basis of shared ethical commitments, 'it would make no claim to inclusiveness (all communities are formed on the basis of some type of exclusion)' (Elam 1994: 109). Gloria Anzaldua echoes this sentiment when she states that '[e]ffective bridging comes from knowing when to close ranks to those outside our home, group, community, nation – and when to keep gates open' (Anzaldua 2002: 3). In other words, and rather paradoxically, a no borders politics at times involves a *strategic use* of borders as a means of protecting and expanding the struggle against borders. To use borders in this way is to keep open the issue of undecidability that I raised above. It's to always ask why a border exists or is made; to ask what its function is, who it excludes and why.

Strategically using borders doesn't mean abandoning ideological positions or being reformist. There are strong ethical and experiential reasons why people come to a radical political praxis like the one I'm arguing for. Rather, navigating inequalities even as we seek out equality means using different practices and strategies depending on what the situation requires. A no borders politics is open to using whatever strategies are likely to bring about greater autonomy and equality. It requires of us to be ideological nomads or, borrowing from Hakim Bey, 'rootless cosmopolitans' (Bey 2003 [1991]: Communiqué #7): undogmatically attached to any one means of action (Croydon Migrant Solidarity n.d.).

Thinking of a no borders politics as a strategic negotiation of borders also involves recognizing that bordering (and engagement with the state can be seen as a form of this) is not an end in itself, but part of a process or a becoming that aims towards achieving greater freedoms. It's a point in an *ongoing* and constant movement, and a 'warding off' of dominating structures or behaviours. It means being mindful that our struggle towards autonomy can always be recuperated by the state. This means two things. First, it means being constantly aware that our capacity to develop hierarchies is always there. We need to create communities that see the state as a ghost or a demon we always need to be wary of (Graeber 2004). Second, it means always keeping an orientation towards autonomy, which is an ever-changing thing. It means 'we can never allow ourselves to think that we are "done"' (Day 2005: 200).

Like Chandra Mohanty in the way that she describes her feminism as a feminism without borders, it's a politics that's attentive to borders, while seeking to transcend and/or negate them (Mohanty 2003). I think this makes a no borders politics a queer politics, by which I mean a constant negation of 'the norm' that produces different, deviant ways of being (Colebrook 2009; Nigianni and Storr 2009). I end with a beautiful summary of what queer means to the Mary Nardini Gang, which for me really reflects what a no borders politics is also about.

> [Q]ueer is not a stable area to inhabit. Queer is not merely another identity that can be tacked onto a list of neat social categories, nor the quantitative sum of our identities ... Queer is a territory of tension, defined against the dominant narrative of white-hetero-monogamous-patriarchy, but also by an affinity with all who are marginalized, otherized and oppressed. Queer is the abnormal, the strange, the dangerous. Queer involves our sexuality and our gender, but so much more. It is our desire and fantasies and more still. (Mary Nardini Gang n.d.)

AFTERWORD

Returning to Calais

I've been back to Calais several times since I started writing this book. Every time the situation has been different from the time before. After the summer and autumn of protests from the new Calais jungle, all the remaining spaces where people stayed in the city were evicted and cleared. The people living in those spaces were marched to the new jungle. In November that year, the minister of the interior, Bernard Cazeneuve, announced intentions to reduce the number of people living in the jungle to 2,000. Attempts to realize this plan involved a number of things. First, the OFFI ramped up its work to persuade people living in the jungle to either claim asylum in France or relocate to the many hastily opened respite centres across the country. In the first weeks of this initiative several hundred people a week were taking buses from the jungle to various centres across France. After a few weeks, the numbers taking these buses dropped precipitously, as word spread that people were often living in poor conditions, stranded in the middle of nowhere with no plans for the future. In this way, the respite centres simply dispersed the 'problem' away from Calais. This was accompanied by mass arrests at the Eurotunnel (reports suggest around fifty people a night, several time a week), with the arrested often being detained far from Calais.

In January the first part of the state-run container camp was open, and some 150 people – mainly families with children – moved in. However, most people in the jungle remained opposed to moving there, seeing the wire fence surrounding the camp and the palmprint recognition system for entering it as proof that this was a further securitization measure that would undermine their ability to cross.

Soon after the opening of the camp, large areas of the jungle were evicted. This took place in stages, beginning with a wide stretch of land running parallel to the highway, and continuing to include the whole of the south side of the jungle. Faced with the destruction of their homes (workers coming in to clear such structures being 'defended' by lines of riot police), some took the decision to move into the camp.

At the time of writing, the container camp is almost full, but the state has failed to reduce the jungle to a population of 2,000. Spring is here, and people are arriving from their journeys across the Mediterranean once more.

Beyond the jungle, work has begun to double the size of Calais port, matching similar expansion plans in Dover. This has included construction of a new fence that extends around the port and its major access roads, making access to traffic more difficult for people trying to cross (Nord Littoral 2015). With expansion comes increased security measures, such as this new fence, but also increased traffic (and chances to cross) (Price 2014).[1]

Returning to Athens

I've not been back to Athens since I started writing this book. My last trip there was in 2012. At that time, the economic crisis was really starting to bite. People were getting acquainted with things being talked about in terms of austerity. This was the time after the squares occupations that had started in Egypt and Spain and spread to Greece; after a summer when mass unrest, strikes and occupations were commonplace. Austerity had been maintained regardless. It felt like a moment of great change; equal parts possibility and despair. Everything was pressurized. I admit I was relieved to leave.

It felt like a time of change for the struggle for mobility too. The summer before had held the possibility of positive change after 'The 300'. But it had been followed by waves of repression and violence, with regular attacks against people of colour. It felt quite likely that support for the Golden Dawn would grow, and that this would happen alongside increased expressions of state racism against migrants too.

What happened next was that the Golden Dawn took a nosedive. Connections made between high-ranking members of the party and the murder of anti-fascist rapper Pavlos Fyssas in September 2013 saw the party fall from favour among many Greeks (Lowen 2013). At the political level, the party was increasingly marginalized by more mainstream parties which saw their radicalism as increasingly unpalatable. At the same time, though, the Greek government, with EU financing, vastly increased border controls at its external eastern land border with Turkey,[2] and continued construction of a detention estate that aimed to make 10,000 spaces available across the country (previously the country had no specific detention prisons, and relied on 'regular' prison facilities) (Clandestina 2012). This expansion was accompanied by the sweep operation 'Xenios Zeus' that I discussed in Chapter 3.

Since then, things have changed once more. The 2015 election victory of the radical left coalition Syriza brought with it hope for a radical change to Greece's stance on immigration. But then all these great intentions were overshadowed by the movement of people into Europe. In 2015 more than one million people arrived in Europe clandestinely, many coming via Greece (BBC 2016). Many were escaping the conflict in Syria, but the response of most European countries was far from welcoming, and took place within a discourse of flooding and crisis.

People kept coming in similar numbers throughout that year. Most people arriving in Greece wanted to continue their journeys farther into western Europe, travelling along what is officially referred to as the Balkan Route (a route that starts in Turkey and continues through Greece, Macedonia, Croatia, Serbia, Slovenia and Hungary, before people disperse on to Austria, Germany and Scandinavia). Many were able to pass through Greece relatively freely. However, numerous countries on the route started implementing strategies to stop the flow of people, or else move them on as quickly as possible. Germany, Austria and Slovakia all suspended the EU's Schengen zone by introducing border checks, while Hungary built a razor-wire fence on its frontier with Serbia and brought in new laws that criminalized crossing the border. Croatia and Slovenia periodically opened and closed their borders too. Despite all this, people continued to come and many found ways around these attempts at disciplining their unauthorized movement. In places where the main means of travel had been closed down in attempts to stop people's onward travel (for example, in Hungary, where some routes out of the main train station in Budapest were closed, or between Croatia and Slovenia, where rail lines were also shut), people continued their journeys on foot.

In Greece people continued to arrive in large numbers, but attempts at stopping their movement by other states on the Balkan route meant that many increasingly found themselves stuck in Greece. At these bottlenecks, self-made camps started to emerge. The EU response was to designate some of these places as 'hot spots': spaces 'characterized by specific and disproportionate migratory pressure, consisting of mixed migratory flows, which are largely linked to the smuggling of migrants'. In establishing the 'hot spot' approach, systems were put in place in these places that attempted to further discipline people's movement. Essentially this amounted to systems that triaged people through the European migration regime, through a series of registration centres. Victoria Square in Athens, which had previously been a space shared by migrants and anarchists, became such a place – Antonis Vradis described it as witnessing the NGO colonization of Victoria (Vradis 2016).

In reality, the reception centres set up at these newly named 'hot spots' have been hugely underfinanced and under-resourced, with people surviving in terrible conditions. Faced with all this, as people tried to assert their right to free movement, conflict often erupted between people trying to move and the police.[3]

By early spring 2016 the EU was looking at another year of massive 'irregular immigration'. Faced with this, the Commission hurriedly sought to find ways to close the external border. An EU–Turkey deal, completed at the end of March, agreed that all new 'irregular' migrants crossing from Turkey to the Greek islands would be returned to Turkey and that, for every Syrian returned that way, another Syrian would be resettled to the EU. This was in exchange for financial support for migrants in the country, acceleration of visa liberalization for Turkish citizens and revitalization of the accession process (Schinas and Bertaud 2016). Behind the headlines of this deal, previous months had seen the EU rush through an agreement to designate Turkey as a safe third country, thereby creating the legal basis for protecting the EU from accusations of refoulement. In practice, Turkey has already refouled around thirty Afghans back to their country of origin since this agreement was put in place (Amnesty 2016). Furthermore, although the agreement specified a one-to-one swap of Syrians, the numbers to be accepted by the EU have been capped at 72,000 per year, far short of the 108,000 a year recommended by international aid agencies (Rankin 2016).

According to the International Organization for Migration, in 2015 at least 3,770 people died crossing the Mediterranean to reach Europe (International Organization for Migration 2016). The 'boat crisis' in Greece has been mirrored in Italy too, with people travelling across from Libya. Things appear bleak, the possibilities for autonomy limited. But people *still* move, and gaps in the system continue to emerge. Outsides exist. People continue to refuse in different ways, to be outside, to be other. They have to. And as this happens, 'the weaker and more full of holes it [the neoliberal order] becomes' (Day 2005: 205). Places like Calais and Athens are full of holes. Perhaps one day these holes will close up, but if they do, the struggle will continue elsewhere, wherever the freedom of movement is contested.

> Imagine a society like a ripped sheet, each hole being a space of freedom destined to grow larger. As long as it is being pierced, those who find themselves caught in the material will not choke. They will be able to choose to migrate towards these interstices and to cultivate the freedom to exist without being consigned to slavery. As long as these harbours of freedom, whether manifested as spaces (squats, caves, forests, hide-outs and shelters of all forms), or imagined (underground movements, political resistance), this totalitarianism will not succeed and will be subject to attacks. We need to push these walls ... (Anon., Contre Faites 2011: 8)

NOTES

Introduction

1 It is estimated that more than one million people arrived in Europe clandestinely across the Mediterranean in 2015, and just over 170,000 in the first three months of 2016 (UNHCR 2015, 2016). The International Organization for Migration (IOM) claimed 2015 to be the deadliest on record for 'irregular migrants', with over three thousand deaths in the Mediterranean, compared to 207 the year before, which had, until that point, been the deadliest year on record (Di Giacomo 2015; Szabo 2016).

2 It was around this time that EU governments began introducing visa requirements for people from Africa and the Middle East, along with externalized border controls in places like Morocco, Libya and Senegal (DeHaas 2008; Lutterbeck 2006).

3 Despite the fact that many states are dependent on a plentiful flow of insecure workers for cheap labour for their economies (Mitropoulos 2006; Walia 2013).

4 It is worth noting that only a fraction of people travelling on these routes end up in Calais, with the intention of reaching the UK.

5 For further discussions on these difficulties, see Gillen and Pickerill (2012); Pickerill (2008); Plows (2002).

6 Some authors that inspired me in their thinking on the responsibility towards those we represent in our scholarship are Aull-Davies (2002); Dauphinee (2007); England (1994); Fuller (1999); Gordon (2012); Harraway (1988); Maxey (1999); Rose (1997).

7 The sense that hierarchically structured social relations function through alienating us remains central to anarchistic conceptualizations of the social world. For further reading on how dominant structures create and (re)produce alienation, see, for example, Debord (1967); Holloway (2010); Invisible Committee (2009); Vaneigem (2003 [1967]).

8 I say this mindful of how the distinction between legality and illegality is far from distinct or fixed. People slip between legalized and illegalized statuses all the time, for example (Düvell 2006; Kasli and Parla 2009).

9 Yet it's also worth noting that not everybody who struggles against the border regime is trying to cross or is without papers. There are many people in Calais who have claimed asylum in France and still find themselves living in camps and struggling against the border regime.

10 Certainly there have been many interpretations of anarchism that present it as a grand 'theory-of-everything', but I think this misses the point of anarchism, the logic of which rejects being a singular and unified ideology that must be practised in a certain way, from a certain tradition or in a certain place. I see anarchism in the plural; as a diverse range of different practices of non-domination that emerge from and draw inspiration from the environment and experiences we find ourselves in, as much as they do from any canonical texts, for example (cf. Evren 2012). I like Surya

Evren's way of thinking about anarchism, as 'a combination of ideas and practices constantly reshaped in various locations according to local problems, local priorities and local conditions, always in touch with the international, global linkages that keep them within the range of (anarchist) radicalism. Anarchism is not the thing that was shipped from a place of origin, but a multitude of shipments, connections, relations, exchanges and intersections' (ibid.: 308).

11 To the degree that incorporation into dominant social reality can be thought of as recuperation, then acts of naming and representing have the potential to be recuperative. Naming and representing make visible and acceptable that which previously seemed invisible or strange. In naming a no borders politics, have I exposed it to recuperation? I have thought a lot about this. I think that recuperation by the state in this case is limited by the 'slippery' logic of a no borders politics. To a large degree this is a politics that makes sense and becomes visible only through practice and participation. Perhaps this is one reason why radical activist movements have been targeted with police infiltrators and why the threat of agents provocateurs is one of the biggest threats to such movements. It involves living out ways of being that are in opposition to the very practices of dominant social reality through which recuperation takes hold. In that way, what I describe here is less a description of a particular way of acting, and more an ethic from which it is up to us how to act on. Unless the state wants to change its own ethic, I don't see how it can recuperate this one.

1 What is a no borders politics?

1 There are a number of limits to what these studies have to say about the struggle for the freedom of movement. The tribes which Clastres and others studied were often numerically small and deeply homogenous, and neither of these things really applies in contemporary society. Equally, we cannot say that hierarchy was entirely absent from these societies. Many of them had deep differences between men and women, for example. What would it have mattered that the Tupi-Guarani tribe, for example, had no organized form of hierarchy, if you were a woman in that tribe whose fertility was something than men could use to trade with? They were far from perfectly egalitarian, and violent to many, yet they crucially organized in a way that ruled against the accumulation of dominant power in the hands of any individual.

2 Day defines these movements as the newest as a way of distinguishing them from those – presumably all those that have gone before – that have organized to be a counter-power. But I would argue that actually organizing non-hegemonically is something that has been common to all kinds of anarchistic experiments throughout history.

3 See also Isiah Berlin's notion of positive liberty (Berlin 1969).

4 Here I'm referring to the way desire is used most prominently in the work of Deleuze and Deleuze and Guattari, who use it in two different and related ways. For them desire refers to conscious and unconscious psychological complexes that manifest in either active or reactive forms. Active desire can be said to represent a deep or innate expression of self that is not shaped by pre-existing understandings of what it's possible or desirable to want or need (Deleuze 2004). In some sense active desire emerges from communing with our 'gut instinct'. As a kind of communion with our selves as divine, it has taken on a mystical tone in the work of scholars such as Hakim Bey. Active desire is a becoming (Deleuze and Guattari 2004 [1987]: 106, 470–71). In contrast reactive desire is the outcome of

our alienation from our desire. Reactive desire entails a desire turned upon itself; one part blocks desire in general, another part resists this block but often comes out in attenuated or distorted form. Reactive desire is often expressed as a desire for the things we think we should desire. Whereas active desire is associated with becoming, reactive desire is associated with being.

5 I have previously talked about how Rancière defines equality, as something 'beneath' rights: as parity between people qualified by nothing other than the fact of us all being human.

2 No borders politics in practice

1 Visit infomobile.w2eu.net/tag/hunger-strike/ for more information.

2 Five days of rioting in the city took place after the shooting by police of a fifteen-year-old boy in the neighbourhood of Exarcheia, a neighbourhood with strong connections to the radical left in Greece.

3 Neighbourhood assemblies exist in many districts across the capital, and in other cities in Greece. They are forums where residents can come together and discuss the issues of importance to them in their locale. Many have been around for years, but the December 2008 insurrection and the occupations of squares in 2011 resulted in a proliferation of neighbourhood assemblies across the country (Mi 2010). Often, they bring together local people who aren't involved with any explicit radical political project with other locals who are.

4 Information and perspectives on the strike come from interviews I conducted with strikers and their supporters, and from the numerous conversations I had with people in the months after it. For further coverage of the strike, go to en.contrainfo.espiv. net/2011/02/09/gathered-links-about-the-300-migrant-hunger-strikers/.

5 The strikers had a number of demands: that all the strikers be granted full residence and labour permits; that residence permits be no longer connected to work credits; that all who lost their permits because of the increase in work credits be legalized again; that everyone whose application was rejected in 2005 be legalized; and finally that a process be put in place for the legalization of all migrants in Greece.

6 An important reduction in social security credits, connected to employment.

7 For example, prisoner solidarity forms a big part of the movement's practice where the prisoners are those detained for acts of resistance as part of the movement's struggle.

8 For example, see 'Statement from a group of libertarian communists' (Libertarian Communists 2011); 'Statement of the Assembly of Anarchists' (Assembly of Anarchists 2011); or 'Statement from the collectives and neighbourhood assembly of Kypseli-Patissia-Acharnon' (Collectives and neighbourhood assembly of Kypseli-Patissia-Acharnon 2011).

9 See www.calaismigrantsolidarity. wordpress.com.

10 In 2012 CMS released its first dossier of examples of police violence against people trying to cross which was presented to the French Defender of Rights. There has been a further dossier since then. The first is available at www. calaismigrantsolidarity.wordpress.com. Beyond that, in 2015 Calais Migrant Solidarity released a montage video of its monitoring of police violence in the city that resulted in the French Defender of Rights opening a case on this alleged violence. The video is available at www. youtube.com/watch?v=0Ln4DP2J5ME& oref=https%3A%2F%2Fwww.youtube. com%2Fwatch%3Fv%3D0Ln4DP2J5ME&h as_verified=1.

11 Within the wider no borders movement the affirmation of the freedom of movement has been interpreted in different ways. For some, such a demand is expressed as a call for open borders, rather than no borders (see, for example, Hayter 2004).

12 It's worth noting that standpoint theory – or positionality – has been criticized for essentializing fixed categories of identity such as race, gender and sexuality, of being overly structurally deterministic and hence ruling out agency (Robertson 2002). Jennifer Robertson, for example, argues that, because of this, positionality is useful only insofar as we also reflect upon those categories that we use to explore positionality (ibid.). I think it's true that we cannot be reduced to our subject positions only, but I also think that standpoint theorists don't make this claim anyway, but rather provide some tools for thinking about identity.

13 Here, I focus on white supremacy so as to offer concrete examples, though it is not necessarily more of an 'issue' than patriarchy or class or any other form of oppression.

14 The term cis refers to people who identify with the gender that they were assigned to at birth, as opposed to trans, which refers to people who do not.

3 The struggle for mobility in Athens

1 For detailed accounts of the history of immigration to Greece see, for example, Cavounidis (2002); Kasimis and Papadopoulos (2005); Kasimis and Kassimi (2004); Kiprianos et al. (2003); Konsta and Lazaridis 2010; Triandafyllidou (2009, 2012).

2 Two important waves of mass emigration took place after the formation of the modern Greek state in the early 1830s, one from the late nineteenth to the early twentieth century, and another following the Second World War. More than one million Greeks migrated in this second wave (Kasimis and Kassimi 2004).

3 The militarization of Greece's borders and the defensive stance of Greece towards immigration issues should be considered in light of the historic and ongoing antagonistic relationship between Greece and its neighbours, particularly Macedonia and Turkey. In the context of the Balkan wars of the nineties, the 'Macedonian question' took on a new importance in public and political consciousness, with a feeling that the war could spread into Greece (Engstrom 2002). Macedonia claims the region of north-western Greece (also called Macedonia) to be part of the Macedonian nation (Triandafyllidou 2009). Relations between Turkey and Greece have also long been strained. Indeed, among the first migrants to arrive in Greece en masse were ethnic Greeks expelled from Turkey who managed to escape the ethnic cleansing of Greeks in the 1920s (Baldwin-Edwards 2006). Mines are still found along the Greece–Turkey border despite demining since 2004 (ibid.).

4 Law 1975/91, the 'Police Control of Border Passages, Ingression, Residence, Employment and Expulsion of Foreigners and Immigrants, Identification Proceeding'. This law was then replaced in 2001, 2005, 2007 and 2008 (Konsta and Lazaridis 2010). The number of times this law has been replaced illustrates the speed with which the system of immigration and asylum controls is being institutionalized. In particular, this is due to efforts to bring Greek immigration and asylum policy in line with EU directives, at least in law, if not in practice.

5 For example, following the 1997 amnesty, 371,641 migrants were registered, but only 201,882 were granted temporary residency (Kasimis and Papadopoulos 2005).

6 The other route to legalization is asylum.

7 The EU quango Frontex has played a central role in this, by coordinating special border missions that have flooded this border with extra guards and control technologies. In 2010 Frontex established its first regional office in the port of Piraeus, Athens. Three border missions have been coordinated by Frontex in Greece since then. These include two joint operations (Poseidon and Attica), both carried out in the eastern Mediterranean, and one rapid border intervention team (RABIT) mission in the Evros region which saw an additional 200 border guards from other member states deployed there. This last mission, which initially was to last four months, has since become a permanent joint operation in that region (called operation Poseidon Land). To the extent that Frontex is tasked with stopping 'illegal migration' (and therefore does not account for how many who flee are forced to travel clandestinely, for instance), it has been criticized on many fronts for failing to uphold human rights. In particular, it has been criticized for increasing the illegalization of people's movement (Karakayali and Rigo 2010), for acting as a barrier to anyone wishing to access asylum procedures, for refoulement of people crossing in boats and for diluting the responsibilities of elected governments of member states (Keller et al. 2011).

8 During my initial fieldwork for my PhD, which I carried out in Slovenia, a conversation with a German border guard who was on a joint operation revealed how, as systematic checks are not allowed, the strategy is to conduct 'random' checks at hot spots on roads, railway lines and transport hubs. The challenge then comes in maintaining the randomness that is required in Union law, even if such randomness is increasingly symbolic.

9 The creation of this border 'zone' was a means of reinstituting border controls, but in a way that could not be said to amount to the reintroduction of controls at the borders of EU states, as this contravenes the Schengen Acquis. It amounts to a form of internal border controls, or compensatory measures, that are increasingly commonplace across the EU. We find such 'ad hoc' controls in the checking of documents at many major transit routes and nodes; at train stations, along motorways, or in city squares, and in other places of everyday life, such as workplaces or places of worship (Indra 2011).

10 In fact Susan Bilier Coutin (2010) has talked about how the European migration regime transforms states into zones of confinement for some, and gives national territories a carceral quality.

11 The Dublin Regulation – currently in its third incarnation – relates to asylum claims and identifies responsibility among EU member states for processing such claims. It prohibits any person from claiming asylum in more than one EU state and requires people to claim asylum in the 'first safe country' they arrive at or else be returned there should there be evidence that they have been there (Europa 2015). Greece is the 'first safe country' for many who come to Europe and seek sanctuary. As such, many who travelled through Greece were liable for return there. Returns to Greece under the Dublin II Regulation were suspended in 2011 after it was ruled that people were being kept in inhuman and degrading conditions in the country's detention prisons, or were liable to refoulement to inhuman and degrading conditions elsewhere (see the case *M.S.S.v. Belgium and Greece* of 21 January 2011).

12 Indeed, there have been a number of cases where tourists have been

arrested as part of these operations. In November 2012, the US embassy in Greece updated its country-specific information on Greece to warn US visitors about 'confirmed reports of US African-American citizens detained by police authorities conducting sweeps for illegal immigrants in Athens' (Cossé 2013: 4).

13 Notably, a revolt in Fylakio detention prison in September 2011, another in Cyprus in October 2011, a fire in Amegdaleza, Attiki, in November 2011, a hunger strike at the Alikarnassos police department in Heraklion, Crete, in December 2011, an uprising in Komotini in November 2012, a hunger strike in Corinth that same month, a wave of hunger strikes in April 2013, a hunger strike in Amegdaleza that started in November 2014 and continued into 2015, a hunger strike of Syrians outside parliament in November 2014, a hunger strike in Paranesti in March 2015 and a hunger strike in Corinth that same month (cf. Anon 2015a; Anon 2015b; Clandestina 2011; InfoMobil 2011).

14 This testimony is taken from numerous times spent with Ahmed over the course of my fieldwork.

15 It's worth noting that Antonio Samaras, leader of the right-wing New Democracy party that won the most seats in the 2012 election, also campaigned to retrieve cities from immigrants (Human Rights Watch 2012: 35).

16 www.tanea.gr/news/greece/article/4332198/?iid=2; www.iospress.gr/ios1998/ios19980927c.htm.

17 In a conversation with the author of the Human Rights Watch report into racism in Greece, Eva Cossé commented how in the same year the Greek government recorded just two cases of racially motivated violence. A culture that fails to take racism seriously within the judiciary means those who are accused of racist crimes are liable to be released, or given low sentences. Equally significant is the fact that the possibility of continually delaying trials means that trials are often not completed within a time limit and those accused are released as a result of this administrative loophole.

18 For example, the number of days applicants had to demonstrate they had been in paid employment had risen to around three hundred days out of every year, in addition to the requirement to pay an application fee of several hundred euros.

19 To me, the number 300 carries obvious symbolic references to the 300 Spartans who fought a battle against the Persians and were the subject of a Hollywood movie (called *300*) that came out three years before the strike. However, I have found no official recognition of this coincidence. Interviewees pointed simply to the fact that 300 represented what they thought was the number of people that would maximize exposure of the strike without creating endless logistical problems for the strikers and their supporters.

20 Despite these affinities, the Network was initially hesitant to get involved. There were several reasons for this. The relationship between the Network and the Forum of Immigrants in Chania, which had until that point been the main group involved in supporting the strikers, was difficult. The Forum had previously come out attacking the proliferation of cultural events that they saw as weakening the movement by amounting to spectacular and one-off events that failed to connect to the lived experience of migrants. As one member of the Forum commented, 'that's not the way I do anti-racism, because it's not in the streets' (Anon., Forum of Immigrants, Chania). The Network, as the main organizer of the Athens Anti-racist Festival, were included in

this critique by association. At the same time, despite 'The 300' publicly refuting this accusation, the Network was not alone in doubting the degree to which the decisions of the strikers had been influenced by the politics of the Forum, something that the Assembly of 'The 300' denied (for example, they stated, '[w]e take our decisions by ourselves during the assemblies we hold, and we do not get influenced by external factors. Nobody is hiding behind our backs or fronts. And we do not receive "guidance" by anybody' ('The 300', 27 January 2011)). Beyond this, the Network had doubts as to whether the different groups in Athens, those within and beyond the anti-racist movement, would be capable of cooperating. Previous experiences of failed collaborations across political dialects (such as the attempt to start a No Border Network) undermined hopes of success this time.

21 This was particularly the case during the squares movement. On 25 May 2011, following ongoing and high-profile mass occupations of squares in Egypt and Spain, Syntagma Square in Athens was occupied and remained so for forty days. During that time, the number of people who participated in the occupation – those camping in the square and visiting – regularly exceeded 10,000. There was a wave of large-scale demonstrations, including a two-day general strike. Over the course of that summer, an estimated 120 similar occupations sprang up across the country, calling for 'Real democracy Now!' Operating through open assemblies, and prohibiting the presence of political parties and party propaganda, the occupations reflected a general sense of anger at the state of politics and society after a year of extremely harsh austerity measures, with more to come. For a time, all eyes were on the squares, and it felt as if politics had been concentrated into something

that happened only in those spaces. But migrants and migration issues were largely absent. 'Even at its best moments, the "Indignados" movement had little reference to migrants' issues. Even people with the best intentions were reluctant to speak about solidarity with the sans Papiers, fearing that this way they would jeopardise their "contact to the crowds"' (Clandestina 2011: 13). In preparing for the annual anti-racist festival, the Network had made the last-minute decision to cancel it, opting instead for a one-day 'migrants' day' in the square instead, one of the few activities that addressed these issues in that space. After the summer, the squares movement was translated into numerous neighbourhood assemblies that continue to meet and discuss politics within their communities.

4 The struggle for mobility in Calais

1 The opening of the Eurotunnel near Calais in 1987 added to the importance of Calais in the journeys of trucks, and therefore of people without papers.

2 Many people do pay to use smugglers to help them cross, but many arrive in Calais without any money, and go there to cross independently.

3 Not forgetting compensatory measures which have been in place across the Schengen zone since the inception of Schengen. See Chapter 3 for a further discussion of compensatory measures.

4 Of course, it made it easier for people to reach all the other European countries too. But the UK's colonial history and post-colonial presence in many countries around the world have had an effect. People from Afghanistan, Sudan, Syria, Eritrea, Ethiopia and elsewhere talked of wanting to come to the UK because of the familiarity of Anglo culture, because they can speak English, because their relatives are there, because there is work on the black market

there, and because England often lies at the end of the line of journeys that have seen people pass through innumerable countries that don't want them, and which treat them as outcasts. The UK, for many, offers the hope of being different from these places.

5 The British government has had a big influence over border control in Calais; 2009 saw the creation of a coordination centre in the British coastal town of Folkestone, near Dover, and the establishment of a €15 million fund for the securitization of Calais port from the British government. Currently it is estimated that the security systems in Calais port cost some €12 million a year (Coordination Française Pour Le Droit d'Asile 2008).

6 See, for example, Calais Migrant Solidarity (2011).

7 Article L622-1 of the French Penal Code makes it illegal to assist, directly or indirectly, the arrival, movement or residence of persons irregularly present on French territory. The offence is punishable by a €30,000 fine or up to five years in prison. While what became known as the 'anti-solidarity' law is primarily used to convict people engaged in people trafficking, it had been used to repress humanitarian assistance to people trying to cross. In a number of cases people from local charities were brought to trial over such activities. In recent years the code has rarely been enforced, largely because of the terrible image it created, the French government finding it difficult to defend a code that essentially criminalized people feeding the hungry and homeless.

8 Coming from the West, there perhaps seemed more reason why I would be drawn to the church and not the mosques (despite the fact that my family is Jewish and I'm an atheist), but it was rather accidental. The congregation requested a microphone and an amp for their Sunday service and Calais Migrant Solidarity provided them. Delivering them was my access to the space.

9 This account is based on my own experiences of staying for a few weeks on rue Victor Hugo in January 2014, interviews with some of those who were more heavily involved, and on two anonymous articles (one unpublished) by those involved reflecting on the project. It's a summary of what was a very complex and non-linear process. Sadly, owing to lack of space, many of these complexities have been left out here.

10 French law states that if you can prove that a squatted building is your primary residence, and if you can show you have been there for a significant amount of time (in practice this works out as forty-eight hours, although this is not written into the law), then the police cannot legally evict you until the case has been resolved in a civil court. This allows for the occupants of the building to present their case as to why they should be able to retain possession of the building and also have clarity about when they must leave. In spring 2015, in a direct attempt to counter squatting in Calais, this law was overturned, making all squatting effectively illegal (Calais Migrant Solidarity, forthcoming).

11 Many of these struggles were over the access of men to the space, and the relationships between the women and men trying to cross that made any exclusive restriction on access to men difficult to uphold. Few of the women in Victor Hugo were travelling alone. Many were dependent on men in one way or another to travel to the UK. They had husbands or male relatives also living rough in Calais that they wanted to support or that they were reliant on for their crossing. Many had contacts with smugglers in the city that they were reliant on too, and had to maintain good relations with. These interdependencies

between the women in the house and the men in the wider community of crossers made restricting access to women difficult, when the house itself was seen by the women as a resource they could or had to share with men. It was made even more difficult by the inclusion of particularly vulnerable men and by male CMS activists. All this confusion over which men could have access meant that many men not connected to the women in some way also often gained access by pretending to be so connected.

12 For example, the women trying to cross didn't feel they were in a position to 'defend' the space from men who were effectively in the same position as them, or that they were dependent on in some way. As a result, CMS activists took on the responsibility of being on the door – 'policing' access to the house – with the other residents sharing responsibility for other aspects of daily life, such as cooking or cleaning.

13 At times the issue of male CMS activist access was discussed, at others it went unquestioned, at others it was allowed mindful of how problematic it could be.

14 The new day centre provides temporary accommodation to 100 women and children, a meal a day, phone charging, and has around twenty shower cubicles. Since December 2015 Médecins sans Frontières have run a clinic next to the day centre. The centre did not provide anything new to people trying to cross. Rather it gathered together already existing services under one roof. Charities providing such services were forced to comply. For example, in January 2015 the anti-solidarity law was again reimposed and it became a criminal offence to distribute food to people on the streets in Calais.

15 It took a further three months for all the previous spaces to be emptied. Many people left the Galloo squat and the jungle known as the 'Leaderprice jungle' but a number of people stayed (tens in each case). In June that year, both places were finally raided by CRS and cleared. This came at the same time as raids on a number of squats in Paris, also home to people without papers.

16 For example, 2015 also saw the beginnings of construction of a new fence around an enlarged port space, and barriers erected around surrounding roads, part of a wider expansion plan of the ports of Calais and Dover.

17 Many people from sub-Saharan Africa had travelled to Libya to live and work with no intention of continuing their journeys. When civil war in Libya took hold, thousands of people were forced to move again.

18 In some way this can be seen as using the system as a means of continuing to enact strategies, if not of movement, then at least of self-determination. That many had not claimed asylum before doesn't mean they weren't in need of protection. Rather, many saw a better chance in remaining free from any categorization, including that of refugee status, the concept of which is decided by the state and skewed in its favour. The right to asylum is a crucial human right, and yet it is also within the migration regime. State asylum systems are a part of the border control regime and a part of the continuum of categorizations that define and limit who has access to rights. Although asylum is a crucial means of protection for those fleeing persecution, there is a tension. A refugee is narrowly defined as an individual suffering abuse by a state power. Hence, refugee status excludes many forms of forced migration (such as escape from poverty or environmental degradation). Asylum protects, but it also reinforces the distinction between forced and voluntary; deserving and undeserving; just and criminal; rightful and rightless. For those

who meet the definitions necessary to be granted refugee status (i.e. persecution by their state for reasons of race, religion, nationality, political opinion or membership of a particular social group), asylum often exists as the only route out of illegality.

19 For example, from jungles in Dunkirk or Hazebrouck.

20 Until that point CMS had received a small amount of donated material that people associated with the group distributed. Many felt that this work was tangential to the struggle against the border, but at the time there were few groups visiting places like the jungles and doing such work.

21 A good example of this is the newspaper *Merhaba*. See merhaba. noblogs.org/post/category/journaux/.

22 It has always been somewhat frustrating to me that the general discourse around the jungle at that time was that it was a space of such squalor that people should not have to live in such conditions, yet much as this might have been true, this was still the first jungle to ever have any kind of amenities (Portaloos and running water throughout the camp, for example). The attention on Calais at that time generated these critiques of the jungle, but this attention had not been present during the preceding decades, when people were living in far worse conditions.

23 Some common slogans during that time were 'No jungle No jungle!', 'Jungle for animals. We are not animals' and 'Open the border'. In addition, there were also a number of more specific protests. For example, people from Syria organized a series of protests on their own, to articulate their specific demands to access the UK. During this time there was also the first (and so far only) women's demonstration in Calais, organized by women living in the jungle.

24 Indeed, local and state-level government and media argued that such protests were entirely caused by agitating 'no borders' activists and 'British anarchists' who were painted as the puppet masters of the jungle.

25 For example, the Facebook group 'Calais – people to people – solidarity action from the UK' was set up as a deviation from the no borders politics of CMS. It took the form of a broader grassroots charity project to deliver aid, adopting a far less critical and rigorous approach to solidarity, relinquishing many of the political approaches – particularly the critique of humanitarianism – developed by CMS, in favour of mobilizing large quantities of material donations.

26 Indeed, although many people living in the jungle were deeply thankful to the volunteers, many were also highly critical of and cynical about the aid effort. There was more than one occasion when I witnessed discussions about taking action where one of the demands was that 'the humanitarians' left the jungle.

Conclusions

1 Eurodac is a database that stores the fingerprints and records of all asylum claimants over the age of fourteen within the Union, as well as people apprehended while 'irregularly' crossing the external border or found to be present in a member state 'illegally'.

2 Although I have met numerous people who have left places like the jungle and then yearned to be back there. Perhaps this is connected to some kind of unprocessed trauma, but equally it can also be a yearning to be part of a place where there is a strong sense of community. I also feel this yearning for the community life the jungle embodies. Many who have left the jungle find themselves living alone as refugees in state-funded accommodation and such a situation can be extremely isolating.

3 As an extreme case, in the early days of the No Border presence in Calais, rumours spread that female activists were prostitutes and this created real safety issues for people.

4 For many people, the trauma of being in Calais long-term results in them never returning. Some, as a way of being able to remain involved in Calais sustainably, have taken a step back from 'full immersion' in Calais, either by living somewhere else in the city and spending less time in places like the jungle, or by focusing much more on friendships, or by coming for shorter, predefined periods of time. Again, this raises other dilemmas around introducing other hierarchies through this added difference in daily experience.

5 This point was raised in another notable struggle that took place at the same time as that of 'The 300'; an occupation by Afghan refugees of another university site. During their struggle, despite ongoing attacks, large numbers of people from Afghanistan continued to gather in Victoria Square. I asked Ismail, one of the elected representatives of the Afghan occupation, why those from the square were not present at the occupation. His response was, 'the ones in Victoria Square want to leave Greece. In Greece you have no rights, you just take a pink card and go your own way. Most want to get the pink card and just leave Greece. They tell us the only demand we have is for the government to open the borders.'

6 I experienced this myself within the movement in Athens. Meetings were really macho and aggressive. I felt intimidated and uncomfortable. Friends within the movement commented on this too, but felt that it was rarely discussed publicly.

7 An article in the Green anarchist journal *Do or Die* contains one of the best descriptions of the rhizome in this context. 'The concept of rhizomes, modelled on the strange root systems of certain plants, was introduced by the French philosophers Gilles Deleuze and Felix Guattari. They're opposed to the tree ... The tree exists in a hierarchical order of a central trunk with larger and smaller branches. The trunk forms the connection between all parts, thus in a way limiting connections. A rhizome, on the contrary, can be connected with any other at any point. A tree can be cut down, whereas rhizomes are much less subject to destruction. Rhizomes can grow again along another line if broken at some point. Rhizomes are abundant; if weeded out in one place, they will definitely show up somewhere else. Rhizomes are endless, as are desire and the imagination' (Anon. 1999: 140).

Afterword

1 Freight traffic between Dover and Calais is expected to rise by 40 per cent by 2030.

2 For example, 1,800 Greek police officers were stationed at the Greek–Turkish border at this time.

3 For example, 15 September 2015 – pressure built at the border through Tuesday, and on Wednesday Hungarian police used tear gas and water cannon on refugees on the Serbian side (Jeffrey et al. 2016).

BIBLIOGRAPHY

A few of the many anarchists in St. Louis (2015) 'Another word for white ally is coward', anarchistnews.org/content/another-word-white-ally-coward, accessed 13 June 2016.

Agamben, G. (1995) *Homo Sacer: Sovereign power and bare life*, Stanford, CA: Stanford University Press.

— (2005) *State of Exception*, Chicago, IL: University of Chicago Press.

Agnew, J. (1994) 'The territorial trap: the geographical assumptions of international relations theory', *Review of International Political Economy*, 1(1): 53–80.

Alcoff, L. (2008) *Visible Identities: Race, gender and the self*, Oxford: Oxford University Press.

Alkis (2010) 'December as a result of social and political processes going back many years, Part 1', in A. G. Schwarz, T. Sagris and Void Network (eds), *We Are an Image from the Future: The Greek revolt of December 2008*, Edinburgh: AK Press.

Allen, T. (1994) *The Invention of the White Race*, vol. 1: *Racial Oppression and Social Control*, London: Verso.

Amnesty (2016) 'Turkey "safe country" sham revealed as dozens of Afghans forcibly returned hours after EU refugee deal', *Amnesty International*, online, www.amnesty.org/en/latest/news/2016/03/turkey-safe-country-sham-revealed-dozens-of-afghans-returned/, accessed 1 April 2016.

Anderson, B., N. Sharma and C. Wright (2012) '"We are all foreigners": No Borders as a practical political project', in P. Nyers and K. Rygiel (eds), Citizenship, Migrant Agency and the Politics of Movement, London: Routledge.

Anderson, M. (2000) 'The transformation of border controls: a European precedent?', in P. Andreas and T. Snyer (eds), *The Wall around the West: State borders and immigration controls in North America and Europe*, Washington, DC: Rowman & Littlefield.

Andrew x. (2000) 'Give up activism', *Do or Die*, 9: 160–71, www.doordie.org.uk/issues/issue-9.html, accessed 29 July 2015.

Andrijasevic, R. (2009) 'Sex on the move: gender, subjectivity and differential inclusion', *Subjectivity*, 29: 389–406.

Anon. (1999) 'Desire is speaking: utopian rhizomes', *Do or Die*, 8, www.eco-action.org/dod/no8/index.html, accessed 27 August 2011.

— (2001) 'Never cry wolf', *Killing King Abacus*, 2, n.p.

— (2011) *Deconstructing Walls: Narratives, analytical texts and photos from the borders of south-eastern Europe*, Zine, n.p.

— (2015a) Infomobil, http://infomobile.w2eu.net/, accessed 12 September 2016.

— (2015b) Clandestina, https://clandestinenglish.wordpress.com/, accessed 12 September 2016.

— (n.d.) *Calais 9: Freedom of Movement for all*, Zine, n.p.

Anzaldua, G. (2002) 'Preface: (Un)natural bridges, (un)safe spaces', in G. Anzaldua and A. Keating (eds),

This Bridge We Call Home: Radical visions for transformation, New York: Routledge.

Arendt, H. (1973 [1951]) *The Origins of Totalitarianism*, 2nd edn, New York: Harcourt Brace Jovanovich.

Assembly of Anarchists. (2011) 'Against fear, State terrorism, impoverishment and social cannibalism: common struggles of locals and immigrants for life, equality and freedom', *ContraInfo*, 30 May, online, en.contrainfo.espiv. net/2011/05/30/against-fear-state-terrorism-impoverishment-and-social-cannibalism/, accessed 29 July 2015.

Athwal, H. and J. Bourne (2007) 'Driven to despair: asylum deaths in the UK', *Race & Class*, 48(4): 106–14.

Aull-Davies, C. (2002) *Reflexive Ethnography: A guide to researching selves and others*, London: Routledge.

Baldwin-Edwards, M. (2006) 'Migration between Greece and Turkey: from the "Exchange of Populations" to the non-recognition of borders', *South East Europe Review*, 3: 115–22.

Balibar, É. (2002) *Politics and the Other Scene*, London: Verso.

— (2004a) *We the People of Europe? Reflections on trans-national citizenship*, Princeton, NJ: Princeton University Press.

— (2004b) 'At the borders of Europe', *Makeworlds*, 4, online, www. makeworlds.org/node/80, accessed 13 February 2013.

Balibar, É. and E. Wallerstein (1991) *Race, Nation, Class: Ambiguous Identities*, London: Verso.

Barbagallo, C. and N. Beuret (2008) 'Bang to rights', *Mute*, 2(7), www.metamute. org/editorial/articles/bang-to-rights, accessed 29 July 2015.

Bauder, H. (2006) 'Commentary: And the flag waved on: immigrants, protests, geographers meet in Chicago', *Environment & Planning A*, 38: 1001–4.

BBC (2016) 'Migrant crisis: migration to Europe explained in seven charts', *BBC News*, 4 March, online, www.bbc. co.uk/news/world-europe-34131911, accessed 1 April 2016.

Bell, B., J. Gaventa and J. Peters (eds) (1990) *Myles Horton and Paulo Freire. We make the road by walking. Conversations on education and social change*, Philadelphia: Temple University Press.

Berlin, I. (1969) 'Two concepts of liberty', in I. Berlin, *Four Essays on Liberty*, Oxford: Oxford University Press.

Bey, H. (2003 [1991]) *The Temporary Autonomous Zone: Ontological Anarchy, Poetic Terrorism*, Autonomedia New Autonomy Series.

— (2009) 'Primitives and extropians', online, www.hermetic.com, accessed 1 April 2016.

— (n.d.) 'Pirate utopias', online, hermetic. com/bey/pirate-utopias/pirate-utopias.html, accessed 1 April 2016.

Bigo, D. (2002) 'Security, immigration: towards a critique of the governmentality of unease', *Alternatives*, 27: 63–92.

— (2011) 'Freedom and speed in enlarged borderzones', in V. Squire (ed.), *The Contested Politics of Mobility: Borderzones and irregularity*, London and New York: Routledge.

Bojadžijev, M. and S. Karakayali (2010) 'Recuperating the sideshows of capitalism: the autonomy of migration today', *Flux e-journal*, online, www.e-flux.com/journal/ view/154, accessed 29 July 2015.

Bonanno, A. (2010 [1987]) *Propulsive Utopia (work in progress)*, London: Elephant Editions.

Bonnett, A. (2000) *Anti-racism*, London: Routledge.

Braidotti, R. (1994) *Nomadic Subjects: Embodiment and sexual difference in contemporary feminist theory*, New York: Columbia University Press.

— (2002) *Metamorphosis: Towards a Materialist Theory of Becoming*, Cambridge: Polity.

— (2006) 'The becoming-minor of Europe', in I. Buchanan and A. Parr (eds), *Deleuze and the Contemporary World*, Edinburgh: Edinburgh University Press.

Butler, J. (1990) *Gender Trouble: Feminism and the subversion of identity*, New York: Routledge.

Butler, J. and G. Spivak (2007) *Who Sings the Nation-State? Language, politics, belonging*, Oxford: Seagull.

Calais Migrant Solidarity (2011) *This Border Kills: Documented police violence, June 2009–June 2011*, calaismigrantsolidarity.files. wordpress.com/2011/09/english-dossier.pdf, accessed 25 September 2013.

— (2015) 'Another death last night', Calais Migrant Solidarity, online, calaismigrantsolidarity.wordpress. com/2015/10/27/another-death-last-night/, accessed 1 April 2016.

— (forthcoming) 'Trapped at the border: a brief history of solidarity squatting practices', in P. Mudu and S. Chattopadhyay (eds), *Migration, Squatting and Radical Autonomy: Resistance and destabilization of racist regulatory policies and b/ordering mechanisms*, London: Routledge.

Casas-Cortes, M., S. Cobarrubias, N. De Genova, G. Garelli, G. Grappi, C. Heller, S. Hess, B. Kasparek, S. Mezzadra, B. Neilson, I. Peano, L. Pezzani, J. Pickles, F. Rahola, L. Riedner, S. Scheel and M. Tazzioli (2015) 'New keywords: migration and borders', *Cultural Studies*, 29(1): 55–87.

Castoriadis, C. (1987) *The Imaginary Institution of Society*, Cambridge: Polity.

Cavounidis, J. (2002) 'Migration in southern Europe and the case of Greece', *International Migration*, 40(1): 45–70.

Chasse, R., J. Horelick and T. Verlaan (1969) 'Faces of recuperation', *Situationist International*, 1, June, www.cddc.vt.edu/sionline/si/faces. html, accessed 28 July 2015.

Chatterton, P. (2008) 'Demand the possible: journeys in changing our world as a public activist-scholar', *Antipode*, 40(3): 421–7.

Cholewinski, R. (2007) 'The criminalisation of migration in EU law and policy', in H. Toner, E. Guild and A. Baldaccini (eds), *Whose Security, Justice and Freedom? EU Immigration and Asylum Law and Policy (Essays in European Law)*, Oxford: Hart.

Cissé, M. (1996) *The Sans-Papiers: A Woman Draws the First Lessons*, London: Crossroads Books.

Clandestina (2011) 'In the struggle between yourself and the world, back the world', Paper presented at the No Border Camp, Bulgaria, 25–29 August, www.anarkismo.net/article/20482, accessed 29 July 2015.

— (2012) 'The first immigrant detention camp will be built in Attiki', 31 March, online, clandestinenglish.wordpress. com/2012/03/31/the-first-migrant-detention-camp-will-be-built-in-attiki/, accessed 24 September 2013.

Clastres, P. (1977) *Society against the State: Essays in Political Anthropology*, Oxford: Blackwell (Mole Editions).

Clayton, G. (2006) Textbook on Immigration and Asylum Law, 2nd edn, Oxford: Oxford University Press.

Cleaver, H. (2008) 'Kropotkin, self-valorization and the crisis of Marxism', Paper presented to the Conference on Pyotr Alexeevich Kropotkin organized by the Russian Academy of Science on the 150th anniversary of his birth, Moscow, 8–14 December 1992, libcom.org/

library/kropotkin-self-valorization-crisis-marxism, accessed 29 July 2015.

Cohen, J. (2008) 'Safe in our hands? A study of suicide and self-harm in asylum seekers', *Journal of Forensic & Legal Medicine*, 15(4): 235–44.

Cohen, J. and A. Arato (1992) *Civil Society and Political Theory*, Cambridge: MIT Press.

Colebrook, C. (2009) 'On the very possibility of queer theory', in C. Nigianni and M. Storr (eds), *Deleuze and Queer Theory*, Edinburgh: Edinburgh University Press.

Colectivo Situaciones (2007) 'Something more on research militancy: footnotes on procedures and (in)decisions', in S. Shukaitis and D. Graeber (eds), *Constituent Imagination: Militant investigations/collective theorization*, Oakland, CA: AK Press.

Coleman, L. M. and K. Tucker (2011) 'Between discipline and dissent: situated resistance and global order', *Globalizations*, 8(4): 397–410.

Collectives and Neighbourhood Assembly of Kypseli-Patissia-Acharnon (2011) 'We should not allow fascist–racist pogroms in our neighbourhoods', *ContraInfo*, online, 13 June, en.contrainfo.espiv.net/2011/06/13/we-should-not-allow-fascist%E2%80%93racist-pogroms-in-our-neighbourhoods/, accessed 29 July 2015.

Contre Faites (2011) *Deconstructing Walls: Narratives, analytical texts and photos from the borders of south-eastern Europe*, Self-published text.

Coordination Française Pour Le Droit d'Asile (2008) 'The Law of the "Jungles": the situation of exiles on the shore of the Channel and the North Sea', Report, cfda.rezo.net/download/The%20law%20of%20Jungles%20recommendations%2009%2008.pdf, accessed 30 July 2015.

Cossé, E. (2013) *Unwelcome Guests: Greek police abuses of migrants in Athens*, Report for Human Rights Watch, www.hrw.org/sites/default/files/reports/greece0613_ForUpload.pdf, accessed 23 September 2013.

Courau, H. (2003) '"Tomorrow, Insallah, chance!" People smuggler networks in Sangatte', *Immigrants & Minorities*, 22(2/3): 374–87.

Coutin, S. B. (2000) 'Denationalization, inclusion, and exclusion: negotiating the boundaries of belonging', *Indiana Journal of Global Legal Studies*, 7(2): 585–93.

— (2010) 'Exiled by law: deportation and the inviolability of life', in N. Peutz and N. de Genova (eds), *The Deportation Regime: Sovereignty, Space, and the Freedom of Movement*, Durham, NC: Duke University Press.

Crass, C. (n.d. a) *Towards an Anti-Racist Politics and Practice: A radical autobiography*, www.coloursofresistance.org/581/towards-anti-racist-politics-and-practice-a-racial-autobiography/, accessed 29 July 2015.

— (n.d. b) 'Looking to the light of freedom: lessons from the civil rights movement and thoughts on anarchist organizing', *Colours of Resistance Archive*, online, www.coloursofresistance.org/556/looking-to-the-light-of-freedom-lessons-from-the-civil-rights-movement-and-thoughts-on-anarchist-organizing/, accessed 29 July 2015.

— (n.d. c) 'Beyond the whiteness – global capitalism and white supremacy: thoughts on movement building and anti-racist organizing', *Colors of Resistance Archive*, online, www.coloursofresistance.org/492/beyond-the-whiteness-global-capitalism-and-white-supremacy-thoughts-on-movement-building-and-anti-racist-organizing/, accessed 29 July 2015.

Crenshaw, K. W. (1989) 'Demarginalizing the intersection of race and sex: a black feminist critique of antidiscrimination doctrine, feminist theory and antiracist politics', *University of Chicago Legal Forum*, 140: 139–67.

— (1991) 'Mapping the margins: intersectionality, identity politics, and violence against women of colour', *Stanford Law Review*, 43(6): 1241–99.

CrimethInk (n.d.) 'Undermining oppression', online, www.crimethinc.com/texts/atoz/underminingoppression.php, accessed 1 April 2016.

Croydon Migrant Solidarity (n.d.) *Radical Migrant Solidarity: Initiatives, observations and ideas from the struggle against the border regime*, Zine, www.scribd.com/doc/78038248/Radical-Migrant-Solidarity, accessed 29 July 2015.

Cunningham-Sabot, E. and S. Fol (2007) 'Shrinking cities in France and Great Britain: a silent process?', Presentation given at the conference 'Shrinking Cities: The Future of Shrinking Cities – Problems, Patterns and Strategies of Urban Transformation in a Global Context', February, Center for Global Metropolitan Studies, Institute of Urban and Regional Development and the Shrinking Cities International Research Network.

Dauphinee, E. (2007) *The Ethics of Researching War: Looking for Bosnia*, Manchester: University of Manchester Press.

Day, R. (2005) *Gramsci Is Dead: Anarchist currents in the newest social movements*, London: Pluto.

Debord, G. (1967) *Society of the Spectacle*, Eastbourne: Soul Bay Press.

DeGenova, N. (2002) '"Migrant illegality" in everyday life', *Annual Review of Anthropology*, 31: 419–47.

— (2011) 'Alien powers: deportable labour and the spectacle of security', in V. Squire (ed.), *The Contested Politics of Mobility: Borderzones and irregularity*, London and New York: Routledge.

— (2015) 'Border struggles in the migrant metropolis', *Nordic Journal of Migration Research*, 5(1).

DeHaas, H. (2008) 'Irregular migration from West Africa to the Maghreb and the European Union: an overview of recent trends', Report prepared for the International Organization for Migration (IOM), Geneva.

Deleuze, G. (2004) *Difference and Repetition*, London: Continuum Impacts.

Deleuze, G. and F. Guattari (2004 [1987]) *A Thousand Plateaus: Capitalism and Schizophrenia*, Minneapolis: University of Minnesota Press.

Della Porta, D. (2000) 'Immigration and protest: new challenges for Italian democracy', *South European Society & Politics*, 5(3): 108–32.

Di Giacomo, F. (2015) 'IOM calls for international investigation of Mediterranean shipwreck deaths', International Organization for Migration, 8 May, online, www.iom.int/news/iom-call-international-investigation-mediterranean-shipwreck-deaths, accessed 28 July 2015.

Doctors of the World (2015) 'Refugee crisis reaches a tipping point', Doctors of the World, online, www.doctorsoftheworld.org.uk/blog/entry/refugee-crisis-reaches-a-tipping-point, accessed 1 April 2016.

Doppler, L. (2015) '"A feeling of doing the right thing": forming a successful alliance against Dublin deportations', *Movements: Journal of Critical*

Migration and Border Regime Research, 2(2).

Düvell, F. (2006) 'Illegal migration in Europe: patterns, causes and consequences', Talk given at the University of Stockholm seminar on 'Irregular, Sans Papiers, Hidden, Illegal and Black Labour', 29 November.

Edkins, J. and V. Pin-Fat (2004) 'Introduction: Life, power, resistance', in J. Edkins and V. Pin-Fat (eds), *Sovereign Lives: Power in global politics*, New York: Routledge.

Edwards, A. (2015) 'Pressure growing on Greek island of Lesvos, as 2015 refugee and migrant crossings of the Mediterranean top 100,000', UNHCR Briefing Notes, online, www.unhcr. org/5576bd836.html, accessed 30 July 2015.

Elam, D. (1994) *Feminism and Deconstruction*, London: Routledge.

England, K. (1994) 'Getting personal: reflexivity, positionality and feminist research', *Professional Geographer*, 46(1): 80–89.

Engstrom, M. (2002) 'The power of perception: the impact of the Macedonian Question on inter-ethnic relations in the Republic of Macedonia', *Global Review of Ethnopolitics*, 1(3): 3–17.

Europa (2015) 'Country responsible for asylum application (Dublin)', ec.europa.eu/dgs/home-affairs/what-we-do/policies/asylum/examination-of-applicants/index_en.htm, accessed 29 July 2015.

Evren, S. (2012) 'There Ain't no black in the anarchist flag! Race, ethnicity and anarchism', in R. Kinna (ed.), *The Continuum Companion to Anarchism*, London: Continuum.

Faulks, K. (2000) *Citizenship*, London: Routledge.

Fekete, L. (2011) 'Accelerated removals: the human cost of EU deportation policies', *Race & Class*, 52(4): 89–97.

Fernandez, C., M. Gill, I. Szeman and J. Whyte (2006) 'Erasing the line, or, the politics of the border', *Ephemera: Theory & politics in organization*, 6(4):466–83.

Firth, R. (2010) 'Critical utopian studies: theory and practice', PhD thesis, University of Nottingham.

— (2012) 'Transgressing urban utopianism: autonomy and active desire', *Geografiska Annaler: Series B, Human Geography*, 94(2): 89–106.

Fjellberg, A. (2015) 'What to do about the refugees in Calais?', *New York Times*, online, www.nytimes. com/2015/09/29/opinion/what-to-do-about-the-refugees-in-calais. html?_r=0, accessed 1 April 2016.

Flacks, R. (2004) 'Knowledge for what? Thoughts on the state of social movement studies', in J. Goodwin and J. M. Jasper (eds), *Rethinking Social Movements: Structure, meaning and emotion*, Lanham, MD: Rowman & Littlefield.

Fotiadis, A. and A. Ciobanu (2013) 'Closing Europe's borders becomes big business', Inter Press Service News Agency, online, 9 January, www.ipsnews.net/2013/01/closing-europes-borders-becomes-big-business/, accessed 29 July 2015.

Foucault, M. (1982) 'The subject and power', in H. L. Dreyfus and P. Rabinow (eds), *Michel Foucault: Beyond Structuralism and Hermeneutics*, Brighton: Harvester Press.

— (1998 [1978]) *The History of Sexuality, an Introduction*, vol. I: *The Will to Knowledge*, London: Penguin.

Frassanito Network (2004) 'Movements of migration', Paper prepared for the European Social Forum, London.

Freeman, J. (1970) *The Tyranny of Structurelessness*, struggle.ws/pdfs/tyranny.pdf, accessed 29 July 2015.

Freire, P. (2005 [1970]) *Pedagogy of the Oppressed*, London: Continuum.

groundless solidarity

Frontex (2010) 'Current migratory situation in Greece', *Situation in Greece*, Frontex press kit, update 29 November.

Führer, D. (2014) 'The supporter-stigma as a tool for escapism? An interview with Rex Osa (The Voice Refugee Forum)', *Transact*, 6, online, transact.noblogs. org/files/2014/02/transact6_en.pdf, accessed 1 April 2016.

Fuller, D. (1999) 'Part of the Action, or "going native"? Learning to cope with the "politics of integration"', *Area*, 31(3): 221–7.

Fuller, D. and R. Kitchen (eds) (2004) *Radical Theory/Critical Praxis: Making a difference beyond the academy?*, Vermont: Praxis (e)Press Critical Topographies Series.

Gentleman, A. (2015) 'The horror of the Calais refugee camp: "We feel like we are dying slowly"', www.theguardian. com/world/2015/nov/03/refugees-horror-calais-jungle-refugee-camp-feel-like-dying-slowly, accessed 1 April 2016.

Gillen, K. and J. Pickerill (2012) 'The difficult and hopeful ethics of research on, and with, social movements', *Social Movement Studies*, 11(2): 133–43.

Glick-Schiller, N. (2009) 'A global perspective on transnational migration: theorizing migration without methodological nationalism', COMPAS Working Paper WP-09-67, online, www.compas.ox.ac.uk/fileadmin/files/Publications/working_papers/WP_2009/WP0967%20Glick%20Schiller.pdf, accessed 29 July 2015.

Goldberg, D. T. (1993) *Racist Culture: Philosophy and the politics of meaning*, Oxford: Blackwell.

— (1996) 'In/visibility and super/vision', in L. R. Gordon, T. Denean Sharply-Whiting and R. T. White (eds), *Fanon on Race, Veils and Discourses of Resistance*, Oxford: Blackwell.

Gordon, U. (2008) *Anarchy Alive! Anti-authoritarian politics from practice to theory*, London: Pluto.

— (2012) 'Participant observation', in R. Kinna (ed.), *The Continuum Companion to Anarchism*, London: Continuum.

Graeber, D. (2004) *Fragments of an Anarchist Anthropology*, Chicago, IL: Prickly Paradigm Press.

— (2009) *Direct Action: An ethnography*, Edinburgh: AK Press.

— (2011) *Debt: The first 5000 years*, Brooklyn, NY: Melleville-House Publishing.

Grelet, S. (2001) 'The art of flight: an interview with Yann Moulier-Boutang', *Rethinking Marxism*, 13(3/4): 227–35.

Grubačić, A. (2004) 'Towards another anarchism', in J. Sen, A. Escobar and P. Waterman (eds), *World Social Forum: Challenging Empires*, New Delhi: Viveka Foundation.

Harding, S. (1993) 'Rethinking standpoint epistemology: "What is strong objectivity?"', in L. Alcoff and E. Potter (eds), *Feminist Epistemologies*, New York: Routledge.

Hardt, M. and A. Negri (2000) *Empire*, Cambridge, MA: Harvard University Press.

Harraway, D. (1988) 'The science question in feminism and the privilege of partial perspective', Feminist Studies, 14(3): 575–99.

Social Centre of Albanian Migrants (2010) In A. G. Schwarz, T. Sagris and Void Network (eds), *We Are an Image from the Future: The Greek revolt of December 2008*, Edinburgh: AK Press.

Hayter, T. (2004) *Open Borders: The case against immigration controls*, 2nd edn, London: Pluto.

Heckert, J. (2010) 'Intimacy with strangers/intimacy with self: queer experiences of social research', in K. Browne and C. J. Nash (eds), *Queer*

Methodologies in Social and Cultural Research, Aldershot: Ashgate.

Held, D. (1995) *Democracy and the Global Order: From the modern state to cosmopolitan governance*, Cambridge: Polity Press.

Hess, S. (2003) 'I am not willing to return at this time ...', *Makeworlds*, 3, online, www.makeworlds.org/node/19, accessed 23 September 2013.

Hill Maher, K. (2002) 'Who has a right to rights? Citizenship's exclusions in an age of migration', in A. Brysk (ed.), *Globalization and Human Rights*, Berkeley: University of California Press.

Holloway, J. (2002) *Change the World without Taking Power: The meaning of revolution today*, London: Pluto.

— (2010) *Crack Capitalism*, London: Pluto.

hooks, b. (1982) *Ain't I a Woman: Black women and feminism*, Massachusetts: Pluto.

— (1984) *Feminist Theory: From Margin to Center*, Boston, MA: South End Press.

— (1991) *Yearning: Race, Gender, and Cultural Politics*, London: Turnaround.

— (1994) *Teaching to Transgress: Education as the practice of freedom*, London: Routledge.

Hoy, D. C. (2004) *Critical Resistance: From post-structuralism to post-critique*, London: MIT Press.

Human Rights Watch (2012) 'Hate on the streets: xenophobic violence in Greece', www.hrw.org/reports/2012/07/10/hate-streets-0, accessed 24 September 2013.

— (2013) 'Unwelcome guests: Greek police abuses of migrants in Athens', www.hrw.org/sites/default/files/reports/greece0613_ForUpload.pdf, accessed 23 September 2013.

Huysmans, J. (1995) 'Migrants as a security problem: dangers of securitizing societal issues', in R. Miles and D. Thränhardt (eds), *Migration and European Integration: The dynamics of inclusion and exclusion*, London: Pinter.

Hyndman, J. (2010) 'Introduction: The feminist politics of refugee migration', *Gender, Place and Culture*, 17(4): 453–9.

Indra, J. X. (2011) 'Borderzones of enforcement: criminalization, workplace raids, and migrant counter-conducts', in V. Squire (ed.), *The Contested Politics of Mobility: Borderzones and irregularity*, London and New York: Routledge.

InfoMobil (2011) 'You always wish it's your last day here in Komunisia', Interview, *InfoMobil*, 1 June, online, infomobile.w2eu.net/2011/06/01/%E2%80%9Cyou-always-wish-it%E2%80%99s-your-last-day-here-in-komunisia-%E2%80%9D-interview/, accessed 24 September 2013.

International Organization for Migration (2016) *Latest Global Figures*, IOM, online, missingmigrants.iom.int/latest-global-figures, accessed 1 April 2016.

Invisible Committee (2009) *The Coming Insurrection*, London: MIT Press.

Isin, E. (2002) *Being Political: Genealogies of citizenship*, Minneapolis: University of Minnesota Press.

— (2008) 'Theorizing acts of citizenship', in E. Isin and M. Neilsen (eds), *Acts of Citizenship*, London: Zed Books.

— (2009) 'Citizenship in flux: the figure of the activist citizen', *Subjectivity*, 29: 367–88.

Iulia (2010) 'Do you join the party to fuck or do you fuck to join the party?', in A. G. Schwarz, T. Sagris and Void Network (eds), *We Are an Image from the Future: The Greek revolt of December 2008*, Edinburgh: AK Press.

Jandl, M., D. Vogel and K. Iglicka (2008) 'Report on methodological issues', Paper prepared for the Clandestino Project, November.

Jany-Catrice, F. (2009) 'The French

regions and their social health', *Social Indicators Research*, 93: 377–91.

Janz, B. P. (2002) 'The territory is not the map: place, Deleuze, Guattari and African philosophy', *Philosophia Africana*, 5(1):1–17.

Jeffrey, S., P. Scruton, C. Fenn, P. Torpey, C. Levett and P. Gutierez (2016) 'Europe's refugee crisis – a visual guide to developments in 2015', *Guardian*, online, www.theguardian.com/world/ng-interactive/2015/sep/18/latest-developments-in-europes-refugee-crisis-a-visual-guide, accessed 1 April 2016.

Johnson, H. (2012) 'Moments of solidarity, migrant activism and (non)citizens at global borders: political agency at Tanzanian refugee camps, Australian detention centres and European borders', in P. Nyers and K. Rygiel (eds), Citizenship, Migrant Agency and the Politics of Movement, London: Routledge.

Juris, J. (2007) 'Practicing militant ethnography with the Movement for Global Resistance in Barcelona', in S. Shukaitis and D. Graeber (eds), *Constituent Imagination: Militant investigations/collective theorization*, Oakland, CA: AK Press.

Kaplan, C. (1987) 'Deterritorializations: the rewriting of home and exile in western Feminist discourse', *Cultural Critique*, 6: 187–98.

Karakayali, S. and E. Rigo (2010) 'Mapping the European space of circulation', in N. DeGenova and N. Peutz (eds), *The Deportation Regime: Sovereignty, space and the freedom of movement*, Durham, NC, and London: Duke University Press.

Karakayali, S. and V. Tsianos (2012) 'Die frohe botschaft der autonomie der migration', *Linksnet*, online, www.linksnet.de/de/artikel/27255, accessed 29 July 2015.

Karatzogiani, A. and A. Robinson (2010) *Power, Resistance and Conflict in the Contemporary World: Social movements, networks and hierarchies*, London: Routledge.

Kasimis, C. and C. Kassimi (2004) *Greece: A history of Migration*, www.migrationinformation.org/Profiles/display.cfm?ID=228, accessed 29 July 2015.

Kasimis, C. and A. Papadopoulos (2005) 'The multifunctional role of migrants in the Greek countryside: implications for the rural economy and society', *Journal of Ethnic and Migration Studies*, 31(1): 99–127.

Kasimis, C., A. G. Papadopoulos and C. Pappas (2010) 'Gaining from rural migrants: migrant employment strategies and socio-economic implications for rural labour markets', *Sociologica Ruralis*, 50(3): 258–76.

Kasli, Z. and A. Parla (2009) 'Broken lines of il/legality and the reproduction of state sovereignty: the impact of visa policies on immigrants to Turkey from Bulgaria', *Alternatives*, 34: 203–27.

Katsiaficas, G. (2007) *The Subversion of Politics: European autonomous social movements and the decolonization of everyday life*, Edinburgh: AK Press.

Katsiaficas, G. and K. Cleaver (2001) *Liberation, Imagination and the Black Panther Party: A New Look at Their Legacy*, Routledge

Keating, A. (2002) 'Forging El Mundo Zurdo: changing ourselves, changing the world',. in G. Anzaldua and A. Keating (eds), *This Bridge We Call Home: Radical Visions for transformation*, New York: Routledge.

Keller, S., U. Lunacek, B. Lochbihler and H. Flautre (2011) 'Frontex Agency: which guarantees for human rights?', A study conducted by Migreurop on the European External Borders Agency in view of the revision of its mandate, www.migreurop.org/IMG/pdf/

Frontex-PE-Mig-ENG.pdf, accessed 29 July 2015.

Kingsley, P. (2015) '700 migrants feared dead in Mediterranean shipwreck', *Guardian*, 19 April, online, www.theguardian.com/world/2015/apr/19/700-migrants-feared-dead-mediterranean-shipwreck-worst-yet, accessed 28 July 2015.

Kiprianos, P., S. Balias and V. Passas (2003) 'Greek policy towards immigration and immigrants', *Social Policy & Administration*, 37(2): 148–64.

Konsta, A.-M. and G. Lazaridis (2010) 'Civic stratification, "plastic" citizenship and "plastic subjectivities" in Greek immigration policy', *Migration & Integration*, 11: 365–82.

Koopmans, S. (2008) 'Imperialism within: can the master's tools bring down empire?', *ACME Journal*, 7, online, www.acme-journal.org/vol7/SKo.pdf, accessed 25 September 2013.

Krasner, S. (2000) 'Problematic sovereignty', in S. Krasner (ed.), *Problematic Sovereignty: Contested rules and political possibilities*, New York: Columbia University Press.

Kropotkin, P. (1912) *Modern Science and Anarchism*, London: Freedom Press.

— (2006 [1902]) *Mutual Aid: A factor of evolution*, Mineola, NY: Dover.

Kumar Rajaram, P. (2002) 'Humanitarianism and representations of the refugee', *Journal of Refugee Studies*, 15(3): 247–64.

Lamble, S. (2001) 'Building sustainable communities of resistance', in J. Chang (ed.), *RESIST! A Grassroots Collection of Stories, Poetry, Photos and Analysis from the FTAA Protests in Québec City and Beyond*, Fernwood Publishing.

Landauer, G. (1983 [1911]) *For Socialism*, St Louis, MO: Telos Press.

— (2005 [1910]) 'Weak statesmen, weaker people', in G. Landauer, *Anarchism in Germany and Other Essays*, Barbary Coast Collective.

Landstreicher, W./Feral Faun (2003) 'Revolutionary solidarity: a challenge', in Anon. (eds) (2005), *Revolutionary Solidarity*, Pamphlet.

— (2009) *Wilful Disobedience*, Ardent Press.

Lara, D., D. Greene and C. Bejarano (2009/10) 'A critical analysis of immigrant advocacy tropes: how popular discourse weakens solidarity and prevents broad, sustainable justice', *Social Justice*, 36(2): 21–37.

Lentin, A. (2004) *Racism and Anti-racism in Europe*, London: Pluto.

Libertarian Communists (2011) 'Greece: urgent call for international solidarity!', *ContraInfo*, 19 May, online, en.contrainfo.espiv.net/2011/05/19/greece-urgent-call-for-international-solidarity/, accessed 13 June 2016.

Lorde, A. (2007 [1984]) 'An open letter to Mary Daley', in A. Lorde, *Sister Outsider: Essays and Speeches*, Berkeley: Crossing Press.

Lowen, M. (2013) 'Greece's Golden Dawn: "Don't say a word or I'll burn you alive"', *BBC News Online*, 2 October, www.bbc.com/news/world-europe-24363776, accessed 13 June 2016.

Lutterbeck, D. (2006) 'Policing migration in the Mediterranean', *Mediterranean Politics*, 11: 59–82.

Luu, H. (2004) 'Discovering a different space of resistance: personal reflections on anti-racist organizing', in D. Solnit (ed.), *Globalize Liberation: How to Uproot the System and Build a Better World*, City Lights.

Malik, K. (1996) *The Meaning of Race: Race, history and culture in western society*, New York: NYU Press.

Marcos. S. (2004) *Ya Basta! 10 Years of the Zapatista Uprising Writings of Subcomandante Insurgente Marcos*, Edinburgh: AK Press.

Maritime and Coastguard Agency (2014) 'Guidance: Dover Strait crossings: Channel Navigation Information Service (CNIS)', www.gov.uk/government/publications/dover-strait-crossings-channel-navigation-information-service/dover-strait-crossings-channel-navigation-information-service-cnis, accessed 13 June 2016.

Martignoni, M. and D. Papadopoulos (2014) 'Genealogies of autonomous mobility', in E. Isin and P. Nyers (eds), *Routledge Handbook of Global Citizenship Studies*, London: Routledge.

Martin, B. and S. Mohanty (2003) 'What's home got to do with It?', in C. Mohanty, *Feminism without Borders: Decolonizing theory, practicing solidarity*, Durham, NC: Duke University Press.

Martinez, E. B. (2002) 'Where was the color in Seattle? Looking for reasons why the Great Battle was so white', colorlines.com/archives/2000/03/where_was_the_color_in_seattlelooking_for_reasons_why_the_great_battle_was_so_white.html, accessed 29 July 2015.

Mary Nardini Gang (n.d.) *Towards the Queerest Insurrection*, Zine, www.weldd.org/resources/towards-queerest-insurrection, accessed 29 July 2015.

Maxey, I. (1999) 'Beyond boundaries? Activism, academia, reflexivity and research', *Area*, 31(3): 199–208.

May, T. (2010) 'Wrong, disagreement, subjectification', in J.-F. Deranty (ed.), *Jacques Rancière: Key Concepts*, Durham: Acumen.

McAdam, D., S. Tarrow and C. Tilly (2001) *Dynamics of Contention*, Cambridge: Cambridge University Press.

McKenzie, M. (2014) '4 ways to push back against your privilege', *Black Girls & Dangerous*, online, www.

blackgirldangerous.org/2014/02/4-ways-push-back-privilege/, accessed 13 June 2016.

McNevin, A. (2009) 'Doing what citizens do: migrant struggles at the edges of political belonging', *Local, Global: Identity, Security, Community*, 6: 67–77.

— (2011) *Contesting Citizenship: Irregular Migrants and New Frontiers of the Political*, New York: Columbia University Press.

Melucci, A. (1989) *Nomads of the Present: Social movements and individual needs in contemporary society*, Philadelphia: Temple University Press.

Menz, G. (2008) *The Political Economy of Managed Migration: Nonstate Actors, Europeanization, and the Politics of Designing Migration Policies*, Oxford: Oxford University Press.

Mezzadra, S. (2004a) 'The right to escape', *Ephemera*, 4(3): 267–75, www.copenhagenfreeuniversity.dk/mirror/righttoescape.pdf, accessed 29 July 2015.

— (2004b) 'Citizenship in motion', *Makeworlds*, 4, online, www.makeworlds.org/node/83, accessed 23 September 2013.

— (2011) 'The gaze of autonomy: capitalism, migration and social struggles', trans. R. Nunes, in V. Squire (ed.), *The Contested Politics of Mobility: Borderzones and irregularity*, London and New York: Routledge.

Mezzadra, S. and B. Neilson (2003) 'Ne qui, ne altrove: migration, detention desertion: a dialogue', *Borderlands e-journal*, 2(1), online, www.borderlands.net.au/vol2no1_2003/mezzadra_neilson.html, accessed 29 July 2015.

Mi (2010) 'The new neighbourhood assemblies', in A. G. Schwarz, T. Sagris and Void Network (eds), *We Are an Image from the Future: The Greek revolt of December 2008*, Edinburgh: AK Press.

Millner, N. (2011) 'From "refugee" to "migrant" in Calais solidarity activism: re-staging undocumented migration for a future politics of asylum', *Political Geography*, 30(6): 320–28.

Mitropoulos, A. (2006) 'Precari-us?', online, eipcp.net/transversal/0704/mitropoulos/en, accessed 28 July 2015.

— (2007) 'Autonomy, recognition, movement', in S. Shukaitis and D. Graeber (eds), *Constituent Imagination: Militant investigations/collective theorization*, Oakland, CA: AK Press.

Mitropoulos, A. and B. Neilson (2006) 'Exceptional times, non-governmental spacings, and impolitical movements', *Vacarme*, online, www.vacarme.org/article484.html, accessed 1 April 2016.

Mohanty, C. (2003) *Feminism without Borders: Decolonizing theory, practicing solidarity*, Durham, NC: Duke University Press.

Moss, P. (2004) 'A "politics of local politics": praxis in places that matter', in D. Fuller and R. Kitchen (eds), *Radical Theory/Critical Praxis: Making a Difference beyond the academy?*, Vermont: Praxis (e)Press Critical Topographies Series.

Motta, S. and A. Robinson (2010) 'On the possibilities of autonomy', Unpublished article.

Moulin, C. and P. Nyers (2007) '"We live in a country of UNHCR": refugee protests and global political society', *International Political Sociology*, 1: 356–72.

Nallu, P. (2015) 'The real winners of Greece's elections: refugees', *IRIN: Humanitarian news and analysis*, online, www.irinnews.org/report/101047/the-real-winners-of-greece-s-elections-refugees, accessed 30 July 2015.

Newman, S. (2011) 'Post-anarchism and radical politics today', in D. Rouselle and S. Evren (eds), *Post-Anarchism: A reader*, London: Pluto

Nigianni, C. and M. Storr (2009) 'So as to know "us" better. Two theories, one concept, one book, many authors', in C. Nigianni and M. Storr (eds), *Deleuze and Queer Theory*, Edinburgh: Edinburgh University Press.

No Borders UK (n.d.) *A No Borders Manifesto*, noborders.org.uk/news/no-borders-manifesto, accessed 29 July 2015.

Nolin, C. (2006) *Transnational Ruptures: Gender and forced migration*, Aldershot: Ashgate.

Non, A. (n.d.) *Calais Calais*, eyfa.dysnomia.ecobytes.net/wp-content/uploads/sites/4/2015/03/Calais_Calais_EN_Download1.pdf, accessed 13 June 2016.

Nord Littoral (2015) 'Migrants: des grilles pour sauver l'économie calaisienne', *Nord Littoral*, 28 May, online, www.nordlittoral.fr/faits-divers/migrants-des-grilles-pour-sauver-l-economie-calaisienne-iaob0n211736, accessed 1 April 2016].

Nyers, P. (2003) 'Abject cosmopolitanism: the politics of protection in the anti-deportation movement', *Third World Quarterly*, 24(6): 1069–93.

— (2006) 'The accidental citizen: acts of sovereignty and (un)making citizenship', *Economy and Society*, 35(1): 22–41.

— (2008) 'In solitary, in solidarity: detainees, hostages and contesting the anti-policy of detention', *European Journal of Cultural Studies*, 11(5): 333–49.

— (2010) 'No one is illegal between city and nation', *Studies in Social Justice*, 4(2): 127–43.

— (2015) 'Migrant citizenships and autonomous mobilities', *Migration, Mobility and Displacement*, 1(1).

Nyers, P. and K. Rygiel (2012) 'Citizenship, migrant activism and the politics of movement', in P. Nyers and K. Rygiel (eds), *Citizenship, Migrant Agency and the Politics of Movement*, London: Routledge.

Offe, C. (1985) 'New social movements: challenging the boundaries of institutional politics', *Social Research*, 52(4): 817–68.

Papadimitropoulos, P. (2010) 'You talk about material damages, we speak about human life: perceptions of violence among Greek anarchist groups', in A. G. Schwarz, T. Sagris and Void Network (eds), *We Are an Image from the Future: The Greek revolt of December 2008*, Edinburgh: AK Press.

Papadopoulos, A., C. Chalkias and L.-M. Fratsea (2010) 'Clustering the migration-related-NGOs and immigrant associations in Greece. A quantitative approach', Paper prepared for the 17th European Colloquium on Quantitative and Theoretical Geography.

Papadopoulos, D. and M. Martignoni (2014) 'Genealogies of autonomous mobility', in E. Isin and P. Nyers (eds), *Routledge Handbook of Global Citizenship Studies*, Routledge, pp. 38–48.

Papadopoulos, D., N. Stephenson and V. Tsianos (2008) *Escape Routes: Control and subversion in the 21st Century*, London: Pluto.

Papadopoulos, D. and V. Tsianos (2013) 'After citizenship: autonomy of migration, organisational ontology and mobile commons', *Citizenship Studies*, 17(2): 178–96.

People in Solidarity with Migrants (2010) *Solidarity to the Immigrants Is Our Weapon*, Pamphlet.

Pickerill, J. (2008) 'A surprising sense of hope', *Antipode*, 40(3): 719–23.

Piven, F. and R. Cloward (1977) *Poor People's Movements: Why They Succeed, How They Fail*, New York: Vintage.

Plows, A. (2002) 'Praxis and practice: the "what, how and why" of the UK Environmental Direct Action (EDA) movement in the 1990's', PhD thesis, University of Wales, Bangor.

Porcu, P. (2005)) 'Revolutionary solidarity', in Anon. (eds), *Revolutionary Solidarity*, Pamphlet.

Price, C. (2014) 'Port of Dover and Calais sign agreement to ensure both invest creating a freight corridor for Europe in memorandum of understanding', *Kent Business*, 14 April, online, www.kentonline.co.uk/kent-business/county-news/ports-perfectly-placed-for-future-15844/, accessed 1 April 2016.

Pupavac, V. (2008) 'Refugee advocacy, traumatic representations and political disenchantment', *Government and Opposition*, 43(2): 270–92.

Rabinowitz, G. (2012) 'Greece's Jewish community warns of return to fascism', *JTA News*, 8 May, online, www.jta.org/2012/05/08/news-opinion/world/greeces-jewish-community-warns-of-return-to-fascism, accessed 24 September 2013.

Rajaram, K and C. Grundy-Warr (2004) 'The irregular migrant as Homo Sacer: migration and detention in Australia, Malaysia and Thailand', *International Migration*, 42: 33–64

Rancière, J. (1999) *Disagreement: Politics and Philosophy*, Minneapolis: University of Minnesota Press.

— (2004) 'Who is the subject of the Rights of Man?', *South Atlantic Quarterly*, 103(2/3): 297–310.

— (2006) *On the Shores of Politics*, London: Verso.

— (2010) *Dissensus: On politics and aesthetics*, London: Continuum.

Rancière, J. and D. Panagia (2000) 'Dissenting words: a conversation with Jacques Rancière', *Diacritics*, 30(2): 113–26.

Rankin, J. (2016) 'EU strikes deal with Turkey to send back refugees', *Guardian*, online, www.theguardian.com/world/2016/mar/18/eu-strikes-deal-with-turkey-to-send-back-refugees-from-greece?CMP=share_btn_twEU, accessed 1 April 2016.

Red Sunshine Gang (1999 [1971]) *Anti-Mass Methods of Organization for Collectives*, Kersplebedeb Publishers.

Rigby, J. and R. Schlembach (2013) 'Impossible protest: noborders in Calais', *Citizenship Studies*, 7(2): 157–72.

Rigo, E. (2005) 'Citizenship at Europe's borders: some reflections on the post-colonial condition of Europe in the context of EU enlargement', *Citizenship Studies*, 9(1): 3–22.

Robertson, J. (2002) 'Reflexivity redux: a pithy polemic on positionality', *Anthropological Quarterly*, 75(4): 785–92.

Robinson, A. (2010a) 'Symptoms of a new politics: networks, minoritarianism and the social symptom in Žižek, Deleuze and Guattari', *Deleuze Studies*, 4(2): 206–33.

— (2010b) 'In theory autonomism: the future of activism?', *Ceasefire*, ceasefiremagazine.co.uk/in-theory-5-autonomism/, accessed 29 July 2015.

Rodriguez, N. (1996) 'The battle for the border: notes on autonomous migration, transnational communities, and the state', *Social Justice*, 23(3): 21–37.

Roediger, D. (1994) *Towards the Abolition of Whiteness: Essays on race, politics and working-class history*, London: Verso.

Rose, G. (1997) 'Situating knoweldges: positionality, reflexivities and other tactics', *Progress in Human Geography*, 21(3): 305–20.

Routledge, P. (2004) 'Relational ethics of struggle', in D. Fuller and R. Kitchen (eds), *Radical Theory/Critical Praxis: Making a difference beyond the academy?*, Vermont: Praxis (e)Press Critical Topographies Series.

Ruhs, M. and B. Anderson (2007) 'The origins and functions of illegality in migrant labour markets: an analysis of migrants, employers and the state in the UK', Paper produced for the project 'Changing status, changing lives? The socio-economic impact of EU enlargement on low-wage migrant workers in the UK', online, www.compas.ox.ac.uk/fileadmin/files/Publications/Research_projects/Labour_markets/Changing_status/Illegality%20paper%20-%20Martin%20Ruhs%20and%20Bridget%20Anderson%201%20Dec%202007.pdf, accessed 28 July 2015.

Rygiel, K. (2011) 'Governing borderzones of mobility through e-borders: the politics of embodied mobility', in V. Squire (ed.), *The Contested Politics of Mobility: Borderzones and irregularity*, London and New York: Routledge.

Sajed, A. (2012) 'Securitized migrants and postcolonial (in)difference: the politics of activisms among North African migrants in France', in P. Nyers and K. Rygiel (eds), *Citizenship, Migrant Activism and the Politics of Movement*, London: Routledge.

Sakellaropoulos, S. (2012) 'On the causes and significance of the December 2008 social explosion in Greece', *Science & Society*, 76(3): 340–64.

Sandoval, C. (1991) 'U.S. Third World feminism: the theory and method of oppositional consciousness in the postmodern world', *Genders*, 10: 1–24.

sasha, k. (n.d.)'*Activism' and 'Anarcho-purism*', theanarchistlibrary.org/library/sasha-k-activism-and-anarcho-purism, accessed 29 July 2015.

Sassen, S. (1998) *Globalization and Its Discontents: Essays in the New Mobility of People and Money*, New York: New Press.

— (2006) *Territory, Authority, Rights: From Medieval to Global Assemblages*, Princeton, NJ, and Oxford: Princeton University Press.

Scheel, S. (2012) 'Biometric re-bordering of the Schengen visa regime: autonomy of migration despite its securitization?', Paper prepared for the annual *Millennium* conference 'Materialism and World Politics', 20/21 October.

Schinas, N. and N. Bertaud (2016) 'European Commission fact sheet: EU–Turkey deal', European Commission, 19 March, online, europa.eu/rapid/press-release_MEMO-16-963_en.htm, accessed 1 April 2016.

Schmitt, C. (2005 [1922]) *Political Theology: Four Chapters on the Concept of Sovereignty*, Chicago, IL: University of Chicago Press.

Scholz, S. (2007) 'Political solidarity and violent resistance', *Journal of Social Philosophy*, 38(1): 38–52.

Schwarz, A. G, T. Sagris and Void Network (2010) 'Chronology: 19th–20th century', in A. G. Schwarz, T. Sagris and Void Network (eds), *We Are an Image from the Future: The Greek revolt of December 2008*, Edinburgh: AK Press.

Scott, J. C. (1985) *Weapons of the Weak: Everyday Forms of Peasant Resistance*, New Haven, CT: Yale University Press.

— (1990) *Domination and the Arts of Resistance: Hidden Transcripts*, New Haven, CT: Yale University Press.

Sengupta, S. (2003) 'Borders: walking across, as opposed to flying above', *Make World*, 2, online, www.makeworld.org/node/46, accessed 13 November 2012.

Sharma, N. (2009) 'Escape artists: migrants and the politics of naming', *Subjectivity*, 29(4): 467–76.

Shukaitis, S. and D. Graeber (2007) 'Introduction', in S. Shukaitis and D. Graeber (eds), *Constituent Imagination: Militant investigations/collective theorization*, Oakland, CA: AK Press.

Snyder, T. (2005) 'The wall around the West', *Eurozine*, online, www.eurozine.com/articles/2005-01-06-snyder-en.html, accessed 29 July 2015.

Spurlin, W. (2001) 'Broadening postcolonial studies/decolonizing queer studies', in J. C. Hawley (ed.), *Postcolonial, Queer: Theoretical intersections*, Albany: State University of New York Press.

— (2006) *Imperialism within the Margins: Queer representation and the politics of culture in southern Africa*, Gordonsville, VA: Palgrave Macmillan.

Squire, V. (2011) 'Politicising mobility', in V. Squire (ed.), *The Contested Politics of Mobility: Borderzones and irregularity*, London and New York: Routledge.

Squire, V. and V. Bagelman (2012) 'Taking not waiting: space, temporality and politics in the City of Sanctuary movement', in P. Nyers and K. Rygiel (eds), Citizenship, Migrant Agency and the Politics of Movement, London: Routledge.

Statewatch (2012) 'Commission wants drones flying in European skies by 2016', *Statewatch*, 14 September, online, www.statewatch.org/news/2012/sep/eu-com-drones.htm, accessed 29 July 2015.

Stierl, M. (2012) '"No one is illegal!" Resistance and the politics of discomfort', *Globalizations*, 9(3): 425–38.

Sunderland, R. and E. Cossé (2012) 'Hate on the streets: xenophobic violence in Greece', Report by Human Rights Watch, www.hrw.org/reports/2012/07/10/hate-streets-0, accessed 24 March 2014.

Syndicate of Anti-racist and Immigrant

Organizations (n.d.) *We Want a World of Many Worlds: Anti-racist, pro-immigrant struggles*, migrant.diktio. org/node/95, accessed 29 July 2015.

Szabo, D. (2016) 'Latest global figures', Missing Migrants Project, International Organization for Migration, online, missingmigrants. iom.int/latest-global-figures, accessed 1 April 2016.

Tagaris, K. (2015) 'Greece pledges to shut immigrant detention centers', Reuters, 14 February, online, www.reuters.com/ article/2015/02/14/us-greece-politics-immigrants-idUSKBN0LI0MJ20150214, accessed 30 July 2015.

Tarrow, S. (1994) *Power in Movement: Social movements, collective action and politics*, Cambridge: Cambridge University Press.

Tazzioli, M. (2015) 'Migrants' uneven geographies and counter-mapping at the limits of representation', *Movements*, 1(2).

Thompson, A. K. (n.d.) 'Making friends with failure: a critical response to Richard Day's *Gramsci Is Dead: Anarchist currents in the newest social movements*', *Upping the Anti*, online, uppingtheanti.org/journal/03-making-friends-with-failure/, accessed 24 September 2013.

Tisserand, C. (2015) 'Calais migrants: towards a permanent police presence at the reception centre?', *La Voix du Nord*, 25 May, online, www. lavoixdunord.fr/region/migrants-de-calais-vers-une-presence-policiere-ia33b48581n2847337, accessed 28 July 2015.

Triandafyllidou, A. (2009) 'Greek immigration policy at the turn of the 21st century: lack of political will or purposeful mismanagement?', *European Journal of Migration and Law*, 11: 159–77.

— (2012) 'Greece: how a state in crisis manages its migration crisis?', 'Migration policies and international relations' series, Center for Migrations and Citizenship.

Triandafyllidou, A. and R. Gropas (eds) (2007) *European Immigration: A sourcebook*, Aldershot: Ashgate.

Tronti, M. (1964) *Lenin in England*, First published in *Classe Operaia*, 1, www. marxists.org/reference/subject/ philosophy/works/it/tronti.htm, accessed 29 July 2015.

UNHCR (2015) 'Over 1 million sea arrivals reach Europe in 2015', UNHCR, online, www.unhcr.org/5683d0b56. html, accessed 1 April 2016.

— (2016) 'Refugees/migrants emergency response – Mediterranean', UNHCR, online, data.unhcr. org/mediterranean/regional.php, accessed 1 April 2016.

Ünsal, N. (2015) 'Challenging "refugees" and "supporters": intersectional power structures in the refugee movement in Berlin', *Movements, Journal for Critical Migrations and Grenzregimeforschung*, 2(2): 1–18.

Vaneigem, R. (2003 [1967]) *Revolution in Everyday Life*, London: Rebel Press.

Vatikiotis, P. (2011) 'Networking activism: implications for Greece', *Estudos em Comunicação*, 10: 169–85.

Vaughan-Williams, N. (2009) *Border Politics: The limits of sovereign power*, Edinburgh: Edinburgh University Press.

Vradis, A. (2016) 'Upside down Athens', *Open Democracy*, online, www. opendemocracy.net/can-europe-make-it/antonis-vradis/upside-down-athens, accessed 1 April 2016.

Walia, H. (2013) *Undoing Border Imperialism*, Oakland, CA: AK Press.

Walsh, D., M. Taulbut and P. Hanlon (2009) 'The aftershock of deindustrialization: trends in mortality in Scotland and other parts of post-industrial Europe', *European Journal of Public Health*, 20(1): 58–64.

Walters, W. (2008) 'Acts of demonstration: mapping the territory of (non-) citizenship', in E. Isin and M. Neilsen (eds), *Acts of Citizenship*, London: Zed Books.

Ward, C. (2008 [1973]) *Anarchy in Action*, London: Freedom Press.

Welcome to Europe (2011) 'You always wish it's your last day here in Komunisia', Interview, *InfoMobil*, 1 June, online, infomobile.w2eu. net/2011/06/01/%E2%80%9Cyou-always-wish-it%E2%80%99s-your-last-day-here-in-komunisia-%E2%80%9D-interview/, accessed 30 July 2015.

Wolfram Cox, J. and S. Minahan (2004) 'Unravelling Woomera: lip sewing, morphology and dystopia', *Journal of Organizational Change Management*, 17(3): 292–301.

Yuval-Davis, N. (2012) 'Dialogical epistemology – and intersectional resistance to the "Oppression Olympics"', *Gender & Society*, 26(1): 46–54.

Zavos, A. (2008) 'Moving relationships/ shifting alliances: constructions of migration in the leftist anti-racist movement in Athens', *Annual Review of Critical Psychology*, 6.

Zetter, R. (1988) 'Refugees and refugee studies: a label and an agenda', *Journal of Refugee Studies*, 1(1): 1–6.

Zolberg, A. (1981) 'International migrations in political perspective', in M. Kritz, C. Keely and S. Tomasc (eds), *Global Trends in Migration: Theory and Research on International Population Movements*, New York: Migration Studies Center.

INDEX